DISARMING
MANHOOD

DISARMING MANHOOD

ROOTS OF ETHICAL RESISTANCE

DAVID A. J. RICHARDS

SWALLOW PRESS

ATHENS

Swallow Press / Ohio University Press, Athens, Ohio 45701
www.ohio.edu/oupress

Swallow Press / Ohio University Press books are printed on acid-free paper ⊗ ™

12 11 10 09 08 07 06 05   5 4 3 2 1

Part of chapter 4 appeared as
"Ethical Religion and the Struggle for Human Rights:
The Case of Martin Luther King, Jr.,"
72 *Fordham Law Review* 2105–52 (2004).

LIBRARY OF CONGRESS CATALOGING-IN-PUBLICATION DATA

Richards, David A. J.
Disarming manhood : roots of ethical resistance / David A. J. Richards.
    p. cm.
Includes bibliographical references and index.
ISBN 0-8040-1074-9 (alk. paper)—ISBN 0-8040-1075-7 (pbk. : alk. paper)
1. Passive resistance—Case studies. 2. Feminist theory. 3. Violence in men. 4. Tolstoy, Leo, graf,
1828-1910. 5. Garrison, William Lloyd, 1805-1879. 6. Gandhi, Mahatma, 1869-1948. 7. King,
Martin Luther, Jr., 1929-1968. 8. Churchill, Winston, Sir, 1874-1965. I. Title.
HM1281.R53 2005
303.6'1—dc22

2005000333

For CAROL GILLIGAN

Ye have heard that it hath been said, An eye for an eye, and a tooth for a tooth; But I say unto you, That ye resist not evil: but whosoever shall smite thee on thy right cheek, turn to him the other also.

MATT. 5:38–39 (KING JAMES VERSION)

Ye had heard that it hath been said, Thou shalt love thy neighbour, and hate thine enemy.
But I say unto you, Love your enemies.

MATT. 5:43–44 (KING JAMES VERSION)

//CONTENTS

CONTENTS

RN: The Index on pages
265 to 271 will not be read.
End RN.

//ACKNOWLEDGMENTS

My interest in both the subject matter and the interdisciplinary method of this work arose from ongoing conversations with Carol Gilligan in a seminar on gender and democracy we have cotaught at the New York University School of Law for the past five years. At the beginning of our collaborative teaching, Carol was working on the book that would be published as *The Birth of Pleasure* (Alfred A. Knopf, 2002), and her thinking about tragic stories of love, rooted in patriarchy, stimulated my own thinking about my long-standing passion for the music dramas of Verdi; in turn, this led me to write *Tragic Manhood and Democracy: Verdi's Voice and the Powers of Musical Art* (Sussex Academic Press, 2004). Subsequently, at my request, we began a close study and discussion in the seminar of important advocates of nonviolent nonresistance, the genesis of the current work. It was Carol's brilliant critical eye and ear that guided my research and writing and gave me a resonance for my work on this project. Throughout this effort, she could not have been more generous, more supportive, and more loving. I am deeply grateful to her and to the helpful comments of our remarkable students, including Emily Bushnell, Kathy Poldneff, Julia Milstein, Jessica Kramer, Ashika Singh, Sandra Farkas, Ron Raveh, Zabrina Aleguire, Tara Herman, Lori Barret, Susanne Kandel, Catherine Hardee, and Maggie Lindsey. I am grateful as well to my friend Nicholas Bamforth, fellow in law at Queen's College, Oxford University, whose advice, during his sabbatical at the New York University School of Law, crucially assisted my research on and writing of the chapter on Churchill, which was added some time after I had completed the rest of the book; I must also thank James Gilligan for related conversations that illuminated my research. Finally, I must acknowledge the help and heartening support in revising the manuscript that I received from Gillian Berchowitz of Ohio University Press, together with the comments of a reader, as well as the comments of editors and readers I received from other presses, in particular from Elizabeth Knoll of Harvard and Douglas Mitchell of Chicago.

The book was researched and written during a presabbatical leave and during summers, supported by generous research grants from the New York University School of Law Filomen D'Agostino and Max E. Greenberg Faculty Research Fund.

A work of this sort, so rooted in my personal history, also arose in conversations with those closest to me. My partner of some thirty years, Donald Levy, indispensably assisted both my research and writing, and his love for me nurtured the voice of this book. My sister, Diane Rita Richards, generously read earlier drafts of the manuscript for me, and her advice and support, as well as her love, have been vitally important to my work on it.

INTRODUCTION

Ethical Voice and Resistance

The inquiry of this work arises within the context of our growing historical understanding of the linkages between violence, including war and terrorism, and appeals to manhood.[1] My interest here is in countertraditions that arise from resistance to these linkages, a resistance made possible by an ethical voice that questions, either implicitly or explicitly, dominant conceptions of gender, especially the aggressive violence of an insulted patriarchal manhood directed at any challenge to its authority. I focus in particular on the thought and psychology of men who notably resisted such dominant conceptions of violent manhood. Four of them—William Lloyd Garrison, Leo Tolstoy, Mohandas Gandhi, and Martin Luther King—form a tradition of thought, with each earlier figure influencing those who came later. All of them found their ethical voice of resistance through the advocacy of forms of nonviolence (including the pacifism of Tolstoy and Gandhi) that challenged certain dominant conceptions of violent masculinity, appealing, as I show, to the authority of Jesus of Nazareth. But the fifth man I study, Winston Churchill, found his voice in arguing that the dominant pacifism of Britain in the interwar period disastrously failed to resist—and thus encouraged—violent forms of totalitarian manhood. Nonetheless, on the same basis of thought and psychology as the others, Churchill found a voice that, when fascist dictatorships took power in Italy and Germany, recognized and called for resistance against their aggressive violence and in terms that prophetically urged the early need for some measure of resisting response (including the relatively small level of proportionate force required for deterrence) before the violence escalated to the catastrophic levels of World War II. While some of these men famously disagreed (as Churchill and Gandhi did on India's independence from British colonialism), they all shared something extraordinary among men of their periods, namely, a distinctive thought and psychology capable of both understanding and resisting injustice based on violence, which in turn enabled them to mobilize and lead remarkably successful and sometimes nonviolent movements of public resistance to this injustice. It is very much part of my project to understand how and why their thought and psychology had such an unexpected resonance in terms of empowering others to adopt historically transformative means of resisting injustice.

The Indian novelist Arundhati Roy has recently expressed concern that our contemporary situation, the war on terror, has marginalized such modes of resistance, involving a loss of memory that legitimates pogroms of religious hatred in India (the home of Gandhi) and nuclear threats between India and Pakistan: "Peaceful resistance is treated with contempt. Terrorism's the real thing. The underlying principle of the War Against Terror, the very notion that war is an acceptable solution to terrorism, has ensured that terrorists in the subcontinent now have the power to trigger a nuclear war."[2] We need now, more than ever, to remind ourselves of the traditions that Roy worries we may forget—traditions of nonviolence that, as in the American civil rights movement of the 1960s, were brilliantly successful at a cost in human life that, though deplorable, was small compared with "a single day of battle in the Civil War or World War II."[3] Nonviolence, in comparison to violence, may advance and secure justice at a lower cost: there are often alternative, better ways to achieve justice than violence. Today, as never before, we must understand how such valuable forms of thought and psychology arise, are sustained, and can be encouraged.

I am gripped, as many contemporary men are, by admiration for these men—for the ways in which they endowed their lives with enduring meaning for themselves and others. When so much in the conception of manhood about them pulled them in more conventionally violent directions, they resisted that pull and spoke in a new ethical voice of resistance to injustice that appealed to and moved not only other men but women as well. Four of these men—Garrison, Gandhi, King, and Churchill—found in themselves a voice that empowered important democratic movements of resistance to injustice, and the fifth—Tolstoy—found an artistic voice that, in *War and Peace* and *Anna Karenina,* spoke truthfully to men and women of their false and broken lives. How do men live so well? Why are such struggles with manhood so ethically creative yet so difficult, sometimes even personally disastrous? What explains their

p. 3

2

personal psychology as men and how and why it empowered a political psychology of social movements in which women prominently defied conventional gender roles to become moral and political agents?

This work has been written out of a sense that these questions may absorb others as much as they do myself, giving us a better sense of the choices we now have and how we might better make choices in the future. Such resistance in each of their cases arose from the new kind of voice these men found in their associations and experiences with women and developed in ways that made possible a new kind of resisting voice in others. Their innovations both reflected and created views of manhood that blurred the lived sense of sharp psychological lines between the gender binary of manhood and womanhood.

The phrase *disarming manhood* describes the psychological impacts of this shift. The most politically palpable shift was in the psyches of the men who advocated and practiced such forms of resistance. Disarmed of the role violence traditionally played in a man's sense of vindicating insults to his honor, these men spoke in a more truthful voice about injustice, and they experimented in new arts of voice and reasonable persuasion, including literature (Tolstoy) and interpretive history (Churchill). Their experiments encouraged in themselves and in others (often women) a new kind of personal and political imagination, empowering creative forms of moral and political agency (for example, public civil disobedience). Such voices of resistance strengthened the resisting voices of others, suggesting unexpected resources of resistance to injustice in the personal and political psychology of men and women alike.

The study of Garrison in chapter 1 explains how I arrived at the thesis of this work, reflecting on Garrison and his relationship to the abolitionist feminists (the subject of a previous book of mine). I discovered in Garrison's thought and psychology a relationship to the ethical voice of his antipatriarchal mother, the basis of his own remarkable resistance to injustice and his appeal to the women who joined him in resistance. It was the attempt to explain these connections that led me to formulate the thesis I offer in chapter 1 and then to explore the explanatory value of the thesis in understanding the resistance of the other men I study in this work. The extended studies of Tolstoy in chapter 2 and Churchill in chapter 5 present a fascinating contrast between the lives of two remarkable men—one ascetic and tragic, the other marked by pleasure and relationship; in a sense, these are the twin pillars on which this book's

architecture is built. Both were aristocrats who, as young men, were courageous soldiers in the wars of their respective imperial states. Both found
their voices in writing—Tolstoy in literature, Churchill in journalism
and histories (notably, of the various wars in which he served either in
the military or as a political leader) and in his remarkable speeches. In both
cases, their thought and psychology arose in unusual relationships with
women, as mothers or maternal caretakers and as wives. Yet no two men
could be more different in terms of the women in their lives. Tolstoy was
tormented by the idealization of women, which fostered his marital misery, celibacy, and pacifism. By contrast, Churchill found his voice in relationship to a mother he knew as a person of powerful sexual voice and
life outside marriage, and he married a woman as complex as he and enjoyed a union of unusual happiness. No men in this study better understood the psychology of men in war nor, through that understanding,
found a more compelling voice that resisted forms of injustice based on
patriarchal violence.

The studies of Mohandas Gandhi in chapter 3 and of Martin Luther
King Jr. in chapter 4 explore how my thesis clarifies the thought and psychology of two creative leaders of important movements of political resistance. It is precisely because Gandhi and King found their ethical
voices in important relationships to the antipatriarchal voices of their
mothers that they were able to form and lead nonviolent movements
which significantly appealed to women, who were mobilized by Gandhi
and King to participate in transformative movements of moral and political agency to resist injustice.

An original feature of my approach is its inductive, textured exploration of these experiments of voice in the form of biography and, when
appropriate, literature and history. This exploration is a new departure for
me. The current work certainly draws on my previous books on political and constitutional theory and interpretive history, but the topic has
required me to work in a rather different way to do justice to its complexities. I explore the development and impact of experiments in voice
as they unfolded in the lives of these men and sometimes clarify my
argument about voice in terms of the relevant novels of Nathaniel Hawthorne, James Baldwin, Richard Wright, and Joseph Conrad. In the
chapter on Tolstoy, the study of his novels is *indispensable* to exploring
psychic shifts and struggles central to my argument. In this connection,
David Lodge has recently argued that the art of the novel offers an in-

valuable means of investigating the complexities of human consciousness, a means that students of human consciousness ignore at their peril.[4]
The method of this book powerfully illustrates Lodge's insight.

What is most original in my story about these men and their political
impact is the primacy I accord gender and voice in an interdisciplinary
theory that combines developmental psychology with feminist liberal
political theory. My argument is that this political theory, usually limited
to the interpretation of constitutional democracies,[5] in fact explains important political leaders and their impact in the context of a voice that
calls on and expands the values of political liberalism, as King's certainly
did in the United States and Churchill's did for Britain and the civilized
world.

Feminism, as a serious development within political liberalism, has been
of growing importance since the liberal political revolutions of the late
eighteenth century, a development reflected in the American struggles
that stretch from the antebellum abolitionist feminists to the recognition
of many of the central claims of justice of feminism under current judicial interpretations of U.S. constitutional law.[6] I analyze the ethical voice
of Garrison, Tolstoy, Gandhi, King, and Churchill as arising, importantly,
in relationship to such developments. Feminism is itself an elaboration of
the principles of political liberalism, as the antebellum abolitionist feminists clearly saw. All these men drew implicitly on these principles when,
as men, they found their ethical voices through criticism of a conception
of patriarchal manhood that legitimated violence as a response to insults,
upholding a code of honor that rationalized forms of structural injustice.
Each of them struggled to a sense of ethical voice, developed on the basis
of the authority of women's voices, that put them in critical opposition
to dominant stereotypes of manhood and thus womanhood. What is so
striking is the power this ethical voice had for all these men, the courage
(inspired by the moral experience of women) they showed in drawing
out its implications, and the price they were willing to pay to follow its
demands. A contemporary feminism will be richer and more profound
when it is able to understand the place of these remarkable men in its
project and when it sees the ethical power of its project in terms of the
price these men have borne to do justice, as they understood justice, to
its liberating insights.

Such a feminism focuses on the impact of unjust gender stereotypes
not only on the voices of women and the men traditionally regarded as

5

feminine (gay men) but also, sometimes ferociously and even catastrophi-cally, on the voices of straight men, rigidly holding them into conform-ity with the requirements of patriarchal authority (deriving from the hierarchical relationships of sons to fathers). These impacts on men and women have been brilliantly investigated in important works on the effect of patriarchy on mothering, including those of Dorothy Dinner-stein and Nancy Chodorow.[7] What this book studies in some depth is a group of remarkable men who did something very difficult for men in such situations to do: they resisted the role accorded patriarchal author-ity in order to follow an ethical voice that arose from the authority they accorded the usually marginalized voices of women, in particular the voices of their mothers or maternal caretakers that placed an ethical value on nonviolent care. At the center of my account is the way these men stayed in real relationship to these women and their voices and how they placed the ethical weight that they did on those voices, which sometimes operated under the radar of patriarchy. Women's voices are often accorded such authority by their sons through the hidden transcript of a personal religion centering on an antipatriarchal interpretation of the life and teaching of Jesus of Nazareth.

My sense that there is an important, unrecognized connection be-tween liberal feminism, voice, and psychology in the life and works of these men arose from collaborative teaching with the developmental psy-chologist Carol Gilligan; with our students, we reflected on many of the texts under discussion in this volume. Gilligan's work is sometimes viewed as largely focusing on issues of gender-inflected voice in the develop-ment of women, but she has always been interested in comparable issues in the development of men. (Her first book, *In a Different Voice,* was originally to be a study of male Harvard students' ethical dilemmas about military service in Vietnam; she turned to the comparable study of ethi-cal dilemmas of a broad range of women, differently situated, in mak-ing the abortion decision when she lost her male sample after Richard Nixon ended the draft).[8] These interests in gender-inflected voice as such (in men as well as women) are quite clear in her recent *Birth of Plea-sure,* framed as a narrative about both Cupid and Psyche, with male and female sexual voices coming into relationship.[9] Our conversations—between a long-married woman with three sons and a gay man in a partnership of some thirty years—were and are a laboratory of experi-ments in voice and relationship, and they have led me to a discovery in the developmental psychology of the voice of certain men. This discovery—that the relationships these men had with their unusual mothers played a critical role in the development of their creative ethical voice—has been missed by others, I believe, in part because the very notion cuts against an ethics and psychology still dominated by patriarchal conceptions that hold such voice in men *must* be linked to other men (in particular, fathers). I use the word *discovery* to express my sense of genuine surprise at what I noticed, and here, I want to capture inductively my excitement at what I discovered, touching on how I came to this finding and what its importance might be. I begin with my order of discovery.

My interest in these five men arose from my work in the history, political theory, and law of constitutional democracy, in particular a long interpretive study of the role of antebellum radical abolitionism in understanding the American constitutional principles embodied in the Reconstruction Amendments.[10] My attention there was on the place of William Lloyd Garrison among these radical abolitionists, including his crucial impact on the development of abolitionist feminism.[11] I will, therefore, begin in chapter 1 with the issues of voice and resistance that I found in Garrison and those he inspired. I will also explore the ways in which these issues led me to develop the working hypothesis about his developmental psychology (including his mother's personal religion based on Jesus) and how this in turn caused me to choose and study the other men closely examined in this work.

(EoF)

27:38.84

7

CHAPTER ONE

Garrison and Antebellum Radical Abolitionism:
Political Theory and Psychology

William Lloyd Garrison, a journalist, was the leading figure among a small group of radical abolitionists who opposed not only slavery but also the cultural racism that they believed underpinned both slavery in the South and unjust forms of racial discrimination in the North.[1] If this stance were not radical enough, Garrison supported and encouraged the work of radical women such as Lydia Maria Child, who offered the most probing analysis of American racism in the antebellum period and carried the argument even further, into the unchartered territory of women's rights. Indeed, it was Garrison who encouraged and published the work of the Grimke sisters, Angelina and Sarah, that gave rise to abolitionist feminism—an ethical analysis of both racism and sexism as reflecting a common form of unjust moral slavery that was later to be elaborated by Lucretia Mott, Elizabeth Cady Stanton, and others; a variant of this analysis underlies the contemporary understanding of rights-based feminism.[2] Garrison supported a number of other radical causes, including nonresistance, the apparently pacifist view that violence was never justified in resisting injustice.[3] His advocacy of such unconventional views before the Civil War placed him well outside the dominant consensus even of antislavery thought. Of course, after the war, his views opposing slavery and racism became mainstream, and Abraham Lincoln (who regularly read his newspaper, *The Liberator*) had Garrison invited among the dignitaries attending the raising of the American flag over Fort Sumter to celebrate the end of the Civil War.[4]

Political Theory

What compelled me about Garrison was that his voice of resistance to forms of injustice sustained by violence was based on a liberal political theory that includes both a robust principle of free conscience and speech and a principle that condemns the political force of irrational prejudice (such as extreme religious intolerance and racism). The two principles are related in the following way.

The principle of free conscience and speech rests on the argument for universal toleration that was stated, in variant forms, by Pierre Bayle and John Locke.[5] That principle forbids a dominant religion or group from unreasonably depriving other groups of their rights of conscience and speech. A prominent feature of the argument for toleration is its claim that religious persecution corrupts conscience itself. Such corruption, a kind of self-induced blindness to the evils one inflicts, is considered a consequence of the political enforcement at large of a conception of religious truth that immunizes itself from independent criticism in terms of reasonable standards of thought and deliberation. Paradoxically, the more the tradition becomes seriously vulnerable to independent reasonable criticism (indeed, increasingly in rational need of such criticism), the more it is likely to generate forms of political irrationalism (including the scapegoating of outcast dissenters) in order to secure allegiance. The worst ravages of anti-Semitism illustrate this paradox of intolerance. Precisely when the dominant religious tradition gave rise to the most reasonable internal doubt (for example, about transubstantiation), these doubts were displaced from reasonable discussion and debate into blatant political irrationalism against one of the more conspicuous, vulnerable, and innocent groups of dissenters (centering on fantasies of the ritual eating of human flesh that expressed the underlying worries about transubstantiation).[6]

The second liberal principle condemns the unjust force in politics of extreme religious intolerance such as anti-Semitism and any form of irrationalist prejudice that arises in the same way (because such irrationalist prejudices rationalize systematic violations of the first principle as well as other principles guaranteeing basic human rights). I call this pattern of structural injustice moral slavery, and I analyze how and why constitutional principles have progressively condemned a politics actuated not only by anti-Semitism but also by ethnic prejudice (including racism), sexism, and homophobia.[7] In all these cases, whole classes of persons have been traditionally excluded from the equal respect derived from basic human rights such as conscience, speech, intimate life, and work on the grounds of dehumanizing stereotypes. And in a viciously unjust circularity, the force of these stereotypes has derived from a tradition of subordination that refused to accord persons respect for their basic human rights. The claim of an analogy among such prejudices (for example, racism and sexism) lies in the similar method of structural injustice inflicted in both cases, namely, "that others have controlled the power to define one's existence."[8] I call this injustice moral slavery because a category of persons, subject to this injustice, has been culturally dehumanized (as nonbearers of human rights) to rationalize their servile status and roles. To cite one example, the long history of Christian Europe's restrictions on Jews was rationalized by Augustine, among others, in the quite explicit terms of slavery: "The Jew is the slave of the Christian."[9]

One important feature of the struggle against any single form of moral slavery (for instance, racism) is that it tends, on grounds of principle, to link its protest to related forms of moral slavery (for instance, sexism), a point central to Garrison's politics of resistance. Thus, the American struggle against racism culminated not only in the constitutional condemnation of segregated education but in antimiscegenation laws as well.[10] Antimiscegenation laws had come to bear this interpretation as a consequence of the Supreme Court's endorsement of the view of the unjust cultural construction of racism first suggested by Garrison's follower Lydia Maria Child in 1833 and importantly elaborated by Ida Wells-Barnett in 1892.[11] Wells-Barnett analyzed Southern racism after emancipation in these terms sustained by antimiscegenation laws and related practices, including lynching.[12] The point of such laws and practices was to condemn not only all interracial marriages (the focus of Child's analysis) but also the legitimacy of all sexual relations (marital and otherwise) between white women and black men; in contrast, illicit relations between white men and black women were, if not legal, certainly socially acceptable or even normative. The asymmetry was rationalized in terms of gender stereotypes: a sectarian sexual and romantic idealized mythology of asexual white women and a corresponding devaluation (indeed, dehumanization) of black women and men as sexually animalistic. Illicit sexual relations of white men with black women were consistent with this political epistemology and thus were tolerable. Both licit and illicit consensual relations of black men with white women were not and thus were ideologically transformed into violent rapes, punishable by lynching. The thought that could not be spoken, for it flouted the concept of the idealizing pedestal on which white women were placed, was that white women had sexual desires at all, let alone sexual desires for black men.

Both Harriet Jacobs (supported by Child as her editor) and Ida Wells-Barnett had analyzed this injustice from the perspective of black women who had experienced its indignities firsthand. Jacobs's slave narrative, *Incidents in the Life of a Slave Girl,*[13] told the story, under the pseudonym Linda Brent, of the indignities she suffered under slavery, her moral revolt against them (leading her to hide for seven years in a small garret), and her eventual escape to freedom in the North. Jacobs importantly examined the role of slaveowning women from the perspective of the slave. Her portrait of the slaveowner's wife (Mrs. Flint) explored "her constant suspicion and malevolence" (31). Pridefully virtuous on her idealized pedestal of Southern womanhood, Mrs. Flint denied any virtue to a woman slave; indeed, "it is deemed a crime in her to wish to be virtuous" (31). The basis of marriage in a slaveholding family was hypocrisy and denial, with white women treated contemptuously as pets on a very tight leash: "the secrets of slavery are concealed like those of the Inquisition"(35). To Brent's certain knowledge, Dr. Flint was "the father of eleven slaves" (35), but the reality was known and not known; as Mrs. Chesnut, a southern white woman of this period, confided to her diary, "Every lady tells you who is the father of all the Mulatto children in every body's household, but those in her own, she seems to think drop from the clouds or pretends so to think."[14] White slaveholding women themselves sustained this mythology by falsely idealizing their virtue and denigrating that of slaves, whose unjust situation, in Jacobs's view, made virtue unreasonably difficult. Thus, Jacobs laid the foundation for later antiracist and antisexist analysis of the role that unjust gender stereotypes, based on the abridgment of basic human rights, played in the dehumanization not only of black women but of white women as well. Resistance to such gender stereotypes often makes possible resistance to forms of structural injustice.

Psychology

The present study resulted from asking myself further questions about Garrison as a man, in particular how his radical resisting voice could have arisen and flourished in a man of his period and place. The impetus to the study came when I found that Garrison's remarkable voice, resisting dominant conceptions of patriarchal manhood that violently

p. 12

targeted such a voice, only made sense when seen as motivated by Garrison's drive to stay in relationship to the antipatriarchal voice of his mother, Frances Lloyd Garrison, and other women who spoke in that voice. Put another way, at the center of Garrison's radical antebellum liberalism of thought and speech lay the need to maintain relationship to his extraordinary mother and forge and sustain comparable relationships with other women. Frances had broken with her Anglican parents to embrace the more personal Christian religion of dissenters, and she herself spoke extemporaneously at prayer meetings (Mayer, *All on Fire,* 5–7); she had married Abijah Garrison, and the couple had moved from Nova Scotia to Newburyport, Massachusetts, where Frances had joined "a populist insurgency that elevated the individual conscience and disdained the ordained clergy, cherished the words of the Bible, and spurned formal theology" (11). With her mariner husband at sea, Frances, the mother of four children, formed a close friendship with another married woman, Martha Farnham, who led prayer meetings that Frances attended. After Abijah abandoned his family, Frances "seemed indomitable to her son, but her churchfolk knew the heaviness of her heart. Her sorrows and her faith made her eloquent in prayer, and she became a familiar voice in the community. 'God's people is a praying people,' she believed, and the weekly female prayer meetings stood as 'the very gate of Heaven to our souls'" (14). Later, when Frances had moved with her son to Baltimore, "she established a women's prayer meeting—the first among evangelicals in Baltimore—and presided over it with passion and eloquence" (21). The son always remembered his mother's "powerful voice in its torrents of pious exhortation" (13). His mother had also given him a compelling counterexample to the dominant racism of his culture in writing of the kindly care she had received from a black woman named Henny: "'Although a slave to man, [she is] yet a free-born soul by the grace of God,' Sister Garrison declared, and she admonished her son to 'remember her for your poor mother's sake'" (69). When Garrison came to recognize the wrongness of cultural racism, a recognition he expressed in his book attacking colonization (the only book he published),[15] it was not only through abstract argument but also through his experience in Boston of the black religious community.[16] Later, on hearing the black woman preacher Maria Stewart, he heard a voice he "knew so well from his mother."[17]

Garrison's developmental psychology led him to place value on his mother's prophetic ethical voice and thus to identify himself as, like her, a preacher inspired by the life and teaching of Jesus of Nazareth.[18] Such Christian speaking witness included, following the example of Jesus, enduring violence. In 1835, after addressing an abolitionist meeting, he was beaten and dragged by a rope, his life at threat, through the streets of Boston by a lynch mob enraged over his radical views.[19] Garrison's patient endurance of this violence was very much inspired by the abolitionist women who had accompanied him; as he put it, "Such a mob—30 ladies routed and . . . demolished by 4,000 men."[20] He had earlier addressed the members of the mob, who were disrupting the abolitionist meeting, in terms that reveal how much the issue of protesting voice had become, for him, a criticism of the conventional understanding of manhood: "His lame joke, 'If any of you gentlemen are ladies in disguise, give me your names . . . and you can take your seats in the meeting,' further dramatized the issue as one that pitted Christian meekness against established power, feminine sentiment against masculine patriotism, with Garrison identified with the women."[21] The importance of this issue to Garrison was dramatized at the World Anti-Slavery Convention in London in the summer of 1840, where he publicly resisted the convention's rule—adopted despite the strong objections of some American leaders—that only male delegates could be seated. Garrison, in protest, sat in the galleries with women, including future feminist leaders Lucretia Mott and Elizabeth Cady Stanton.[22]

Garrison had clearly come to develop and express a sense of his own free ethical voice in protest of slavery and racism by challenging a conventional sense of manhood that unleashed violence on any threat to its sense of honor, an American expression of codes of patriarchal honor.[23] His growing commitment to nonviolence tracked closely his sense that the enormity of the evil of American slavery and racism required both men and women to resist the violent repression of voice that was demanded by a patriarchal manhood threatened by criticism of slavery, racism, and sexism in American society. Garrison nurtured and supported such a free ethical voice in himself and in a woman of the North (Lydia Maria Child) and two women of the South (the sisters Angelina and Sarah Grimke), authors of pathbreaking works that offered an ethical criticism of the linkages between unjust racial and gender stereotypes.[24]

// Nonviolent Resistance

Nonresistance appears to have been an important common position of radical abolitionists such as Garrison, Child, and the Grimke sisters. Garrison achieved his distinctive moral voice based antipatriarchally on the moral authority of his mother's voice. For this reason, his independence from dominant patriarchal conventions took the remarkable form of a passionate support for and interest in the free ethical voices of women. Garrison the journalist thus sought out and offered a radically antipatriarchal resonance chamber for the free voices of women, Child and the Grimkes included. Such women, through their relationships with Garrison, trusted and developed their own sense of free ethical voice, raising increasingly profound questions about how sexism and racism rested on a common structural evil (what I have called moral slavery).

There is certainly a criticism of conventionally accepted political violence implicit in these struggles, but it is not obvious that the criticism reflected an ethically grounded form of pacifism like that of Garrison's American contemporary Adin Ballou.[25] There is, rather, a more specific focus to the criticism, namely, on the forms of political violence, intimidation, and social sanctions imposed on any voice that contested the patriarchal demands of gender stereotypes. These forms of violence, broadly understood, included not only killing (in the case of Elijah Lovejoy), beatings (Garrison), and public abuse, insult, and thrown objects (the Grimke sisters) but also a range of social sanctions, including withdrawal of support (Child), shaming and bullying, contempt and opprobrium, and the like. Nonviolence was rooted in a criticism of the role such patriarchally rooted violence pervasively played in both personal and political psychology in antebellum America, directed against any voice in a woman or man that would reasonably test the unjust terms of dominant patriarchal conceptions of political authority, including extreme religious intolerance, racism, and sexism. The repudiation of violence in this domain made it possible to speak in and hear a new kind of free ethical voice. Garrison's nonresistance spoke to women in particular because it dignified their ethical voice and intelligence as equals. It made possible new forms of democratic political action in which women emerged as equal moral and political agents in collaboration with men.[26]

This disarming of patriarchal manhood may also have opened to Garrison a psychology of manhood more responsive to the humanity of women *personally,* as well as politically. Garrison was a companionate husband and a tender and supportive father: "He took upon himself 'burdens which most husbands and fathers shun,' . . . 'His shining quality was that of nurse,' Fanny [his daughter] emphasized, feeding and tending the children with such 'unbounded love' and skill that the little ones were 'drawn to him as if by a magnet.'"[27] People who had only read Garrison's provocative and uncompromising rhetoric as an abolitionist journalist expected to encounter an intransigent, difficult man; they were shocked on meeting the person. One notable example was Harriet Beecher Stowe, who "confided that while she had once considered Garrison a wolf in sheep's clothing, she now knew that he was really a lamb in a wolf's disguise."[28]

In the harmonious and hopeful days of 1833, the Declaration of Sentiments of the American Anti-Slavery Convention, authored by Garrison, could articulate a common abolitionist view of the relationship between political theory and the Constitution.[29] According to that document, slavery was morally wrong, though constitutionally protected. Abolitionists would limit advocacy for change to making moral arguments; all other means were "carnal weapons" and therefore illegitimate.[30] That claim may have made some larger political sense in 1833 when abolitionists might reasonably have believed that American constitutional principles of free speech would be extended on fair terms to them. But the age of Andrew Jackson (with its repression of abolitionist advocacy both by law and by mobs sponsored by civic leaders) led many Americans, including Lincoln, to question whether public opinion still adequately sustained constitutional principles and institutions, including fundamental rights of free speech.[31]

The key to the early insistence of moral abolitionists such as Garrison that they eschewed "all carnal weapons" was their clear-eyed public statement that, absent immediate abolition, slaveowners "*know* that oppression must cause rebellion."[32] A clear statement of the legitimacy of revolution was rendered at least strategically palatable by Garrison's apparently anarchist denial that coercion could ever be justified in principle for any cause or reason. Garrison's position may, however, have been even more strategic: nonresistance was a way of denying the inference that any fundamental challenge to the justice of American constitutional institutions could be ruled out as subversive advocacy (ending slavery), when such advocacy was precisely what the American public needed most to hear. Garrison was making a valid point about the scope of free speech protection under American constitutionalism, a view now judicially accepted in the United States.[33] Part of the reason why the notion is accepted is that the antebellum period so conspicuously displayed the disastrous consequences of a conception of free speech that rules out subversive advocacy of that type from the scope of constitutionally protected speech. Garrison's practice as a journalist and advocate is of such enduring value to American constitutionalism because he insisted on this point. That he himself did not conceive nonresistance, in contrast to Adin Ballou,[34] as an ultimately pacifist position is suggested, as the nation moved to secession and civil war, by Garrison's shift in his position on nonresistance, especially when the conflict led to the abolition of slavery.[35]

Garrison's great interest (and that of the radical abolitionists he led and inspired) was the role accorded nonviolence in understanding the proper scope of free speech and in new forms of democratic resistance to injustice that were later to inspire, for example, Tolstoy and Gandhi.[36] Garrison was no philosopher and had no formal education, but his journalistic skills and his personality empowered new forms of resistance, notably, "nonresistance societies" in which women participated equally with men.[37] These societies were, in fact, new forms of resistance to injustice that empowered the moral and political agency of women on equal terms with men. In founding such a nonresistance society in 1838, Garrison told his wife, Helen, that it "took its mandate from the Sermon on the Mount" (Matt. 5:38–39).[38] Its inspiration was the life and teaching of Jesus on the repudiation of patriarchal violence, which Garrison and the radical abolitionist women allied with him saw so conspicuously all about them—not only in Southern slavery and violence but also in the Northern mobs of Boston and even, eventually, on the floor of Congress when a leading abolitionist senator, Charles Sumner of Massachusetts, was beaten nearly to death by a Southerner.[39]

In the antebellum period, nonresistance activities took a variety of forms, including the refusal of Frederick Douglass to sit in a Jim Crow car on a railroad in the North and refusals to comply with the requirements of the Fugitive Slave Act in the name of what the New England Anti-Slavery Convention called its "theory of civil disobedience."[40] In 1848, the Concord writer Henry David Thoreau lectured in the town lyceum on the topic "The Rights and Duties of the Individual in Relation to Government," expressing his views that "[if a law] requires you to be the agent of injustice to another, then, I say, break the law. Let your life be a counter friction to stop the machine"; the lecture was published as an essay the next year.[41] Born of Thoreau's opposition to slavery and the Mexican War (leading to a refusal to pay taxes and imprisonment) and informed by the Garrisonian spirit of his household, the lecture was a passionate protest against the loss of moral voice that allowed such injustices to continue.

Thoreau would never have joined nonresistance societies of the sort Garrison sponsored. His later enthusiastic support of John Brown showed a position on legitimate political violence much closer to that of Theodore Parker than to that of Garrison, and his defense of resistance was grounded in an individual's refusal of complicity, not a more political empowerment of associational practices of resistance.[42] In his masterpiece, *Walden,* Thoreau wrote of higher laws, but for him they were laws discovered not through association but through an austere autarky.[43]

In contrast, Garrison's ethical genius was not only journalistic but also relational and associational, like that of Gandhi and King. My suggestion is that this genius was rooted in a developmental psychology in which, unlike more conventionally patriarchal men of his time, Garrison stayed in close relationship to his mother's prophetic ethical voice as well as the comparable voices of the abolitionist women he supported and inspired. Garrison's interest in securing a forum for these women's voices was more than an issue of the principle of free speech (though it was certainly that, too). It was also a conviction that something fundamental about the evil of American slavery and racism could *only* be learned by bringing the ethical voices of these women into the public discussion. Garrison was, to be sure, concerned with removing the forms of censorship that encumbered women's basic human and constitutional rights of free exercise of conscience and free speech. But he was also concerned with forging a cultural sense of resonance that strengthened women's otherwise traditionally silenced ethical voices, emboldening a creativity and brilliance of voice by being an audience that heard and valued that brilliance. All these women carried the argument into places Garrison could not himself have gone, seeing connections and drawing inferences that expressed and advanced humane intelligence about issues the culture could barely acknowledge, let alone discuss. His passion for truthful voice against lies took, then, the form of encouraging the voices of such women as crucially necessary for the truth to be spoken and heard, acknowledging their roles as ethical prophets. One masterpiece of ante-bellum American literature supports and illuminates my reading of Garrison's voice—Nathaniel Hawthorne's *The Scarlet Letter*.[44]

Hawthorne on Sexual Voice

My interest in Hawthorne's novel, published in 1850, centers on the way it treats prophetic ethical voice.[45] The novel is set in the harshly patriarchal Puritan community of seventeenth-century Boston. The novel's heroine, Hester Prynne, is married to an older man, Chillingworth, whom, as he well knows, she has never loved. During the long absence of her husband, Hester has a passionate love affair with her minister, Dimmesdale, leading to the birth of a daughter, Pearl. Dimmesdale conceals the affair, and Hester refuses to identify the father of her child to the community. Her punishment is a ritual of public shaming, requiring her to stand in public with an *A* on her dress and then wear the *A* through the rest of her life. Chillingworth returns as his wife is being punished and insists that she not tell anyone who he is. Suspicious that Dimmesdale had been his wife's lover, he forms a close friendship and living arrangement with the minister, both to confirm his suspicions and to inflict psychological and other punishment. Dimmesdale meets with Hester with a view to sailing abroad with her, but Chillingworth learns of their plan and proposes to join them. At the yearly election sermon, Dimmesdale finally publicly confesses his wrongdoing and, a broken man, dies. Hester and Pearl live abroad, but Hester eventually returns and becomes an esteemed member of the community. Pearl, who has married, continues to live abroad.

The narrative of *The Scarlet Letter* deals, of course, with a question—the punishment of an adulteress—that is the subject of John 8:1–11. In that passage, Jesus saves an adulteress from the death by stoning that was to be inflicted on her and indeed forgives her. Such violence is at the heart of patriarchy, and Jesus is, here and elsewhere, raising ethical questions about the force such patriarchal violence has in our lives. Hawthorne's *Scarlet Letter* reflects on an allegedly deeply Protestant Christian culture that both politically and personally perpetuates such violence—precisely the violence that Jesus of Nazareth questions. Hawthorne puts the question of love at the center of the novel because Hester, who comes to regard her loveless marriage to Chillingworth as her "crime" and his "fouler offense . . . than any . . . done him," loves Dimmesdale and the daughter of their union, Pearl.[46] Paradoxically, the only character in the novel who speaks with a prophetic authority, like that of Jesus, is Hester herself, and that is very much Hawthorne's point about how, if at all, we can any longer reasonably understand the life and teaching of Jesus.

Hawthorne's developmental history is similar to that of Garrison. He had a close and nurturing relationship with his mother and indeed married a woman, the artist Sophia Peabody, whose sister, Elizabeth, was a leading abolitionist feminist. Hawthorne had come to value the prophetic ethical voice of his mother and women generally, and he explores such voice in *The Scarlet Letter,* a book written in the period of recovery after his mother's death and his own resulting illness.[47] ⌐— 41.11.01

As the years pass, the community that had once condemned Hester Prynne to ignominy comes to admire her goodness to others in emergencies. Even the *A* she wears takes on a new public significance: "They said that it meant Able; so strong was Hester Prynne, with a woman's strength" (Hawthorne, *Scarlet Letter,* 141). An outcast from her community, Hester finds strength in her situation to question the "iron framework of reasoning" of its patriarchal religion and politics (143). Her line of thought is compared to "Ann Hutchinson, as the foundress of a religious sect. She might in one of her phases, have been a prophetess" in which "the same dark question often rose into her mind, with reference to the whole race of womanhood" (144). She questions whether gender arrangements are in the nature of things, querying if "as a first step, the whole system of society is to be torn down, and built up anew. Then, the very nature of the opposite sex, or its long hereditary habit, which has become like nature, is to be essentially modified, because women can be allowed to assume what seems a fair and suitable position" (144).

When Hester returns to New England, leaving her daughter abroad, the scarlet letter worn on her bosom "ceased to be a stigma which attracted the world's scorn and bitterness, and became a type of something to be sorrowed over, and looked upon with awe, yet with reverence too" (227). People now sought her counsel, and "she assured them . . . a new truth would be revealed, in order to establish the whole relation between man and woman on a surer ground of mutual happiness" (227). She no

43.32.19

longer supposes, as she had as a younger woman, "that she herself might be the destined prophetess," having "long since recognized the impossibility" (227). However, she still believes "the angel and apostle of the coming revelation must be a woman, . . . showing how sacred love should make us happy, by the truest test of a life successful to such an end!" (228).

Hester's search for prophetic ethical voice is Hawthorne's moving tribute to his relationship to his mother and the value he placed on her ethical voice, the psychological and moral inspiration of Garrisonian radical abolitionism, including that of the abolitionist feminists. Hawthorne, as great artists do, raises important questions that radical abolitionism was not yet prepared to address, in particular the role of free sexual voice in love.

The Psychology of Resistance

Hawthorne's romance suggests that any nontragic alternative will require taking seriously women's free sexual voice as women, and my study of Garrison has shown at least one man who had apparently found a way to open himself to the voices of women, with happy consequences for both his public life and his private life. Were there others? Do their lives, in contrast to Garrison's, reveal internal conflicts that clarify how and why such resistance is so difficult for men? The argument of this book is propelled forward by the evolving set of questions that arise from and are complicated by the evidence presented, including the final question posed by the Churchill chapter: are the problems in Tolstoy's and Gandhi's and King's relationships with women and their own sexuality reflective of an idealization of motherhood that in turn reflects the patriarchal split between good and bad women?

This book explores my answers to these questions in the lives and psychology of four other men, all of whom have an important place in the history of constitutional democracy as voices of resistance to fundamental injustices such as extreme religious intolerance (anti-Semitism) and racism. What I discovered was a developmental pattern of voice in all these men, a struggle for their distinctively creative ethical voices (voices that resisted the violence of patriarchal manhood) that arose from their relationships with their mothers or maternal caretakers and was often later developed in relationships with other women—their wives or followers. What I also discovered, however, was the complexity of such men's relationships with maternal caretakers and how important the quality of these relationships was, in particular how idealized or nonidealized these relationships were. Hawthorne's suggestion that a failure to take women's sexual voices seriously might cripple the psychology of otherwise moral men was confirmed, as we shall see.

To the extent an interpretation of Christian texts played an important role in the development of the ethical voice of four of the men studied here (Garrison, Tolstoy, Gandhi, and King), the interpretive authority arose in relationship to the voices of such women, who found in these texts an ethical voice often quite different from that of established Christian churches. These women, speaking in a different voice from dominant patriarchal models, gave authority to a comparable voice in their sons, with consequences we must examine. There is no reason to believe that such a personal religion of women is limited to Christianity. Leila Ahmed has powerfully shown, for instance, that a personal religion of this type exists among Islamic women, and it is a religion quite different from dominant patriarchal models of Islamic religious authority.[48] The voices of these women, rooted in their own moral experiences as women and maternal caretakers, gave rise to what James Scott has called the hidden transcripts (for example, a woman's highly personal sense of Christian religion or, in Churchill's mother, a sense of sexual voice) through which subordinated groups preserve a sense of ethical resistance.[49] The women's antipatriarchal voices were sufficiently under the patriarchal radar to avoid public acknowledgment, but they riveted the attention of their sons, enabling them to find their own voices creatively in giving public form to insights derived from these transcripts, empowering new means of public resistance for both men and women. How should we understand this psychology?

If gender (as traditionally understood in terms of the binary of man and woman) were a wholly rigid and impermeable aspect of our psychological identities as men or women, there would be, contrary to fact, no psychological basis for the resistance of a person such as Garrison to structural injustice, since so much of that resistance requires resistance as well to conventional gender stereotypes (embodied in codes of honor). Yet Garrison did resist in ways that challenged dominant codes of male honor. I will first address the force of such codes and then turn to developing a hypothesis about the psychology of the resistance offered to those codes by Garrison and other men like him. (EoF)

(P) p. 22   Men, Honor, and Obligatory Violence

Honor codes exemplify the unjust demands of patriarchy on the psychology of men—a patriarchal manhood that places sons and daughters under the hierarchical authority of fathers.[50] These demands take the form of an obligatory violence directed against any voice that challenges in particular the strict social controls over women's sexuality (including arranged marriages), controls that are required to advance patriarchal dynastic ends, to wit, virginity before marriage and monogamous fidelity after marriage. A father's or brother's or lover's or husband's sense of honor, as a man, is defined in terms of his control over the chastity or fidelity of women, irrespective of personal feeling or desire. Historically, any challenge to this control was an insult that triggered violence, as a condition of manhood under patriarchy. Such control was, in dominantly face-to-face and largely illiterate Mediterranean societies, understood in terms of how matters publicly appeared, so that men were vulnerable to dishonor because women (often in fact quite innocent of sexual relations) merely appeared less strictly modest and reticent in their relations with men.[51] Such masculine dishonor, sometimes arising only from gossip, required violence—the killing of wives or daughters.[52] A man's most intimate feelings and relations were, under the code of honor, subject to rules that rested as much on the repression of his personal feeling and voice as they did on those of women.

Codes of honor thus understood are aspects of patriarchal institutions (resting on precisely the mythological idealization of gender stereotypes) that sustain forms of structural injustice through violence directed against any challenge to the terms of such gender stereotypes.[53] Within the framework of patriarchy, women do not exist as persons with moral individuality, let alone sexual agency and subjectivity, independent of the roles assigned them by patriarchy. The patriarchal culture of nineteenth-century Italy illuminates the kind of tragic losses and repressed voices that objectifying gender stereotypes, as a general matter, both inflicted and covered over, namely, the sacrifice of children born out of wedlock.[54] The honor code condemned as intrinsically shameful both sexual relations out of wedlock and the illegitimate children often born of such relations.[55] Enforced by Catholic priests and the police, the code rationalized both bullying unwed mothers to abandon children to public institutions and effectively imprisoning some of these women in these institutions, in some cases as compulsory wet nurses to children other than their own. The babies often died (Kertzer, *Sacrifices for Honor,* 125). Families sometimes protested these separations, citing the mothers' "infinite grief" and arguing that the practice robbed a mother "of the dearest object of her heart." Such pleas express the traumatizing emotional losses that must have been widespread (56). But such losses, consistent with the political psychology of patriarchy, were often not acknowledged but rather covered over with gender-stereotypical idealizations; thus the foundlings in Naples were idealized as "children of the Madonna," although most of them in fact died (107, 122). Meanwhile, their real mothers, if they were wet nurses in the foundling homes, were "treated as livestock" (148).

The atrocity of these patriarchal practices rests on such mythological idealizations in terms of gender stereotypes, denying the personal feeling and voice of the individuals most afflicted by the stereotypes. The high rates of both illegitimacy and abandonment of infants during this period were common knowledge, yet the underlying emotional trauma and loss could be given no voice and weight (55). The tragic music dramas of Verdi so absorbed Italians and others because they gave powerful expression to widespread feelings that could not otherwise be acknowledged.[56]

The Italian system of infant abandonment, echoing the abandonment of Oedipus, illustrates a larger point about the power of idealizing gender stereotypes over the men and women subject to the structural injustice of patriarchy. The unjust power of these stereotypes requires a supporting political psychology that must, in its nature, bury through disassociation the personal emotions of traumatic loss that the hegemonic power of the stereotypes requires.

The developmental psychology that makes possible a conception of manhood that can sustain such patriarchal demands requires the traumatic separation of young boys from their mothers, in contrast to the developmental continuity in such relationships allowed to girls until early adolescence.[57] The marks of this trauma are not only loss of intimate voice and memory but also the kinds of disassociation from intimate relationship that patriarchal manhood requires. Idealizing stereotypes are inherently objectifying, supported by a psychology of disassociation that lends itself to the forms of violence required to hold such stereotypes in place in patterns of structural injustice.

The honor code thus understood is sustained by a system of physical and psychological violence triggered by deviance from its demands; these external demands enter into the psyches of men and women through their loss of protesting voice and their consequent vulnerability to shaming by any appearance of deviating from the honor code and the expression of such shaming in violence, whether physical or psychological. The psychology of this kind of shaming is in conflict with a democratic ethics of reciprocity based on the free and equal voice of all persons, an ethics that expresses itself in ideals of equal respect as the foundation of friendship and love reflecting free and equal voice. The requirements of this ethics enters into our psyches through the experience of love and respect consistent with its demands, and it shows itself in guilt and remorse when one culpably violates the demands of equal respect and the forms of love it makes possible.[58]

Democratic Manhood

This alternative in developmental psychology may underlie the turn to resistance that I discovered first in Garrison and then in each of the other men examined in this work. The story is by no means always the same in each case, and a number of the men, as we shall see, certainly lived with some degree of contradiction between their overall protest of structural injustice and the forms of patriarchy they still allowed to dominate parts of their lives. But there is strikingly similar alternative developmental psychology in their lives that made it psychologically possible for them to adopt a more democratic conception of manhood, one much more sensitive to issues of unjustly suppressed voice (including the voices of women) than is patriarchal manhood.

What is remarkably discernible in the lives of Garrison, Tolstoy, Gandhi, King, and Churchill is that each man, instead of experiencing the more typical developmental trauma of early boyhood separation from a mother, stayed in significant intimate relationship to the loving moral voice, care, and concern of a maternal person (whether a biological mother or an aunt, as in the case of Tolstoy); further, each of these men placed continuing value and weight on the voice and insights of the maternal caretaker as a significant counterweight to traditional patriarchal demands. How should we understand this common experience among these men and its links, if any, to their turn to resistance?

Certainly, Virginia Woolf in *Three Guineas* had suggested links between women's claims to voice and resistance to political violence: "[We are] fighting the tyranny of the patriarchal state as you are fighting the tyranny of the Fascist state."[59] Sara Ruddick has recently refined Woolf's insight in her pathbreaking inquiry into the voices of mothers that have been traditionally silenced by patriarchy.[60] Ruddick is well aware that loving care is, has been, and should be done by men but chooses, for reasons of exposition, to call all such care "maternal work."[61] This work has, for Ruddick, three tasks: preservation, growth, and acceptability, all of which require a loving care that she, drawing on Iris Murdoch and Simone Weil, calls "attentive love."[62] Ruddick certainly sees the complex strands in this work, some of which may be distorted by narcissism or guided by patriarchal aims. But she insists that we take seriously at least the strands of such maternal practice of intimate voice and responsiveness in which mother and child can read one another's human world well after the mother-child attunement of infancy.[63] Ruddick's brilliant insight is to identify in this maternal care the practices of resistance required to maintain connection in the right developmental way, including sustaining life and growth, renouncing one's lethal powers to nurture the vulnerably powerless, limiting aggression to maintain connection, and even being willing to suffer oneself as a developmental strategy of moral education.[64] Implicit in this practice are four ideals: renunciation, nonviolent resistance (where feasible), reconciliation, and peacekeeping.[65]

My hypothesis about the alternative developmental psychology under examination here is that the five men I have studied shared a common developmental psychology that, in contrast to the traumatic break with mothers required by the Oedipal patriarchal story in early boyhood, prominently included staying in significant relationship to the loving voice and care of maternal caretakers, understood as displaying the features of attentive love and implicit ideals of resistance that Ruddick describes so well. This story may be much more common than Sigmund Freud supposed even in his own period, let alone today when, as Ruddick's work shows, feminist women are bringing their convictions to bear on both their private lives as mothers and their public lives as citizens. The unjust political demands of patriarchy would, to the extent patriarchy is hegemonic or at least still very powerful, show themselves by the attempt to suppress or marginalize the developmental experiences that would psychologically threaten the stability of patriarchy.[66]

But of course, not all persons with this background will make of it what the men studied in this volume did. The demands of patriarchy can lead people to repudiate or deny or marginalize psychological propensities that do not appear to have any legitimacy or ethical appeal. To make sense of why some men, among them those I examine here, rather unusually (for men) acted on their sense of psychological truth, we need to address how and why they held on to their sense of lived truth in relationship as one of life's most enduring and sustaining humane values, and were motivated for this reason to resist unjust patterns of structural injustice.

The stability of structural injustice requires, as we have seen, the violent repression of any voices that would reasonably question its authority or legitimacy, which includes the voices not only of women but of men as well. The vehicle of this psychology for men takes the form of a sense of manhood defined by codes of honor. Such codes vary. They do not, for instance, always take the precise form of the Mediterranean honor code discussed earlier; under Icelandic honor codes, to cite one example, "virginity was a non-issue," as men, not women, were placed on a pedestal.[67] But apparently, such codes pervasively enforce gender idealizations in the form of "the widespread presence of something recognizable as the heroic ethic from the cold North Atlantic to the Arabian desert."[68] Their force rests on trauma and disassociation, a psychology prone to violence against any threat to the gender idealizations that sustain structural injustice.[69] Responses to such threats include, as in the early republican period in the United States and in the antebellum South, the practice of dueling to settle insults to masculine honor.[70] James Gilligan's important study of violent criminals shows us how alive this culture of insult to manhood and violence remains today, and Chris Hedges, Mark Juergensmeyer, and others show how powerful it remains as the trigger to ethnic violence and genocide in the former Yugoslavia and elsewhere, including the resort to violence by Islamic and other fundamentalists.[71] Forms of these codes clearly existed in antebellum America, Imperial Russia, Gandhi's India, King's America, and Churchill's Britain.

My hypothesis is that men like those studied in this work resist such disassociation by holding on to the psychological truth of loving association experienced in their relationships of loving care with maternal caretakers. If patriarchal manhood armors itself through disassociation against the voices and feelings that reasonably contest gender idealizations, these men self-consciously disarm themselves of the role violence plays in traditional manhood as a way of remaining truthful to personal voice, relationships, and experiences, with consequences to themselves and others that we must investigate. Four of the men in this study—Garrison, Tolstoy, Gandhi, and King—connected such truth to nonviolence, drawing on the ethical voice of maternal caretakers who gave a quite different interpretation to Christian texts than established churches did. These women spoke in a different voice about religious texts, imparting to their sons what James Scott has called the hidden transcripts (in this case, a highly personal sense of religion rooted in their experiences as women and mothers) through which subordinated groups preserve a sense of resistance to their subordination.[72] These men found their ethical voices through original interpretations of these hidden transcripts, as I explore at some length in the case studies to follow. In this context, it is important to see what it was in the life and teachings of Jesus of Nazareth that these women and their sons, certainly outsiders to the dominant tradition of established Christian churches, interpreted as authority for their original ethical voices. Their interpretations were not hallucinations but made good interpretive sense; indeed, they were, as I try to show in the following discussion, remarkably close to some of the best work now being done on the historical Jesus. It is useful to make this point now because it suggests that antipatriarchal voices may bring our psyches to greater truth not only in politics (as I demonstrate in later chapters) but in religion as well.

Why Jesus?

Ten years before Henry David Thoreau lectured his townspeople on "resistance to civil government," William Lloyd Garrison had called for resistance to unjust laws on the model of Jesus of Nazareth: "If I violate it [the law], I will submit to the penalty, unresistingly, in imitation of Christ, and his apostles, and the holy martyrs."[73] Leo Tolstoy justified his political pacifism on the grounds of the "commandments of the Sermon on the Mount"; Gandhi acknowledged the same inspiration: "If then I had to face only the Sermon on the Mount and my own interpretation of it, I should not hesitate to say, 'Oh yes, I am a Christian'"; and Martin Luther King defended nonviolence by appealing to "these very arresting words flowing from the lips of our Lord and Master: . . . 'Love your enemies, bless them that curse you.'"[74]

The imitation of Christ is a long tradition within Christianity, but it has conventionally been conceived in terms of patience in enduring suffering, not resistance or disobedience.[75] Certainly, a general pacifist position (condemning all uses of violence) was not uncommon in the early church, and it persisted later in the peace churches (of the Quakers and others) and has important advocates today.[76] But the arguments for nonviolence under study here were not always grounded in such pacifism, as Garrison showed when he accepted the legitimacy of the Civil War and Martin Luther King showed when he accepted the legitimacy of defensive, as opposed to preemptively aggressive, self-defense.[77] Nor are these views always grounded in any Christian theology or even in the divinity of Jesus, both of which Tolstoy, a Voltairean rationalist, certainly denied, as did Gandhi.[78]

These thinkers found in the life and teachings of Jesus something much of the Christian tradition did not. My interest in Jesus arose from the interpretive sense these four important advocates of nonviolence made of Jesus, as the authority for their positions. My study of them reasonably led to a further question: did they offer better readings of Jesus's life and teachings than the mainstream Christian tradition did? It was certainly a necessary condition of the originality of their readings that they were skeptical, on grounds of the argument for toleration, of the ways in which the dominant interpretive traditions of Christianity had so formed themselves through a corrupt alliance with political authorities such as the Roman Empire. This skepticism led them to identify and condemn the role anti-Semitism played in the formation of the Christian tradition (unjustly displacing responsibility for the death of Jesus from Rome to the Jews). To this extent, they anticipated the remarkable contemporary consensus among scholars (including Catholics, Protestants, Jews, and agnostics) that recovers the historical Jesus and is motivated by a long overdue skepticism, crystallized by the Holocaust, about the role anti-Semitism played in the formation of the Christian tradition, including the writing of the Gospels themselves (downplaying, for example, Jesus's Jewish background and roots).[79] None of our four advocates of nonviolence knew of this consensus (only King, while at Crozer Theological Seminary, had studied early forms of this scholarship, see chapter 4), but the fact that their original readings were more consistent with good history than much of the dominant Christian tradition supports the ethical power and truthfulness of those readings. The insights of the

p. 29

scholarly consensus bring out certain features of the historical Jesus, as a pious Jew, that also arrested the attention of these thinkers, affording religious and ethical authority to their path to nonviolence. Both the value placed on free moral voice by their political theory and the value they placed on maternal voice as having authority were interpreted as valid because these men were absorbed, indeed compelled, by a life and teaching of Jesus of Nazareth that gave a religious and ethical sense to both these values—a reading of Jesus that, importantly, their maternal caretakers could and sometimes did passionately share. It is certainly plausible that their notably antipatriarchal approach to the interpretation of Jesus may show us a way, as Christians or non-Christians, to make better sense of Jesus's moral authority, one more consistent as well with a reasonable contemporary understanding of the historical Jesus. If so, our study of these men bears not only on our understanding of vital movements of resistance to injustice but also on the enduring authority of the religious and ethical figure who inspired them, as he has many others. For Christians in particular, our inquiry may cast light on the moving appeal of Christianity, as both a historical and an ethical religion.

The contemporary scholarly consensus crucially sees the historical Jesus as a pious, learned Jew of his culture and period, acutely conscious of the prophetic tradition of moral protest that he elaborated, whose life had analogues in his period (Honi, Hanina, and others) and whose teachings were largely well within the range of views current in intertestamental Judaism, including the influence on Jesus's teaching of Hillel.[80] One feature of such pious Judaism was that it essentially focused on the trusting relationship with God conceived as a loving, caring person, not on the theological propositions of later Christian belief.[81] In this connection, Geza Vermes powerfully shows how Jesus avoided addressing God with "the divine epithet, 'King'" that was predominant "in ancient Jewish literature"; rather "the Synoptic Gospels depict him as addressing God, or speaking of him, as 'Father' in some sixty instances, and at least once place on his lips the intimate Aramaic title, *Abba*" (Daddy or Dad).[82] God was addressed as an approachable, solicitous, and loving father, one concerned above all with staying in relationship to his erring children, those outcasts whom "'decent' Jews despised and relegated to pariah status."[83] To a critical query about his joining a meal given by a publican and attended by many of his colleagues, Jesus justified his presence by identifying them as those who were spiritually ill and needed a physician (Mark 2:17; Matt. 9:12; Luke 5:31). There is also a specific report that he allowed a prostitute ("a woman of the city who was a sinner" [Luke 7:37, 39; cf. Mark 14:3; Matt. 26:6–7]) to anoint him. Jesus's practice of accepting the companionship of the despised was sufficiently common knowledge to endow him with the name "friend of tax-collectors and sinners" (Matt. 11:19; Luke 7:34). If his mission as healer and exorcist was for the sick and the dispossessed, he understood himself as primarily bringing God's love to those in the most spiritual need: "I came not to call the righteous, but sinners" (Mark 2:17; Matt. 9:13; Luke 5:32). The overriding concern was the miserable and helpless: "I was sent only to the lost sheep of the house of Israel" (Matt. 15:24); "Go to the lost sheep of the house of Israel" (Matt. 10:6). As Vermes puts the point: "[Jesus] is depicted in the Synoptics as the compassionate, caring, and loving pilot and shepherd who, imitating the merciful, caring, and loving God, guides those most in need, the little ones (Matt. 18:10), the sinners, the whores, and the publicans, toward the gate of the Kingdom of the Father."[84]

Jesus's sense of God as the loving and caring father of his erring children was interpreted by the Jewish philosopher Martin Buber as a model for love in an I-Thou personal relationship—"the equality of all lovers, from the smallest to the greatest and from the blissfully secure whose life is circumscribed by the life of one beloved human being to him that is nailed his life long to the cross of the world, capable of what is immense and bold enough to risk it: to love *man*."[85] Buber, interpreting Jesus's sense of relationship to God as loving father, construes such a loving relationship as one of equality and reciprocity: "Everyone can speak the You and then becomes I; everyone can say Father and then becomes son; actuality abides."[86] But Buber reads Jesus as contesting the patriarchal framing of relationship, for if even the father-son pair must ultimately be understood as in developmental service of a loving and caring relationship of equals, then hierarchy must yield to relational care, sensitivity, and concern, including concern for voice, in all relationships.

The power of Buber's reading of Jesus is the way it clarifies the remarkable role women played in his life and ministry in ways that were, if anything, very much in tension with patriarchal conceptions of gender. In the Synoptics, Jesus is pictured as showing reserve, verging on hostility, to his family, including his mother, Mary (Mark 3:21). And although Jewish men, including holy men, were expected to marry, everything points to Jesus being an unmarried, celibate man (Matt. 19:12).[87] In these respects, Jesus did not conform to a patriarchal conception of gender—he refused to accept the authority of his own family of origin, and he did not define himself by his authority within a family

Jesus nonetheless took a remarkable interest in women, as persons, and they took an interest in him. Women were not only disciples, they were among the most faithful of his disciples, holding on to their relationship with Jesus in a way men did not.[88] While male disciples abandoned Jesus after his arrest or even denied him (Peter), women were with him at his death (see Mark 15:40–41).[89] Moreover, it was to a group of these faithful women that, at his tomb and later, resurrection experiences were first granted, only to be initially disbelieved by the terrified male disciples (see Mark 16:1–14; cf. Matt. 28:1–10; Luke 24:1–49). The women's interest in his teaching was portrayed as something that legitimately engaged their intelligence, as Jesus defended Mary's listening to his teaching from her sister Martha's distracted insistence that he patriarchally tell Martha to help her in the womanly tasks of serving (Luke 10:38–42).

Jesus clearly taught and ministered to women in ways that spoke to their subjective experience, including their experience of suffering as women, even when traditional outcasts. The experience of women, as equally subject to God's loving attention as men, was thus a frequent subject of both the parables and judgment sayings of Jesus, as well as his ministering concern.[90] For example, he spoke at length to a ritually unclean sinning woman from Samaria at a well and brought her to faith (John 4:7–42).[91] The conversation with the woman at the well displays not just unusual openness and interest but also capacities of psychological penetration, as Jesus spoke "to a woman whom he had never met before and appear[ed] to know everything about the emotional chaos of her life—images which cannot be dispelled by scholars calling into question their historical plausibility."[92] A. N. Wilson brilliantly connects such remarkable insight and sympathy into women with the ways in which women, as feminists (including, as we have seen, the abolitionist feminists), have read the Gospels as calling for forms of political liberation ("The words of Jesus to the daughter of Jairus were taken up as a rallying-cry among nineteenth-century feminists. 'Damsel arise!'").[93]

Jesus was, of course, a man, but the interpretive issue raised by his attitude toward women involves the critical position to patriarchy that his attitude suggested. As one careful student of the historical Jesus concludes,

p.32

31

his teaching, at a minimum, "entailed a certain reformation of the patriarchal structure of society."[94] If we take seriously, as contemporary feminist Bible scholars do, the degree to which Jesus's critique of patriarchy was diluted by the sexism of his later followers, a reasonable case may be made that the historical Jesus's critique of patriarchy was probably much more profoundly radical.[95]]35.17 40

One way of understanding the roots of what is ethically radical in Jesus is to relate his attitude toward women to his conception of God, which was itself remarkably antipatriarchal. As we have seen, Jesus always spoke of God as a loving father, but as Buber's interpretation of Jesus shows, gender as such played no fundamental role in his understanding of the relationship as one of reciprocal intimate love and care between equals. Jesus's thought on this point was traditionally Jewish: maternal images of God's love were used by Moses, by Isaiah, and in Qumran hymns.[96] Consistent with this traditionally Jewish way of thinking, all the important features that Jesus ascribed to a loving God are exactly those that Sara Ruddick describes as maternal care, a loving care that holds on to relationship to another, despite frustrations and disappointments, to serve the ends of love—protection, growth, and ethical acceptability. What is remarkable in Jesus's conception of God is how his loving care showed itself to sinners who had not yet repented and the extent to which he defined his life and teaching in precisely such terms—in terms of never breaking relationship to those who have failed one's hopes for them but rather defining the value, indeed the power, of love as its willingness to stay in loving relationship, above all when the beloved fails one. Jesus started, it seems, from the microcosm of caring love that Ruddick describes and then wrote it at large into a sense of ethics and religion. Within that context, the demands of love were interpreted in terms of God's loving care, as expressed in the protection, growth, and ethical acceptability of his recalcitrant children interpreted historically (as a record of their advances to and digressions from growth to moral maturity as a people) through the prophetic tradition, which Jesus assumed and elaborated. As Buber shows, Jesus redefined the scope and demands of ethical concern between and among persons, made in God's image, as a loving concern that is equally available to all persons, certainly to women at least as much as men. As Erik Erikson, the psychoanalyst and historian, perceptively observes about Jesus: "One cannot help noticing, on Jesus' part, an unobtrusive integration of maternal and paternal tenderness."[97]

What arrested Garrison, Tolstoy, Gandhi, and King in Jesus was, I believe, his conception of God along these lines, the sense that our psyches as ethical persons, made in God's image, were rooted in a loving care for persons equally available to men and women and, for that reason, ethically skeptical of conventions and practices inconsistent with such ethical concern. The developmental psychology of these men crucially involved relationships with mothers or maternal caretakers whose care imparted to them the value and importance of loving care, indeed, whose care imparted to them the sense that moral voice was as available to women as to men. Jesus had authority for these men because, on the interpretation they accorded his life and teaching, he spoke of equal voice and concern (in particular in his relations with women); this was a conception of Jesus that their mothers or caretakers had sometimes conveyed to them. But why did these men choose nonviolence?

On this point, one statement of the teaching of Jesus absorbed the attention of all four advocates of nonviolence, namely, the Sermon on the Mount, at Matthew 5–7. In particular, the text directly relevant to nonviolence is Matthew 5:38–42: " I tell you not to resist one who is evil. But if anyone strikes you on the right cheek, turn the other to him as well."[98]

There are compelling reasons for believing that the historical Jesus could not have meant Matthew 5:36–42 to forbid the role that the principle of self-defense plays in criminal law. As David Daube has persuasively argued, Jesus invoked "an eye for an eye" not as a principle of criminal law but in terms of the developing tradition of Jewish civil law, in which varying monetary damages were assigned for different kinds of injuries. Jesus did not question this tradition as it applied to injuries but rather questioned the view that the tradition extended to insults as well, including the Near Eastern insult of striking the right cheek with the back of the hand.[99] In any event, Jesus was criticizing "the urge to resent a wrong done to you as an affront to your pride, to forget that the wrongdoer is your brother before God and to compel him to soothe your unworthy feelings; and [he] advocates, instead, a humility which cannot be wounded, a giving of yourself to your brother which will achieve more than can be achieved by a narrow justice."[100] In effect, men were asked to resist responding to insults by violence as a way of breaking the destructiveness of the patriarchal cycle of violence.

There is, however, a compelling way to understand the extraordinary force the life and teaching of Jesus had for Tolstoy as well as for Garrison,

Gandhi, and King, one quite close to such a reasonable contemporary scholarly interpretation of the historical Jesus. We can thus interpret the antithesis of Matthew 5:43–44 ("You have heard that it was said 'You shall love your neighbor and hate your enemy,' but I tell you to love your enemies and pray for those who misuse you") in terms of Jesus's rejection of the Essene teaching that commanded such hatred.[101] Paradoxically, the Essenes accepted a teaching of nonretaliation analogous to that of Jesus, but that teaching was a strategic expression of apocalyptic faith that, at the last judgment, God himself would wreak vengeance on the hated enemies of the light.[102] John the Baptist, Jesus's mentor, may have been associated with the Qumran Essenes, but the fact that his message, like that of Jesus, appealed to the entire Jewish people, including sinners, suggests that, by the time he appears in the Gospels, John was no longer a member of the secretive, monastically self-isolated sect.[103] Both John and Jesus may have been celibate men, like the Essenes, but Jesus, unlike the ascetic John, embraced open-table fellowship with all as a distinctive feature of his ministry, a "bon vivant existence with robbers and sinners ... more scandalous and ominous than a mere matter of breaking purity rules dear to ... the Pharisees."[104] The scandal is captured at Matthew 11:19: "For the Son of Man came eating and drinking, and you say: 'Behold an eater and drinker, a friend of toll collectors and sinners.'"[105] Accordingly, what distinguishes Jesus's commands "not to resist one who is evil" and to "turn the other [cheek]" is the way he grounded the motivations behind those commands in an inclusive, caring love; that love would ask men in particular to question the force of the Mediterranean honor code in their lives, which required that insults to manhood unleash a cycle of violence. Honor codes of this type, as we have seen, are framed in terms of patriarchal gender stereotypes, and the violence is the way such stereotypes are enforced, for it is keyed to threats to honor defined by patriarchy. Jesus, here as elsewhere, asked men to question the role this violence plays in their sense of manhood.

As noted, one of the remarkable features of Jesus's life and teaching was his ethical sensitivity to the plight of women—something usually covered over by patriarchal gender stereotypes that silenced women's voices through a violence unleashed by any threat to these stereotypes. This theme was touched on in Jesus's defense of an adulteress who was to be stoned (John 8:1–11). Such gender stereotypes repress men's voices as well to the extent that their conventional political force rests on the

34

violent repression of any man's voice that would reasonably contest the demands the stereotypes unjustly impose on both men and women. The incident of the adulteress was put in particularly poignant terms as Jesus confronted a culture of patriarchal male hypocrisy with a question that called for a voice in patriarchal men they did not usually confront:

> Then the scribes and the Pharisees led forward a woman who had been caught in adultery, and made her stand there in front of everybody. "Teacher," they said to him, "this woman has been caught in the very act of adultery. Now, in the Law Moses ordered such women to be stoned. But you—what do you have to say about it?" (They were posing this question to trap him so that they could have something to accuse him of.). But Jesus simply bent down and started drawing on the ground with his finger. When they persisted in their questioning, he straightened up and said to them, "The man among you who has no sin—let him be the first to cast a stone at her." And he bent down again and started to write on the ground. But the audience went away one by one, starting with the elders; and he was left alone with the woman still there before him. So Jesus, straightening up, said to her, "Woman, where are they all? Hasn't anyone condemned you?" "No one, sir," she answered. Jesus said, "Nor do I condemn you. You may go. But from now on, avoid this sin." (John 8:3–11)[106]

There was a Socratic inwardness in Jesus's questioning of these patriarchal men (exemplifying the principle of Matthew 7:1–2, "Do not sit in judgment, lest you yourself be judged, for you will be judged by the same standard which you have used"). This inwardness laid bare voices and desires in men that the injustice of patriarchy violently repressed. Put another way, the men's inability to answer Jesus's searching question as he turned from them, "drawing on the ground with his finger," freed the silenced voices in the male psyche that patriarchy had violently repressed in accord with the demands of the honor code. That code wreaked havoc, of course, on any woman who deviated from its demands, as the stoning of an adulteress showed. Jesus's ethically rooted forgiveness in this case may have been so threatening to the sexism of the early church that it was not accepted into the canon until a more tolerant period.[107]

In terms of my argument in this volume, I am profoundly interested in how Jesus's forgiveness, combined with the prohibition on violence between men in Matthew 5:43–44, confronts us with the ways in which patriarchal conventions of manhood depend on a violence—whether against women or between men—that is provoked by a threat to the gender stereotypes on which the stability of patriarchy depends. Jesus showed how patriarchal violence rests on the repression of a free ethical voice.

No aspect of Jesus's life and teaching was more important than his insistence on the free prophetic ethical voice that, consistent with the tradition of the prophets on which he relied,[108] he himself developed and displayed with an authority that "astonished" his audiences, "for he taught them as one that had authority, and not as the scribes" (Mark 1:22).[109] The historical Jesus may have regarded himself as an eschatological prophet like Elijah[110] and discovered his own remarkable prophetic voice in relationship to a conception of a God whose loving care inspired that voice. Jesus's approach to disagreement with his teaching or his actions was that of a teacher; when disagreement with him expressed itself in the political violence that ultimately ended his life, he asked poignantly: "Are ye come out as against a thief with swords and staves for to take me? I sat daily with you teaching in the temple, and ye laid no hold on me" (Matt. 26:55).[111] Like Socrates, whose method of indirection and introspective inwardness resembled his own, Jesus died for his beliefs and teachings. He himself fell victim to unjust political violence directed against a voice interpreted as challenging that injustice, under the terms of the Roman law that "instigators of a revolt, riot, or agitators of the people" were to be "either crucified, thrown to wild animals, or banished to an island."[112]

Roman political authority was, of course, itself highly patriarchal, resting on a conception of patriarchal manhood that made possible a military life and rule that legitimated aggressive war, imperial rule, and the enslavement of defeated peoples on which the Roman imperium and economy depended.[113] The Roman governor of Judea, Pontius Pilate, who condemned Jesus to death (probably at the insistence of the Sadducee temple officials who were corruptly complicit with Roman rule), exemplified the patriarchal hierarchy and violence—displaying a servile devotion to his superiors, contempt for the people he ruled, cowardice, and cruelty.[114] Jesus may have been as much critical of the patriarchal violence of Rome as he was, or would have been, of the forms of it in Jewish culture, including those forms that would later develop into the violence of the Zealots in the First Jewish Revolt (66–70 C.E.); the Romans would respond within forty years after the death of Jesus with the ultimate destruction of the Second Temple in 70 C.E., leading to the Diaspora.[115] The death of the historical Jesus thus exemplifies what may have been one of his distinctive teachings: that the violence of patriarchal manhood in any of its forms focuses on the unjust repression of free ethical voice. 04:26.02

I believe this interpretation of the life and teaching of Jesus explains the distinctive way Jesus inspired Garrison, Tolstoy, Gandhi, and King. This interpretation was made possible by a distinctive background of context and developmental history that opened up new possibilities in the relations between men and women. The interpretation of Jesus on nonviolence, rooted in the authority of a relationship to caring love, brought forth a new voice in these men, made possible by the caring love they had known in their relationships with their mothers or other maternal caretakers. The experience of such maternal care, in the terms Sara Ruddick has described, was accorded a new kind of moral authority on the ground that it expressed the same kind of caring love that, as Buber argues, Jesus identified with God. The Buddhist technique for developing *bodhicitta* casts light on this process and its consequences:

05:24.02

> One relationship among all others is singled out: that of mother and child. Every being in the universe has been one's human mother in a past life. This relationship is presumably chosen because it is universal. Although everyone in the universe has also been one's child, not everyone has been a parent in this lifetime. But everyone has been a child, and everyone has had a mother. One is instructed to see every being that one encounters as having been one's mother in a past life, to the point that this is the first thought that one has when meeting someone. All of the sacrifices that the mother makes for the child are described in poignant detail, noting that, after all of the pain and discomfort the child causes for the mother during the months of pregnancy, it is surprising that the mother does not simply disregard the child when it ultimately emerges from the womb. Instead, she treats the child with great love, sacrificing her own health for its

welfare, patiently teaching it to walk and to talk, such that every step one takes and every word one speaks for the rest of one's life is the direct result of the mother's kindness.[116]

Mother-child experiences of this sort are, of course, universal, but it is much less universal to accord them the kind of interpretation that, as I am suggesting, some forms of Buddhism and some interpretations of Jesus give them. The interpretation of Jesus under examination here gives ethical priority to the voice of loving care that stays in relationship, despite frustration and disappointment, to secure the aims of love: protection, growth, and ethical acceptability. Skepticism about the role violence plays in patriarchal manhood is a consequence of the priority given to loving voice because violence rests on and perpetuates the traumatic breaking of personal relationship and the repression and loss of this voice in a humane life. All the advocates of nonviolence in this volume were brought by this skepticism to develop, cultivate, and express a new kind of voice in themselves, finding in the life and teaching of Jesus authority for that voice. As I have suggested, the mandate of the historical Jesus "not to resist one who is evil" but rather "to turn the other [cheek]" calls for a new kind of manhood, one that frees itself from the armored psychology of a patriarchal manhood that responds to insult with violence. To this extent, all these men are pioneers of a new kind of voice that can speak from a new psychology of gender (of manhood and thus of its gender binary, womanhood) that values a freer ethical voice and is, as we shall see, skeptical of the role violence plays in the unjust repression of voice both in men and in women.

It is part of the power of religion in general and of the life and teaching of Jesus in particular that our ethical and political intelligence calls on religious images and symbols in ways that Iris Murdoch has brilliantly noted:

> High morality without religion is too abstract, high morality craves for religion. Religion symbolises high moral ideas which then travel with us and are more intimately and accessibly effective than the unadorned promptings of reason. Religion suits the image-making human animal. Think what the image of Christ has done for us through centuries. Can such images *lie?* Do we not indeed adjust our attitudes to them, as time passes,

09.44 71

so as to "make them true"? This continuous adjustment is an aspect of the history of religion.[117]

There is an obvious rhetorical reason why Garrison and the others were so absorbed by Jesus: Christianity was the dominant religion of their audiences (for Garrison and King, the United States; for Tolstoy, Russia; for Gandhi, South Africa and Great Britain). But it is, I believe, much more than rhetorical appeal that led to the ways these thinkers so powerfully used the life and teachings of Jesus in criticizing the ways in which the established churches of Christianity often have been corruptly complicit in supporting fundamental injustice. Murdoch elsewhere suggests "that the central concept of morality is 'the individual' thought of as knowable by love, thought of in the light of the command, 'Be ye therefore perfect.'"[118] The command is from the Sermon on the Mount (Matt. 5:48), and Murdoch's examples of such love are those of maternal care.[119] Interest in the life and teachings of Jesus has the great virtue of enabling us to take seriously aspects of ethics that traditionally have been marginalized, including the examples on which Murdoch focuses—namely, ethics as rooted in the capacity for loving attachments liberated from fantasy.[120]

Because Jesus, as a man, was able to center the authority of his voice in such attachments, he was so remarkably sensitive to the issues of the suppressed voice of women and men on which, as we have come to see, the injustice of much structural injustice depends. The advocates of nonviolence inspired by him did not always believe in him as religious Christians do, but they found in his free ethical voice a means of understanding and cultivating an ethical voice in themselves made possible by a skepticism about the role violence plays in aspects of patriarchal manhood. The way in which the life and teaching of Jesus exemplified how this voice is formed in relationship to the values of maternal care enabled advocates of nonviolence to find in Jesus a teaching that, as Gandhi put it, "went straight to my heart."[121] If Christians have sometimes venerated Jesus as mother, these men found through Jesus a way, as men, to see the values of their early relationships with women as supporting the authority of a new kind of free ethical voice, centered in these relationships.[122]

Jesus's prophetic voice, inspired by a value placed on attentive, caring love in the family, expressed itself in a new conception of relationships among persons as such that required him to leave his family, which was hostile to his new way of life and teaching. It is striking that one of the few times Jesus used violent imagery to describe his teaching ("Do not think that I have come to bring peace to the earth; I have not come to bring peace, but a sword," [Matt. 10:37][123]), he did so to underscore the degree to which his ethical vision required one to contest the authority of members of one's family. Both the sources and the demands of this new conception of ethics inspired advocates of nonviolence to give it an interpretation relevant to politics. On the one hand, intimate relations of maternal care inspired a new kind of free ethical voice; on the other hand, this free ethical voice resisted the demands of family life, including patriarchal hierarchy, calling for protest of forms of structural injustice resting on the violent repression of voice.

Why These Men? Resistance and Blockages to Resistance

Based on my initial work on Garrison, I offer this book in terms of four other case studies to give a textured sense of what I believe I discovered, a certain *pattern* of developmental psychology leading to the distinctive ethical voice each man brought to public life and culture. This approach gives some sense of the remarkable similarities among them but also highlights, and with equal significance, their complex differences. What motivated me to choose Tolstoy as well as Gandhi and King was not only their important sense being inspired by one another and by Garrison but also, in contrast to Garrison, the quite different qualities of their relationships with their maternal caretakers. The study of such different relationships throws light on resistance and on the blockages to resistance that these men experienced, in particular the degree to which the problems in their relationships with women and their own sexuality were reflective of an idealization of motherhood that in turns reflected the patriarchal split between good and bad women. And I end my study with Churchill precisely because his life and psychology reveal yet another form of these relationships, one that rests on a relationship, neither abusive nor idealized, with a sexual mother.

A study of five men does not a scientific sample make. But it may raise important questions and offer illuminating hypotheses that advance a scientific psychology of men's resistance to injustice. I chose the five men under study here both because they exemplify such resistance and because their psychologies are different in precisely the ways that might advance alternative questions and hypotheses. For example, some of these men were psychologically crippled in their resistance to injustice: thus, though Tolstoy and Gandhi certainly resisted religious intolerance and racism, they also inflicted sexist violence in their private lives.

Freud, who had framed male developmental psychology in terms of the Oedipal story of traumatic separation from mothers and alignment with fathers, observed the consequences of this separation in the context of a male heterosexual psychology (which tends to debase a person who is sexually desired) structured by images of women idealized as virginal madonnas or denigrated as whores.[124] All of the men studied here challenged the universality of this psychology by the ways in which they stayed in relationship to their mothers and the role this played in grounding resistance to injustice. But only two of them (Garrison and Churchill) possessed a psychology that challenged the universality of a sexual desire burdened by Freud's idealizing and debasing gender stereotypes. I selected the five men in this volume because a close study of them clarifies these complexities, showing how difficult and corruptible resistance can be even in men who resist injustice based on patriarchal violence. The close study of Tolstoy takes us intimately into the developmental psychology of a man's artistic and ethical voice connected to the voices of maternal caretakers and later lovers and shows us how much his voice is shaped and misshaped by the degree to which these relationships are idealized. Men's ongoing relationships with maternal caretakers, which ground resistance in some spheres, may, if sufficiently idealized, corrupt resistance elsewhere, as the later studies of Gandhi and King also reveal, in different forms. I end with the close study of Churchill because it shows yet another variation on the theme of the relationship between men's resisting ethical voices and those of their mothers. Here, however, the son's voice was framed by a relationship, neither idealized nor abusive, to a mother's highly sexual voice in a flamboyant life of free love. With Tolstoy and Churchill, the comparison in such terms between otherwise similar men could not be more striking or more powerfully suggestive.

My working hypothesis is that idealization covers traumatic loss and that breaking relationships with mothers, as Freud saw, shows itself in the acceptance of gender stereotypes that burden sexual desire with idealization and denigration.[125] I study a range of men who stayed in relationship to maternal caretakers, but some of them also idealized these women in ways that bespoke a breaking of relationship, with consequences I explore. The forms of resistance to injustice I investigate here are not easy for men, resting as they do on unleashing voice when violence is countered as the honorable response to an insulted or shamed manhood. What I believe I have discovered is an alternative psychology involving a manhood that resists injustice, showing both its strengths and perils. The close, inductive study of these men will allow the reader to see how I arrived at my discovery and to subject my thesis to the further discussion, refinement, and testing that it certainly deserves.

The chapter that follows presents an extended exploration of Tolstoy because his life and work (in particular his novels) give us a *uniquely* illuminating path into a complex alternative psychology of manhood. Tolstoy struggled for an artistic and ethical voice that resisted patriarchal violence. But through idealization based on desolating loss, he experienced a crisis of vocation in terms of artistic versus ethical voice. In the end, he found an ascetic ethical voice that, in disowning his artistic voice and achievements, called for nonviolence even as he tragically inflicted violence on people he loved or believed he loved. None of the men in this work is a better example of what happens when a person does not heed Hawthorne's caution that the failure to take seriously women's sexual voice corrupts the ethical resistance of otherwise good men.

// CHAPTER TWO

Tolstoy on Nonviolence

Leo Tolstoy is an important figure in the story of resisting voice, but he is important in a different way from Garrison or Gandhi or King. All the latter were mainly leaders of democratic political movements, remarkable both for their arguments (featuring nonviolence) and for the forms of resistance they inspired and mobilized. Tolstoy certainly actively supported movements of political resistance in Imperial Russia and elsewhere, but his activism was ancillary to the ethical and religious ambitions of his later years.[1] Those ambitions included nothing less than founding a new religion whose ethics required a rather ascetic, celibate way of life devoted to acts of practical goodness and a pacifist skepticism of state power as such. Tolstoy's ethical religion acknowledged the influence of both Garrison and Adin Ballou and was in turn a significant influence, as we shall see, on Gandhi and thus on King.[2] But where the lives and work of Garrison, Gandhi, and King essentially confronted basic issues of injustice and inspired and mobilized nonviolent forms of resistance to that injustice, Tolstoy came to these issues relatively late, in the wake of his towering achievements as an artist of genius in the fields of the novel and short story. He saw in these issues the solution to an ethical crisis of vocation that led him to doubt the value not only of his artistic achievement but also of his artistic gift, indeed, his very voice as an imaginative artist. In consequence, he imposed on himself tasks for which he had little talent—translation of the Christian Gospels from Greek into Russian, Bible interpretation, religious commentary, and even the formulation of a kind of neo-Kantian philosophy. But these tasks also led to his statement of a political theory of pacifism, which made an important contribution to the role nonviolent resisting voice might play in protesting forms of structural injustice, a contribution Gandhi immediately recognized and embraced. We need to make sense of this striking

// p. 44

turn in his life and of his output in this period—the rather rigid, doc-trinaire, and today largely unread works—for they are the works in which he defends the ethical religion, a religion of which, to the grow-ing scorn of his wife, he conceived himself as the latter-day prophet. Nonviolence was accorded a prominent role in Tolstoy's ethical religion.

Tolstoy was a person of extraordinary ambition. It was not enough for him that he had climbed to the summits of the novelistic art in *War and Peace* and *Anna Karenina;* he would as well found a new religion and ethics, challenging politics in general and the theocratic, imperial, czarist absolutism of the Russian state into which he was born and that his fam-ily, as privileged aristocrats, had long served. In a study of the political theory and psychology of resistance, it is our great good fortune that we have in Tolstoy's life and art (for they are closely related) a clearer road map of the psychology of the dilemma of manhood than we have with men who were essentially activists, such as Garrison, Gandhi, and King. Tolstoy shared with these men, as I will show, a common trajectory of political theory and developmental psychology that ended in nonviolence as the way to understand and to remedy structural injustice. And in studying Tolstoy, we can see, stretched out over a lifetime, the stages of psy-chological tension and crisis that all these nonviolent men went through, some more disastrously than others. But what the study of Tolstoy the artist uniquely gives us is a deeper insight into the inner psychological contradictions of the life of a man who moved through this trajectory (contradictions beautifully on display in his great novels, in particular *Anna Karenina*). I begin with Tolstoy's early life and art and then focus on the impact of his marriage on the treatment of gender in *War and Peace* and *Anna Karenina*. Finally, I consider how my argument about his life and art advances the understanding of both his crisis and the works of ethical religion (featuring nonviolence) to which he turned to resolve the crisis.

Tolstoy's Early Life and Art

Tolstoy has been fortunate in his biographers: there are at least two long masterpieces of the biographical form, those of Henri Troyat and A. N. Wilson, and several illuminating shorter studies.[3] All serious analyses of Tolstoy agree that his art drew significantly, both in its characters and in its narratives, on his life—sometimes on people he never really knew (his maternal grandfather and his mother), sometimes on experiences of persons and relationships at remarkably close hand (for example, in both *War and Peace* and *Anna Karenina,* his relatively late marriage and his relationships with his wife and her family). Two features of Tolstoy's background were pivotal in this artistic development: his aristocratic lineage, together with considerable inherited wealth, and his early history of personal familial losses, including the death of his mother when he was two.

Tolstoy's mother was Marya Nikolayevna Volkonskaya—that is, Mary, the daughter and only child of Nicholas Volkonsky (Mary had lost her mother at age two). Nicholas (Prince Nikolay) was an eccentric, difficult man who, at Mary's birth in 1790, was eminent in the service of Empress Catherine the Great. The Volkonskys were an ancient family who considered themselves grander than the Romanovs, and Prince Nikolay had added the distinction of military achievement to that of noble inheritance. He rose to prominence in the Turkish campaign of 1780, and in 1793, his military achievements were rewarded with a diplomatic post: he became the Russian ambassador to Berlin that year. Nicholas was far from a sycophant in relation to his royal patrons, and he was famously outspoken. When Catherine suggested he should marry the mistress of her favorite, Grigory Potemkin, Volkonsky replied: "What made him think I should marry his whore?"[4] (The independence of the family was also shown when Tolstoy's second cousin participated in the unsuccessful 1825 Decembrist uprising against Czar Nicholas I, after which the prince was stripped of his title and estates and exiled to Siberia for thirty years; Tolstoy eventually met him in Italy.) With the death of Catherine the Great in 1796, the career of Prince Nicholas Volkonsky came to an end, and he retired to his estate at Yasnaya Polyana (which Tolstoy was later to make world-famous as his literary home).[5] His world there featured patriarchal authority, culture, and agriculture:

> His severity was proverbial, but his muzhiks were never beaten. At seven o'clock every morning, eight serf-musicians in wide blouses, breeches, white stockings and pumps would assemble in front of their music stands near an ancient elm. A little boy would cry, "He's awake!" as he went by carrying a pitcher of hot water. Thereupon the orchestra tuned up, and the opening chords of a Haydn symphony rose to the windows of the

princely bedchamber. At the end of their *aubade* the musicians dispersed, one going off to feed the pigs, another to knit stockings in the servants' hall, a third to spade in the garden.[6]

On retirement, the prince devoted himself to his daughter's education. A true follower of Catherine the Great and a child of the Enlightenment, he believed (unlike his famous grandson) both in the education of women and in the superiority of European culture over Russian culture. "They spoke to one another in French, the father and his child. He ensured that Mary knew German and Italian, and that she had a good grounding in music and history. They read Rousseau together, and works of the French Encyclopaedists." He died in 1821, leaving his thirty-one-year-old daughter unmarried.

Worried about her inheritance, Mary sought an engagement with a cousin; when he married someone else, she met a less eligible bachelor five years her junior, Prince Nikolay Ilyich Tolstoy. Count Tolstoy was a former army officer. His father was governor of Kazan, but the old man's financial affairs were in such disarray that Nikolay left the army because he was too poor to buy further promotion. Marriage to a rich woman was the solution to his difficulties. The Tolstoys were also a highly esteemed, ancient Russian family, and the Volkonskys consented to the match. The couple was married in 1822. Mary's dowry was eight hundred serfs in the Tula and Oryol districts and the estate of Yasnaya Polyana. The Tolstoys had five children—Nikolay, Sergey, Dimitry, Leo (in 1828), and Marya, born in 1830. Princess Mary never recovered from this last confinement and died five months later. Leo was two years old.

The pattern of loss for the young Leo continued. His father, a widower at the age of thirty-five, tried to manage the estates he inherited from his wife; his occupations were farming and pursuing lawsuits. Like all aristocratic children, the youngsters saw little of their father, though they felt a certain closeness to their Tolstoy grandmother. But in 1837, the children suddenly lost their father, who dropped dead in the street in Tula, and this was followed the next year by the death of their grandmother. Tolstoy was a nine-year-old at his father's death. The children were now put under the guardianship of an aunt, the late count's sister, the Countess Alexandra Ilyinichna Osten-Saken, who, after a disastrous marriage to a homicidal "mad Baltic count" found consolation in the pious exercise of the Orthodox religion. She undoubtedly imparted to the children the stories of the heroes and saints of Orthodoxy, and she entertained at Yasnaya Polyana "the strange, half-crazed wandering pilgrims who traipsed the mud roads that connected town with town in those pre-railway days."[8]

The figure closer to all the children and in particular to Tolstoy himself was a distant kinswoman, Tatyana Alexandrovna Yergolskaya—the beloved Tante Toinette, who "provided a mother-substitute." Tolstoy wrote of her: "Probably she loved my father and he loved her, but she did not marry him when they were young, because she thought he had better marry my wealthy mother, and she did not marry him subsequently because she did not wish to spoil her pure poetic relations with him and with us." We do not know of the truth of what Tolstoy claims here. A. N. Wilson is skeptical because he believes the intensity of Tolstoy's relationship with Tante Toinette may have motivated idealization: "For Tolstoy, it was important to establish his 'little aunt's' purity. Her kisses and caresses were reserved for him. It was from her, and perhaps only from her, that he had any displays of physical affection when he was a young child. It was from her that he learnt 'the spiritual delight of love.'"[9]

It is striking to find in Tolstoy's intense relationship with a maternal caretaker, Aunt Tatyana, not only his first experience of loving care and a loving voice he deeply valued but also something that was, for him, psychologically closely related—the sense of his artistic voice. It was Tante Toinette who apparently nurtured his artistic voice, even suggesting to Tolstoy that he write novels, as he acknowledged to his aunt in a letter from his military service in the Caucasus, where he began his literary apprenticeship: "Do you remember, dear Aunt, a piece of advice you once gave me—to write novels? Well, I'm following your advice and the occupations I speak of consist of composing literature."[10]

Aunt Toinette's voice, which he experienced as nurturing his sense of both loving and artistic voice,[11] was also an ethical voice that challenged "the unconscious egotism of the young lord" when, as a boy at Yasnaya, he said nothing after the steward told him he was taking a groom to the barn to be flogged as punishment: "When he told Aunt Toinette about the incident, she burst out, 'Why did you not prevent it?'"[12] The nagging sense of an inner ethical voice protesting unjust patriarchal violence, which Tolstoy struggled with as an artist and as a prophet of ethical religion, was developmentally connected to the value he had learned to place on the voice of his loving aunt.

Tolstoy was, however, to suffer disruption of this most central of his early personal relationships during a significant period of his young manhood. The death of his guardian, Aunt Alexandra, in 1841 was the fourth major death in Tolstoy's first thirteen years of life, and it was the most crucial in terms of his destiny over the next six years. The loss of Aunt Alexandra uprooted the children from their familiar homes in Yasnaya Polyana and Moscow, and it divided them from the one person for whom they all felt the warmest affection. Aunt Tatyana was only a very distant relative. She had no legal right over the children, and guardianship passed to their father's only surviving sister, the Countess Pelageya Ilvinichna Yushkova, who lived with her husband, Colonel Yushkov, in Kazan. Because of Aunt Pelageya's pathological jealousy regarding the fact that her womanizing husband had once proposed to Aunt Tatyana, she decided that the children would live with her and her husband in Kazan and that Tatyana would remain in Yasnaya. Tatyana complained to a correspondent: "It is a cruel and barbaric thing to separate me from the children for whom I have cared so tenderly for nearly twelve years" (Wilson, *Tolstoy,* 28). Aunt Pelageya and her husband thought they were doing the best for the children, but they disrupted the "ramshackle and rather crazy grandeur of the life under the tutelage of Aunt Alexandra" to replace it with "the moneyed 'comfort' of life with her worldly sister," surrounded by "powdered flunkeys and socialite nobodies, who, because they were in Kazan, were somebodies" (29).

Tolstoy's life for six years in Kazan certainly acculturated him to the terms and perquisites of Russian aristocratic manhood, including its pretensions and fatuities. He was first taken to a brothel by his elder brother Sergey when he was about fourteen years old; he tells us that after he had "accomplished this act," he stood by the bed and wept (43). Tolstoy was eventually "to have plenty of subsequent experiences that could complement the first disillusioning movement with the Kazan tart: parlour maids, gipsies, peasants, eventually a wife were all to share his bed and witness the violent contradictions between his animal appetites and his sense of spiritual revulsion against the sexual act" (43–44). The background to his self-disgust was "that three years of sleeping with prostitutes left Tolstoy infected with gonorrhoea. A V.D. clinic is a better place than most to form feelings of hatred for one's own body" (44). In the enforced solitude that followed, he began to keep a diary, which was to develop in time into the practice of fiction. He did disastrously in his ex-

aminations at the University of Kazan but thankfully came into his inheritance in 1847. After dividing the estate with his brothers and sister,
the nineteen-year-old Tolstoy inherited, with Yasnaya Polyana and several other estates, 4,000 silver roubles and 330 slaves. Now independently
wealthy and a nobleman, he could and did return to "Auntie" at Yasnaya
(47–48).

Tolstoy's return failed to give him any enduring focus for his energies
other than his predatory sexual relations with peasant women and his
growing problem with gambling, which eventually nearly ruined him.
His aunt worried about him, wishing he could settle on something, even
if it were an affair with a rich, married woman (61). Tolstoy began to
work on fictional experiments under the impact of reading the novels of
Laurence Sterne; a close reading of British novels was evidently an important and continuing stimulus to his creativity, even later in his creative
life (64–69). Tolstoy would find focus, as well as experiences on which
his early and later fiction drew, in joining his brother, Nikolay, during his
military service in the Caucasus between 1851 and 1854 and in Tolstoy's
subsequent military service in the Crimean War in 1854 and 1855 (73–98,
101–19). Like his maternal grandfather and father, he took up the traditional role of the Russian aristocracy in military service to the aims of
the imperial, theocratic, absolutist state. His mature novels study war
(*War and Peace*) and military men (Vronsky in *Anna Karenina*) so well because Tolstoy had himself played this role with such apparent enthusiasm
during these years. In this period, he was a passionate patriot, fully on
the side of his own country against other powers, though his duty in the
Crimean War was in service of Nicholas I's "mixture of political opportunism and religious fervour" against unreal threats "by an unholy alliance
of western Protestants and atheists and Turkish infidels" that covered over
the injustice of the czarist regime, "the plight of intellectuals, dissidents,
serfs and other such blots on the Russian landscape" (102). Later in his
life and now a pacifist, Tolstoy would brilliantly analyze and unmask such
a politically corrupt politics built on sectarian religious intolerance, a
politics to which, in his early manhood, he had given himself heart and
soul. (EoF)   0:44:10.84

From his adolescence in Kazan, Tolstoy was, unlike his brothers, "really
obsessed" with the perquisites of manhood—"dress, rank, or personal appearance" (34). He self-consciously thought of manhood in terms of
roles, including roles in the family, and thought of himself and others,

sometimes at the expense of any sense of inwardness, as playing these roles ably and with style.[13] Moreoever, he was a special kind of man, an aristocratic nobleman in a family with a distinguished history of imperial military service; he was also, under serfdom, a slaveowner, who, like his slaveowning brethren in the American South, sexually exploited women held in slavery. His sense of honor included challenging those who insulted him to duels; in a prolonged contretemps of misunderstandings between once close literary friends, one of his challenged rivals was Ivan Turgenev.[14] Tolstoy's sense of manhood during this period was clearly an expression of the patriarchal honor code discussed in chapter 1, and it depended, as such codes do, on its gender binary—womanhood, divided into two types. On one side were good women placed on an idealized asexual pedestal, whom a man's honor required him to protect (including from sexual experience, as Tolstoy allegedly did as a boy in protecting the girl who was to be the mother of the woman he married[15]. On the other side were bad or fallen women, who were often racialized (as Gypsies or peasant women were) and whose sexuality made them freely available to interested men, including, under slavery or its analogues, men who owned them. Tolstoy clearly accepted a rather conventional form of this gender binary; as Troyat incisively observes, "The fact was that Tolstoy, who claimed to be broad-minded, was extremely old-fashioned when it came to women."[16] Until his relatively late marriage at age thirty-four, Tolstoy's sexual experience was almost entirely with women of the fallen variety: Gypsies when he was in the military, women in brothels when he was not, and, at Yasnaya, peasant women he owned or who, after emancipation in 1861, were in his service. Later in his life, after his crisis and conversion to ethical religion, Tolstoy described his sense of manhood during this period as resting on a conception that was easily prone to violence (including killing men in war) and to a certain kind of sexuality: "I killed men in the war, ... I fought duels; playing cards, I squandered money extorted from the peasants, and I punished them cruelly; I fornicated with women of easy virtue and deceived husbands. Lies, theft, adultery, drunkenness and brutality of every sort, I have committed every shameful act; there is no crime I am not acquainted with.[17]

Even during these years, however, we see in the emergence of Tolstoy's early artistic voice the glimmerings of ethical doubt and questioning. One of his first published stories, *The Raid,* written while he was in the Caucasus, draws on his experience there, showing us a battalion of well-trained Russian soldiers—actual people, with lives and personalities, who are quite real for us—harrying some pitiful tribesmen. Even in a period when Tolstoy fully identified, as a man, with the aims of the Imperial Russian state, he asks: "Can it be that there is not room for all men on this beautiful earth under these immeasurable starry heavens? Can it be possible that in the midst of this entrancing Nature feelings of hatred, vengeance, or the desire to exterminate their fellows can endure in the souls of men?"[18] Tolstoy was now writing continuously in circumstances that were, to say the least, distracting. His works in these years showed a special interest in manhood and its growth and demands—for instance, his semiautobiographical exploration of the stages of male development, *Childhood, Boyhood, Youth,* and his starkly journalistic treatment of the experience of men fighting the Crimean War, *The Sebastopol Sketches.*[19] Tolstoy was in the midst of a war experience that he would use in his first unqualified masterpiece, *The Cossacks,* and later brilliantly study in *War and Peace.*[20] There was, however, another experience some years afterward that he was crucially to draw on for his later fiction, namely, his marriage.[21]

Tolstoy's Marriage and His Mature Novels

After service in the Crimea, Tolstoy took some pleasure for the next six years, first in the less regimented life of an increasingly recognized man of letters living in Saint Petersburg and then in extensive travels in Europe.[22] He was, at least in retrospect, emotionally affected by the death of his brother Dmitry from consumption in 1856. In fact, Tolstoy had hardly seen his brother after his eighteenth year and at the time of Dimitry's death was absorbed by the excitement of life in the metropolis. He compared his own withdrawal and lack of feeling to the practical goodness, in ministering to the dying man, of his Aunt Toinette and Masha, the pockmarked girl his brother had rescued from a brothel. He would later memorably use the scene in *Anna Karenina.*[23]

At the end of this period, Tolstoy, now in his early thirties, decided that it was time to get married. As conventional a Russian aristocrat as Tolstoy was, it would be a mistake to underestimate the sheer force of conventional manhood in leading him to this decision. Turgenev had once perceptively complained that Tolstoy was always putting on an act:

"Not one word, not one movement of his is natural! He is eternally pos-
ing before us, and I find it difficult to explain in a clever man this im-
poverished Count's arrogance."[24] As only a man from a family that had
experienced so much traumatic loss can, Tolstoy had, from early on, been
imaginatively absorbed by inventing and playing the role, as he took it,
of a patriarchal male in a flourishing, intact family of the sort he in fact
had never known.[25] Now, he would play such a role for all it was worth.

No artist more perceptively described the conventional pressures surrounding marriage in nineteenth-century aristocratic Russia and its lack
of congruence with—indeed, its conflict with—personal feeling. In *War
and Peace,* Tolstoy shows us how marriages are arranged between people
not in love and actually very ill suited and how people in love often are
conventionally unable to marry. Prince Vasili and his daughter, Helene,
so manipulate matters that the hapless Pierre proposes marriage to Helene, a woman he does not love and who does not love him. And despite
the love of Sonya and Nicholas Rostov for one another, Rostov family
interests, represented by Nicholas's mother, compel Nicholas to marry
the wealthy heiress Princess Mary and manipulatively insist that Sonya,
a family ward, surrender all claim on Nicholas.[26]

The very fact that Tolstoy was such a sensitive observer of these conventional pressures is integral to the truth of his artistic voice, imparting
the very texture and feel of the power of this psychology over men and
women in aristocratic Russia. His sense of its power may have been what
caused him to give only cursory consideration to the possibilities of marriage with respectable women who showed "acquiescence, rather than
ardour" (Wilson, *Tolstoy,* 184). He may have wanted someone who really
wanted to be married to him, indeed, someone who shared "his highly
charged erotic proclivities" (184). He had found such a partner, evidently,
in a twenty-three-year-old married peasant, Aksinya Bazykina, with
whom he had shared "a passionate and long-standing liaison" since 1858,
resulting in the birth of a son, Timofey, at the time Tolstoy had con-
tracted a legitimate union in Moscow (184–85). A liaison with an already
married peasant woman was not what Tolstoy, as a patriarchal aristocrat,
was looking for in marriage. He needed a respectable woman who would
mother legitimate children.

In 1862 Tolstoy married Sofya Bers, one of the three daughters of the
highly respectable, middle-class Bers family; the father was a doctor. Tolstoy had known the mother since his boyhood and the family for years.

As the child of a family that had known so much loss, Tolstoy often fell in love with families, and he was in love with the Berses as a family before the question of marrying one of the daughters had been proposed to him by his old friend and former playmate—their mother, Lyubov Alexandrovna. She had wanted her eldest daughter, Liza, married off first, but Tolstoy actually preferred the youngest sister, Tatyana (or Tanya), who, barely sixteen, possessed an abundance of animation (she is the model for Natasha in *War and Peace*). Tolstoy also found himself drawn to the middle sister, Sofya: "Obviously, there was a powerful sexual attraction between them" (192). There occurred between them the romantic scene "which Tolstoy was later to mythologise in *Anna Karenina,* in the proposal scene between Kitty and Levin" (192). Sofya Andreyevna later described his writing letters in chalk that expressed in code his attraction to her, not her sister (192–93). The incident with the chalk and letters was accorded profound significance by Sofya Andreyevna. She was now head over heels in love and in love with an artist. She herself began to scribble a short story about a fascinatingly repulsive, moody, older man who was quite inconsistent in his opinions and whom she adored; she showed the story to Tolstoy, as one artist to another. A. N. Wilson believes that the incident with the chalk "cannot possibly be true." The imagined story tells its subtext: Tolstoy did not want to marry Sofya, but he felt a surge of sexual interest in her, the kind of interest that, "in the past, he had felt for at least forty women: a feeling which could liberate him from the marriage bond" (194). And unlike his previous partners, the woman in question was a respectable woman and suitable marriage partner who appeared to desire him.

Tolstoy was still very uncertain whether he wanted marriage. He talked with a friend about the impact on him of his brother Nikolay's death and wept. Agitated, he decided what he wanted most was a confidante: "There won't be any secrets for me alone; but secrets for two; she will read everything" (196). He was searching for the intimate loving voice that he had certainly not known in Nikolay but had known from other close male friends and had found in Aunt Toinette and other female relatives. But he was now seeking that voice from a woman—a woman who would be his sex partner and yet not a bad or fallen woman. He was entering into a new kind of relationship that was to be enormously creative for his art but would eventually plunge him calamitously into a life-changing crisis of vocation.

The Bers household was thrown into disarray by Tolstoy's proposal of marriage to Sofya, a marriage that he insisted should take place at once. It is astonishing that Sofya's parents finally agreed to this. The next day, September 17, was her name day, and when her friends came to celebrate, they learned she would be married within the week. The couple hardly knew one another. A. N. Wilson observes, "They were not even sufficiently well-acquainted to know whether they *liked* one another. Probably they never did. He found her strange and fascinating. She found him monstrous and frightening. There was a strong sexual attraction between them. On this basis, they prepared to enter upon one of the most closely documented and one of the most miserable marriages in history" (196).

Consistent with his professed aim of securing an intimate confidante, Tolstoy's present for his future wife's name day was giving her his diaries to read, diaries that included a full description of his sexual history: "the early whoring and wenching, the repeated doses of V.D., the gipsies, the Cossack girls, the quasi-homoerotic devotion to his student friends, the flirtations in drawing rooms—a whole catalogue of active sexual life going back twenty years," including, worst of all, "the discovery that he had, until only a month or two before, been besottedly in love with his peasant mistress" (Sofya would have to bear the indignity of living on an estate where her husband's former mistress and illegitimate son were servants she saw every day) (197, 204–5). Sofya was a sexually inexperienced, rather puritanical, well-brought-up eighteen-year-old when she first read the diaries; she was shocked not only by what they disclosed but also by the callousness of such a disclosure: "These diaries, which he made me read, before our wedding, out of an excessive sense of duty, upset me very much. He shouldn't have done it; it made me cry as I looked into his past.["27]

Early on, she saw that this man she had married apparently had little understanding of the dimensions of feeling women experience, including feeling for their mothers or the trauma of separation from them: "He had never had a real family—neither father nor mother; he was brought up without them; and, in any case, being a man, he could not have understood my feelings.["28] In 1890, twenty-eight years later, she was still poring over Tolstoy's diaries, writing in her own diary, "I don't think I have ever got over the horror I experienced when I read Lyova's diaries before our marriage, and I doubt that the sharp sting of jealousy and my bewilderment at the thought of such filth and debauchery, has ever quite disappeared. May God preserve all young souls from such wounds—for they will never heal."[29]

Sofya had been shockingly introduced into the inner world of a patriarchal aristocratic man but a man who was also a great artist, himself divided between his sense of himself as an aristocratic man and his sense of truthful voice as an artist. Importantly, she was the first reader of Tolstoy's diaries, and she and he would, for some time to come, read one another's diaries as a way of staying in touch with each other's inner world, including the growing unhappiness each felt in the marriage. Since Tolstoy's art fed on his life, including his life with Sofya and her family of origin, reading his wife's diaries gave him a way into a woman's experience he had never known before, itself yielding him material on which his artistic imagination would feed to astonishing artistic effect in *War and Peace* and *Anna Karenina*. Sofya thus gave Tolstoy things even the lovingly supportive voice of Tante Toinette could not—a sense of her inner world as a sexual woman and mother and a resonance for Tolstoy's developing artistic voice, for Sofya was the first audience for the writing and rewriting of the lengthy masterpieces produced during the first decade of their marriage. Sofya was a woman of considerable managerial powers. In addition to her demanding duties as a mother (she bore Tolstoy thirteen children in the first twenty-six years of their marriage[30]), she managed the estate at Yasnaya; she clearly challenged Tolstoy's sexist conception of respectable women as submissive (he complained of her in a letter to an aunt as "a 'man of integrity'—I mean what I say: both 'integrity' and 'man'").[31] But the intimate heart of the marriage was her active participation in Tolstoy's writing, copying and recopying his almost undecipherable handwritten drafts; her son Ilya reported that she copied and recopied *War and Peace* seven times. It was an important expression of the deterioration of the marriage when, later on, one of the Tolstoy daughters supplanted her furious and embittered mother in the role of copyist, a role Sofya had diligently occupied for so many years.[32]

Although their past sexual experiences could not have been more different, Tolstoy and Sofya unfortunately brought to their marriage the same idealizing mythology of gender roles on which patriarchal codes of honor depend. Tolstoy's almost orgiastic sense of guilt about his premarital sexual exploits depended on this ideology, and Sofya's obsessional preoccupation with his diaries was often expressed in a sense of superiority to her husband: "My purity alone saved us from perdition."[33] There is good reason to doubt whether Tolstoy, with his highly charged sense of erotic pleasure, ever took seriously the pleasure of his wife, let alone her free sexual voice as a person. Their first sexual experience together sounds like rape: "That was the night Tolstoy first possessed his young and terrified wife. Brutal and disillusioning combat between an experienced man and a virgin struggling to defend herself, weeping and imploring and then dropping back inert. The act over, he notes, for the record, 'She knows all. Simple. . . . Her terror. Something morbid'" (Troyat, *Tolstoy*, 252).

Sofya apparently always experienced Tolstoy's aggressive sexuality with revulsion (259–60). By her twelfth pregnancy in 1884, she had come to regard "this succession of pregnancies" as a humiliation: "She was no longer a woman, she thought, she was a brood mare, a vase, good only to receive the master's seed and germinate his progeny" (440). She unsuccessfully attempted, without telling her husband, to secure an abortion (441).

Once he was married to a respectable woman appropriately placed on the pedestal that patriarchal gender roles required, Tolstoy assumed—and never really questioned the normative assumption—that sex, which he loved, was only for procreation (440, 474, 623). His wife, of course, bore the consequences. He was even prepared, against the advice of doctors (including his wife's doctor father), to demand in the name of Rousseau that Sofya nurse her first child even though she suffered excruciating pain, and her nipples were soon cracked (266–67). When Sofya engaged a nurse, he could not bear to enter the nursery; no one could make "any dent in Tolstoy's dogged disapproval" (267).

Tolstoy's absolutely rigid views about proper roles for women were ideologically at war with any serious criticism of such roles. "Feminism," for example, "was a crime against nature and it was man's duty to see that his helpmeet [*sic*] did not succumb to this temptation" (326). To Turgenev's fury, he excoriated the life and works of George Sand (131, 283), and one of his most powerfully reasoned indictments of the injustices of Russian urban society, *What Then Must We Do?*, gives vent at its conclusion to a crudely irrationalist, sexist name-calling: "Every woman, however she may dress herself and however she may call herself and however refined she may be, who refrains from child-birth without refraining from sexual relations is a whore."[34] With a deadly accuracy characteris-

p.57

tic of her criticisms of her husband's sexism, Sofya would later observe of his idealization of good women as self-sacrificing, "That is what Lyovochka likes! ...A type of women—a she-animal, slave, lacking in all initiative, interests! Wait on your husband, serve him, bear and feed children!"[35]

Whatever his ideology, however, Tolstoy was also a great artist, developing during this period, under the impact of his relations with his wife and her family (in particular his wife's sister Tanya[36]), the artistic voice of two remarkable novels, *War and Peace* and *Anna Karenina*. His artistic voice, formed in relationship to the caring love of Tante Toinette, grew in power in relationship to Sofya and Tanya and others and took on, in consequence, an increasingly ethical voice as Tolstoy examined aristocratic Russian imperial society, politics, and culture.

We can see the striking impact of these new relationships on Tolstoy's artistic voice in *War and Peace,* a novel John Bayley analyzes as "dominated by the female principle; it is a profoundly feminine view of life."[37] The great protagonists in the plot, Prince Andrew and Pierre, struggle to find meaning in life and in war, all of which ends in their love, whether frustrated or fulfilled, for Natasha Rostov. The plot of the novel pivots on the importance of its women—Natasha with her brimming sense of life and adventure, Princess Mary with her ethical aspiration. Pierre, who had toured as a civilian observer the battlefields of the war and nearly been executed, ends up married to Natasha; Nicholas Rostov, Natasha's brother, who fights in the war, ends up married to Princess Mary, Prince Andrew's sister. Tolstoy concludes his great study of war and its sources and impact "by handing things over to the female ... principle, and by denying and suppressing male authority and initiative and the guilt and anguish about sex and death that troubled him as a male.[38]

In giving voice to Natasha Rostov and Princess Mary, Tolstoy, as an artist, finds new sources for his growing ethical skepticism about the role war played in the aristocratic sense of patriarchal manhood he had known and played at so well in the Caucasus and in the Crimean War. He was drawn to examine the Napoleonic invasion of Russia by his interest in the abortive Decembrist revolt, in which a relative of his had had a prominent role. That generation had challenged czarist absolutism on the basis of European egalitarian ideals absorbed through their military service in the Napoleonic Wars, and Tolstoy thus studied the latter period as a way of understanding them (Pierre might eventually become a Decembrist). But Napoleon's invasion of Russia was regarded by many as an outrage. It had led to slaughter unrivaled in the history of warfare. For the Slavophiles who resisted European influences, memories of the war hardened the view that European culture was essentially hostile to Russian interests.[39]

In *War and Peace,* Tolstoy studies how and why the Russian people had been successful in resisting Napoleon's imperialist ambitions, and he finds the ethical sources of such resistance not in the glittering aristocratic circles of Moscow and Petersburg but in ordinary men and women and their relationships with one another. Indeed, such aristocratic circles are placed in quite sharp antagonism to forming these relationships.

The vulnerability of Natasha Rostov to seduction by Anatole, the wastrel brother of Helene (Pierre's wife), illustrates this point. Tolstoy here uses the touching perspective and voice of an alive and captivating young woman to illustrate the lies and destructiveness inherent in a system of the patriarchal male privilege of soldiers of which he had once been an able practitioner. Natasha and Prince Andrew are engaged to be married, but because of the objections of his aristocratic father, Prince Bolkonski, to the match, Andrew has postponed the marriage for a year and gone traveling abroad in the interim. It is during this painful period of separation that the confused and inexperienced Natasha is introduced to the glittering aristocratic world of Moscow, in which her beauty, on display at the opera, prompts the interest of Pierre's corrupt wife, Helene, and the sexual interest of Helene's wayward brother, Anatole, who is already married. The ingenuous Natasha takes their interest at face value and is drawn in by Anatole's seduction, acceding to an elopement she imagines to be marriage. When plans for the elopement are frustrated, Natasha, who had broken her engagement to Prince Andrew, comes to realize the enormity of the deception and her misjudgment; she is plunged into remorse at the pain unjustly inflicted on Andrew and attempts suicide.[40]

The character of Princess Mary is based on Tolstoy's mother and that of Mary's father, Prince Bolkonski, on his maternal grandfather. The character of Natasha builds on Tolstoy's experience of women he knew, and he also would have been much influenced in his remarkable insight into a young woman by Aleksandr Pushkin's astonishing portrait of Tatyana in *Eugene Onegin.*[41] In contrast, Tolstoy's treatment of the characters of Mary and her father builds on no personal memory at all (his mother died when Tolstoy was two, his grandfather before he was born), and it has no such literary models. The character of Princess Mary is an intensely personal idealization of his mother, born of his sense of loss, as well as of Tante Toinette, the woman who lavished loving maternal care on him and who now lived with Tolstoy and his wife and growing family at Yasnaya (she died in 1874 when he was working on *Anna Karenina*). The idealized virtues are, if anything, heightened by the sense of Mary's patient victimization by an overbearing, irascible, arrogantly aristocratic father in *War and Peace*. Tolstoy's humane grandfather, Nicholas Volkonsky, had served Catherine the Great as a solder and diplomat and was rooted in the French Enlightenment of the eighteenth century; he was correspondingly dedicated, as we know, to the European education of his daughter. Tolstoy did not appreciate what that kind of love might say about a father's caring respect for his daughter's intelligence, and he makes his grandfather into a self-absorbed, jealous tyrant and his daughter into a kind of long-suffering saint. The transformation is very personal, very mythological, and very Tolstoyan.

What the portrait of his mother loses in intellectual and emotional complexity, it gains in the prophetic ethical voice he accords Princess Mary, a voice that marks Tolstoy's growing skepticism about violence and the role it plays in the life of men and nations. In a book that looks so honestly into war and the psychology of the men who fight war, Princess Mary gives voice to the most radical skepticism about men's propensity to violence, even when directed against injustice. Her brother, Prince Andrew, is about to go to war for the second time (he will be fatally wounded) and is quite personally miserable because Natasha has broken their engagement in favor of the seductive rake Anatole Kuragin. Mary speaks to her brother of the violence she knows is in his heart:

> "Andrew! One thing I beg, I entreat of you!" she said, touching his elbow and looking at him with eyes that shone through her tears. "I understand you" (she looked down). "Don't imagine that sorrow is the work of men. Men are His tools." She looked a little above Prince Andrew's head with the confident, accustomed look with which one looks at the place a familiar portrait hangs. "Sorrow is sent by *Him,* not by men. Men are His instruments, they are not to blame. If you think someone has wronged you, forget it and forgive! We have no right to punish. And then you will know the happiness of forgiving."

"If I were a woman I would do so, Mary. That is a woman's virtue. But a man should not and cannot forgive and forget," he replied, and though till that moment he had not been thinking of Kuragin, all his unexpended anger sudden swelled up in his heart.

"If Mary is already persuading me to forgive, it means that I ought long ago to have punished him," he thought. And giving her no further reply, he began thinking of the glad vindictive moment when he would meet Kuragin who he knew and was now in the army (Tolstoy, *War and Peace,* 561).

The power and appeal of Mary's prophetic ethical voice to men appears later in the novel when Prince Andrew, now seriously injured, is in the operating tent: "The doctor bent down over the wound, felt it, and sighed deeply. Then he made a sign to someone, and the torturing pain in his abdomen caused Prince Andrew to lose consciousness. When he came to himself the splintered portions of his thighbone had been extracted, the torn flesh cut away, and the wound bandaged. Water was being sprinkled on his face. As soon as Prince Andrew opened his eyes, the doctor bent over, kissed him silently on the lips, and hurried away" (725).

Andrew then sees in the operating tent Anatole Kuragin, whose leg has just been amputated:

> In the miserable, sobbing, enfeebled man whose leg had just been amputated, he recognized Anatole Kuragin. Men were supporting him in their arms and offering him a glass of water, but his trembling, swollen lips could not grasp its rim. Anatole was sobbing painfully. "Yes, it is he! Yes, that man is somehow closely and painfully connected with me," thought Prince Andrew, not yet clearly grasping what he saw before him. "What is the connection of that man with my childhood and my life?" he asked himself without finding an answer. And suddenly a new unexpected memory from that realm of pure and loving childhood presented itself to him. He remembered Natasha as he had seen her for the first time at the ball in 1810, with her slender neck and arms and with a frightened happy face ready for rapture, and love and tenderness for her, stronger and more vivid than ever, awoke in his soul. He now remembered the connec-

tion that existed between himself and this man who was dimly gazing at him through tears that filled his swollen eyes. He remembered everything, and ecstatic pity and love for that man overflowed his happy heart.

Prince Andrew could no longer restrain himself and wept tender loving tears for his fellow men, for himself, and for his own and their errors.

"Compassion, love of our brothers, for those who love us and for those who hate us, love of our enemies; yes, that love which God preached on earth and which Princess Mary taught me and I did not understand—that is what made me sorry to part with life, that is what remained for me had I lived. But now it is too late. I know it!" (726)

It is a very striking feature of *War and Peace* that men at war experience doubts, sometimes not expressed, about the cult of male honor surrounding war (for example, Nicholas Rostov and Prince Andrew) (364–65, 574–75, 691). Tolstoy comments on the role such codes play in silencing ethical voice, a theme prominently illustrated in the cultic ideology of Napoleonic imperialistic genius that rationalizes ethical atrocities (537, 555, 572, 1001, 1060). Prince Andrew had once admired Napoleon as a hero of the political dimension of the Enlightenment, but after he is injured in battle with him at Austerlitz and is brought before him to enjoy his praises for his courage on the battlefield, he sees Napoleon as "a small, insignificant creature compared with what was passing now between himself and the lofty infinite sky with the clouds flying away"; indeed, "so mean did his hero himself with his paltry vanity and joy in victory appear, compared to the lofty, equitable, and kindly sky which he had seen and understood" (253–54). The image returns in the novel, marking Andrew's awakening ethical voice as, after a conversation with his friend Pierre, "he looked up at the sky to which Pierre had pointed, and for the first time since Austerlitz saw that high, everlasting sky he had seen while lying on the battlefield; and something that had long been slumbering, something that was best within him, suddenly awoke, joyful and youthful, in his soul" (561; see also 558, 685–86).

It is a feature of this ethical voice, as ethical demands arising outside and impartially critical of the patriarchal culture of war, that Andrew ultimately comes to hear and understand its demands (even at the moment

of his death) through the voice of an outsider to the glittering aristocratic world of Petersburg and Moscow—his unworldly sister Princess
Mary (561, 726, 817–18, 868–89)—and that his friend Pierre (who ultimately marries Natasha) hears it from another such outsider—the peasant Karataev (859–61, 895, 977).

Tolstoy had invested twenty years of his life in playing at the competitive game of aristocratic manhood, which included fighting in Russia's
highly questionable imperialistic wars in the Caucasus and the Crimea
and indulging in the corresponding sexual exploits with fallen women.
His marriage to Sofya Bers made possible a shift and growth in artistic
voice, one that raises in *War and Peace,* as we have seen, profound ethical
doubts about the role manhood played in sustaining and glorifying war.
There are two dimensions of his skepticism, one expressed through the
impact on Natasha of a system of male honor centered on the exploitation of women's sexuality and the other expressed through Princess
Mary's questioning of the role such codes of honor played in rationalizing violence. *War and Peace* ends, however, in an unsatisfactory accommodation to the system about which it raises such doubts (Gustave
Flaubert, enthusiastic about the rest of the novel, found its ending a
shocking accommodation to conventionality[42]). Natasha, so lively and
surprising as a young woman, becomes, on her marriage to Pierre, a person whose "soul was not visible at all. All that struck the eye was a strong,
handsome, and fertile woman"; not understanding discussions about
women's rights, she "placed herself in the position of a slave to her husband."[43] The moral complexity of women is now reduced to the terms
of a sexist slogan as they are defined in terms of "the pleasure given by
real women gifted with a capacity to select and absorb the very best a
man shows of himself."[44] Tolstoy may himself have been dissatisfied with
the novel's fatalistic ending.

War and Peace was finished and published in 1869. Tolstoy had every
reason to feel content. He had conquered his gambling habit and written a novel of genius that, thanks to his wife's advice to publish it himself in a volume, had made his fortune. He had both cash and time on
his hands. Happening to see an advertisement of an estate for sale in the
province of Penza, he set off on an impulse to look it over at the end of
August 1869. It was a difficult journey. On September 2, before he got
to Saransk, Tolstoy found himself exhausted and decided to spend the
night at a place called Arzamas. He was too exhausted to sleep. He wrote

a letter to his wife two days later about a nightmarish experience: "Suddenly I was over overcome by despair, fear, and terror, the like of which I have never experienced before."(45) A. N. Wilson urges us to be skeptical about the way Tolstoy himself interpreted the experience (namely, as a religious awakening) in a short story (*Memoirs of a Madman*) fifteen years later. After the night at Arzamas, he did not have a religious conversion; that would occur some years in the future. Rather, Wilson notes two features of the experience that were to recur in Tolstoy's life: first, a mad desire to get away from himself, as in ending his life, and second, a fear of death (*Tolstoy,* 250–51). At the heart of the later short story was a hallucinatory experience that would recur several times over the next few years. There is a kind of psychic confrontation within him of what was in *War and Peace* "an exercise in mythology—a reconstruction of his personal and national history" with "a series of unanswerable questions: . . . Why are we here? In Tolstoy's personal life, this was quickly translated, with the help of Schopenhauer, into 'What is the point of anything?'" (251).

The sources of *Anna Karenina,* Tolstoy's next novel, are often traced to the fact that his own sister, Marya Nikolayevna, had been in a position similar to Anna's, running away from her husband and getting pregnant by a Swedish viscount, as well as the 1872 suicide under a train of Anna Stepanovna Pirogova, the mistress of a landowner neighbor of the Tolstoys who had cast her off for his children's German governess (270, 261). These events would have arrested Tolstoy's creative attention only if they had offered him a way of addressing the kind of suicidal despair he experienced at Arzamas and later, that is, if they gave him a way to answer, consistent with his voice as an artist, his doubts about the fatalistic mythology of gender with which he had ended *War and Peace.*

The plot of *Anna Karenina* is a contrapuntal study of two relationships: one between Anna and Vronsky and another between Levin and Kitty. The Anna-Vronsky relationship is adulterous. Anna is married, with a son, to Karenin, an important civil servant in the Petersburg bureaucracy. Vronsky, a military officer, was initially interested in Kitty, an available unmarried woman, but he pursues Anna, a married woman, instead. The Levin-Kitty relationship ends in a marriage closely modeled on Tolstoy's own, including the putative incident with the tablet and chalk already discussed, and the death of a brother is also mentioned. Kitty's sister, Dolly, is married to Stiva, Anna's brother. The novel begins with

Anna's mediation of a crisis in the marriage of Stiva and Dolly after Dolly discovers that her husband is having an affair with a former French governess. Anna, who comes to Moscow from Petersburg and success-fully mediates the dispute, meets Vronsky; Vronsky, who had initially been interested in Kitty, now aggressively pursues Anna to Petersburg. Anna abandons her son to live with Vronsky and has a daughter with him. At one point, in a spirit of large-hearted generosity, Karenin had offered to divorce Anna, but patriarchally shamed by a religious woman friend (as a man dishonored by his wife's adultery), he withdrew his offer; Anna is cut off from relations with her son. Irrationally suspicious of Vronsky's fidelity, she commits suicide by throwing herself under a train.

The Levin-Kitty relationship closely tracks Tolstoy's own life with Sofya and his growing family, which, as in *War and Peace,* he mytholo-gizes in terms of an alternative to Anna's tragic end. There is, surely, such mythology in the famous opening of the novel: "All happy families are alike; each unhappy family is unhappy in its own way,"[46] as if, contrary to fact, there was or is only one fixed pattern that happy families or in-timate relationships follow. I call this mythology because its statement is clearly not factually true, yet in terms of a certain patriarchal ideology, it must be true and could not *not* be true. The piercing, gripping interest of *Anna Karenina* is that Tolstoy crucially gives artistic voice to Anna, whose experience of an irrationally suicidal despair was one Tolstoy un-derstood all too well at Arzamas and later. It was an experience that, as a happy family man, he *should* not have had. But he did have it, and he un-dertakes to explore it in the voice not of a man but of a woman and moreover of a woman he condemned; we see this aspect of Tolstoy in Levin's "loathing for fallen women," shown in his sense of horror that Anna should meet his wife, Kitty.[47] We earlier saw what Tolstoy, publicly speaking as a moralist, thought of women like Anna, who notably used contraceptives to have no further children by Vronsky.[48] "Every woman . . . who refrains from child-birth without refraining from sexual rela-tions is a whore."[49] The epigraph to *Anna Karenina* expressly refuses to make such an easy moralistic judgment, or rather, it expresses doubt that any man could reasonably make such a judgment: "Vengeance is mine; I will repay."[50] The epigraph certainly echoes and was meant to echo Jesus's refusal to judge the adulteress in John 8:1–11. However, Tolstoy goes well beyond the mere refusal of punitive moral judgment; he takes on and explores Anna's voice as a way of asking questions he could not otherwise explore, moving himself into regions so psychologically perilous for his sense of himself, as a man, that he apparently was plunged into a crisis of vocation. *(EOF)* 0:51:01.94

Anna pursues, as a woman, sexual interests that Tolstoy had, as a man, certainly taken at least as seriously, including in his erotically charged relationship with his wife. As we have seen, he would never have accepted that his own wife might have such interests or might pursue them with the freedom accorded men; his views of a wife's role were, as Wilson puts it, within "the stricter disciplines of old religions such as Islam."[51] Both he and Sofya accepted, as earlier noted, the ideology of the pedestal, whereby women were divided into good or respectable women who had no such interests and often racialized bad or fallen women who did. But Tolstoy may have heard another inner voice in his wife, which gave him a knowledge that, within the limits of his experience (he had never loved a free woman), he explores in *Anna Karenina*. Certainly, Sofya had reached such a point of unhappiness in her marriage later in 1890 that she actually gave expression to that inner voice, protesting the price she paid for her idealization, in a passage in her diaries that Tolstoy would have read: "Purity is beautiful anywhere and in anything—in nature, in the souls and consciences of men, in morals, and in the material life—everywhere. But why did I try so hard to preserve it? Would not the remembrance of even a criminal love be better than my purity of conscience—and this awful sense of void?"[52]

By the time he would have read this, Tolstoy had withdrawn into an ethical religion that, as we shall see, equally condemned sexuality in men and in women. But in the more open-minded days of his work on *Anna Karenina,* he was not only sensitively recording in Anna a woman's interest in free sexual voice akin to that later expressed by his wife but also asking why exactly such a voice—so freely indulged by men like Anna's brother, Stiva—should be accorded so different a weight in women.

At several points in *Anna Karenina,* Tolstoy records conversations and debates about the question of women and their rights, a question brought to the attention of Russians by the prominent role the issue played in European, including British, thought and literature of this period.[53] *Anna Karenina* is his creative response, as an artist, to this genre.[54] As we have seen, Tolstoy was, to say the least, quite unsympathetic to arguments for women's rights, but his growing skepticism about the role violence played in manhood was reflected in the way he gave expression to women's voices in *War and Peace,* suggesting that such voices, when properly understood, afforded an ethically prophetic alternative. His mounting skepticism about manhood carried over to its gender binary, womanhood. However, as in the case of Princess Mary, the alternative in *Anna Karenina* was freighted with highly idealized conceptions of women that drained them, as women, of any intellectual or emotional complexity. In *Anna Karenina*— building undoubtedly on his relationship with Sofya, her family, his sister, and the like—Tolstoy gives expression to a sexual voice in women that takes seriously their complexity and also the repressive forces arrayed against the free exercise of that voice by women. Those repressive forces rest, as Tolstoy shows us with exquisite psychological sensitivity, in women as well as men—in the good women of the novel who viciously turn on Anna and abandon her into a kind of solipsistic exile and in the men, not only Karenin but also Vronsky, who do not give Anna the caring, attentive love she needs. Tolstoy shows us the consequences of such a failure of love in Anna's suicide and also in Vronsky's turning his pain into political violence, as he redeems his injured manhood by fighting in another of Russia's unjust imperialistic wars. The antiwar conclusion (against the Turkish war in which Russia was then engaged) was regarded as so shocking that the publisher, who had been issuing the novel in serialized form, refused to publish it.[55]

We are told very little about Anna's background, other than that her marriage to Karenin was, in the usual Russian way, an arranged marriage, certainly loveless on Anna's part; she is, however, devoted to her young son by Karenin, Seryozha. Anna is, of course, beautiful but also, at the opening of the novel, a sensitive and intelligent interpreter of the human world (a person of "subtle perceptiveness") (*Anna Karenina,* 530). She accurately reads the crisis in the marriage of Dolly and her brother, Stiva, and exquisitely uses her human skills to draw the couple back into a sense of relationship to one another and to their frightened children. She is also a person who values honest feeling, as opposed to a hypocrisy that conceals real feeling: "At least I don't lie" (532). The question posed by the novel is how such a remarkable reader of human relationships can, by the novel's end, be so irrationally and self-destructively cut off from the human relationships and the feelings she had sacrificed so much to achieve—her love for Vronsky and Vronsky's love for her.

After Anna has finished patching up the quarrel between Dolly and Stiva, Dolly pays tribute to her psychological powers ("Your soul is clear and good"), to which Anna responds, "Each of us has his skeletons in his soul, as the English say" (97). Anna has been disturbed by meeting Vronsky, but she now puts that behind her as she returns by train to Petersburg (unknown to her, Vronsky, smitten, is on the train to pursue her). Tolstoy, a novelist whose art depended on eliding the lines between his life and his fiction, depicts Anna on the train as suspicious of fiction. She is reading an English novel to pass the time but finds it difficult to read fiction because it compromises some increasingly urgent need of her psyche:

> Anna Arkadyevna read and understood, but it was unpleasant for her to read, that is, to follow the reflection of other people's lives. She wanted too much to live herself. When she read about the heroine of the novel taking care of a sick man, she wanted to walk with inaudible steps round the sick man's room; when she read about a Member of Parliament making a speech, she wanted to make that speech; when she read about how Lady Mary rode to hounds, teasing her sister-in-law and surprising everyone with her courage, she wanted to do it herself. But there was nothing to do, and so, fingering the smooth knife with her small hands, she forced herself to read. (100)

Anna is reading about the hero of the novel "beginning to achieve his English happiness" and wishes to be with him

> when suddenly she felt that he must be ashamed and that she was ashamed of the same thing. But what was he ashamed of? "What am I ashamed of?" she asked herself in offended astonishment. . . . There was nothing shameful. She went through all her Moscow memories. They were all good, pleasant. She remembered the ball, remembered Vronsky and his enamoured, obedient face, remembered all her relations with him: nothing was shameful. But just there, at the very place in her memories, the feeling of shame became more intense, as if precisely then, when she remembered Vronsky, some inner voice were telling her: "Warm, very warm, hot!" "Well, what then?" she said resolutely to herself, shifting her position in the seat. "What does it mean? Am I afraid to look at it directly? Well, what of it? Can it be

that there exist or ever could exist any other relations between
me and this boy-officer than those that exist with any acquain-
tance?" (100) ⁴⁄

Anna is portrayed in a struggle with herself to feel what she feels, to
center herself in a sexual voice that acknowledges what it feels and how
those feelings of desire make possible a new kind of relationship with the
"boy-officer" she desires. Once having faced herself as a real person, fiction makes no sense; she "now was decidedly unable to understand what
she was reading." Now completely in her body and its feelings, Anna realizes her freedom as a person: "'And what am I? Myself or someone
else?' It was frightening to surrender to this oblivion. But something was
drawing her in, and she was able, at will, to surrender to it or hold back
from it." After she notes that a muzhik comes in as a stoker, she falls into
a dozing, hallucinatory experience—a form of which will recur before
her suicide: "This muzhik with the long waist began to gnaw at something on the wall; . . . then something screeched and banged terribly, as
if someone were being torn to pieces; then a red fire blinded her eyes,
and then everything was hidden by a wall. Anna felt as if she was falling
through the floor. But all this was not frightening but exhilarating" (102).
Tolstoy takes us into the psyche of a married woman of good station
in the aristocratic Russian frame of things, who, like Hester Prynne, is
remarkably open to feelings and thinking outside what Hawthorne
called the "iron framework of reasoning" that held conventional gender
arrangements in place.⁵⁶ But we see Hester's independence of mind as a
development long after her adultery with Dimmesdale and the public
shame to which she was subjected; it leads her to fundamental reflections
on the injustice of patriarchy and the need for resistance. If Anna ever
has such thoughts, Tolstoy does not share them with us. The closest the
novel comes to exploring such intelligence in Anna is a scene late in the
novel when she meets Levin. Levin, who was reluctant even to meet
Anna, an adulteress living openly with her lover ("What would Kitty
say?"), is impressed not only by her "intelligence, grace, beauty" but also
by her "truthfulness." Anna's brother, Stiva, has told Levin that Anna is
writing a book for children that a publisher had said is "a remarkable
thing," but he responds to Levin's evident skepticism with, "'But you'll
think she's a woman author? Not a bit of it. Before all she's a woman
with heart, you'll see that.'" When Levin actually meets Anna, the sub-

ject of her children's book comes up again, but Anna herself characterizes the book not in terms of Hester's idea of liberation from a patriarchal cage but as a kind of prison: "'My writing is like those carved baskets made in prisons that Liza Mertsalov used to sell me. She was in charge of prisons in that society,' she turned to Levin. 'And those unfortunates produced miracles of patience.'" Levin is "completely won over," describing her to Stiva as "'an extraordinary woman! Not just her intelligence, but her heart. I'm terribly sorry for her!'"[57]

In the narrative's patronizing pity, Tolstoy's barely concealed contempt for the very idea of "a woman author" is revealed. If even Stiva must defend his sister's honor against even Levin's visible disgust with such an idea, we have some sense of the degree to which Anna is cut off from any respect or care for her intelligence, as expressed in her writing. Tolstoy shows us the psychological consequences of such a world on Anna's sense of herself as a writer, conceiving her writing as bounded by the terms of the cultural prison in which she is trapped. With all his feeling for Anna, he shows us the terms of her misery as he shows us that the most compassionate persons he can imaginatively create (Stiva, Levin) cannot even acknowledge, let alone respect, a woman's prophetic ethical voice that might challenge, as Hawthorne's Hester Prynne does, the injustice of the patriarchy that condemns her. When Tolstoy himself acknowledges that some women have such a prophetic ethical voice, as in his portrait of Princess Mary in *War and Peace,* he employs a highly idealized, desexualized image of a mother Tolstoy never knew. His mother was very well educated by her Enlightenment father and undoubtedly highly intelligent, but any such intellectual and emotional complexity is drained out of the portrait of her as having prophetic ethical voice. On Tolstoy's understanding of such voice, it could not be connected to a free sexual voice that, as he well knew as a man, supports and sustains creative voice, a sexist problem in men on which Freud commented when he traced the intellectual inferiority in some women "to the inhibition of thought necessitated by sexual suppression."[58] Nathaniel Hawthorne, in contrast to Tolstoy, acknowledged such a creative sexual voice in Hester Prynne. But that was a voice Tolstoy had the greatest difficulty in even recognizing in women, as his increasingly unhappy marriage clearly shows.

The Levin-Anna scene contains, in microcosm, the answer to my earlier question: how should we understand the psychological movement of

Anna from the intelligent reader of human relationships at the novel's opening to her irrational failure to read relationship at the novel's conclusion? In Tolstoy's portrayal of Anna, her journey starts in the previously quoted scene exploring her feelings and thoughts on the train from Moscow to Petersburg, as she comes to recognize and feel the authority of her free sexual voice, a voice she had never previously acknowledged. But for a novel that centers on the astute study of a woman feeling and acting on her sexual voice, it is striking that we never enter into the psychological world of her feelings, sexual and romantic, for Vronsky or his feelings for her. For all his sexual adventures, Tolstoy never had a relationship with a free woman like Anna, and his highly autobiographical fiction does not go where he has never gone himself, namely, into the background and force of such passionate love, based on the free sexual voice of both partners as equals. What we are shown is what Tolstoy knew all too well: how a military man such as Vronsky tended to regard women. This is revealed through the remarkable scene, obviously a metaphor for his relationship with Anna, of his highly erotic feeling for and riding of his horse, Frou-Frou, at a race Anna attended, a race that ends disastrously with the serious injury and ultimately the death of his beloved horse (181–82, 192, 198–200, 544). The scene is much the most erotic one in the novel, and in a novel about sexual voice, it must be accorded great interpretive importance.

If we are never taken into Anna's passion for Vronsky, the Frou-Frou scene takes us into Vronsky's passion for her. It is, of course, a deeply erotic passion, but however tender the passion is, it stems from an eroticism so formed on the model of a military hierarchy of mastery and submission that it may be distorted by patriarchal hierachy in love as in war. Vronsky is always portrayed as feeling and being in love with Anna, as is surely shown by his sacrifice of a promising military career in order to live with the still-married woman. But a love experienced in the way the Frou-Frou incident depicts is vulnerable to being disastrously distracted from the free sexual voice of the partner. Anna certainly feels and acts on the authority of her sexual voice, but Vronsky's love does not, at an emotionally crucial point, give her the resonance for that voice that she needs. What comes between them is Vronsky's code of honor. As a military man, he stands ready to defend what Tolstoy archly calls "the nonexistent honour of the woman he loved" (305) and would prefer that Karenin fight him standing up "for his honour" rather than respond with "this weakness or meanness" that puts Vronsky, as he thinks of it, "in the position of a deceiver, which is something I never wanted and do not want to be" (356). Anna, however, is in a psychic place where considerations of honor or humiliation lack meaning for her. Once she tells her husband of her affair with Vronsky and receives his written refusal of divorce and demand that she continue living with him to keep up appearances (283–84), she goes to Vronsky and would have gone off with him, leaving her son, if, as she expected, "he would say to her resolutely, passionately, without a moment's hesitation: 'Abandon everything and fly away with me!'" (315). However, Vronsky, a man of honor, is thinking about the duel with her husband that he regards as inevitable (it never, in fact, occurs) as well as the price an open liaison with Anna would exact from his military career. Anna misconstrues his sternness as a lack of the feeling of love she expected. Just as Vronsky, at a crucial point in riding Frou-Frou, was disastrously distracted from his usual sensitivity to the horse he loved ("he, not knowing how himself, had made a wrong, an unforgivable movement as he lowered himself into the saddle . . . , and he knew that something terrible had happened"), he does not give Anna the responsiveness she needs at this pivotal moment in their relationship (Frou-Frou's death prefigures Anna's) (199).

Now, she says that she cannot and will not leave her husband if it involves losing her child, to which Vronsky responds that leaving her son would at least be better than "this humiliating situation." Anna disowns such an emotional evasion:

> "You say 'humiliating' . . . don't say it. Such words have no meaning for me," she said in a trembling voice. She did not want him to say what was not true now. All she had left was his love, and she wanted to love him. "You understand that from the day I loved you everything was changed for me. For me there is one thing only—your love. If it is mine, I feel myself so high, so firm, that nothing can be humiliating for me. I'm proud of my position, because . . . proud of . . . proud . . ." She did not finish saying what she was proud of. Tears of shame and despair stifled her voice. She stopped and burst into sobs. (316)

What comes between the lovers at this critical point is their different relationship to the code of honor. Anna, a fallen woman condemned by that code, breaks down in grief at her sense of shame; her honor has been irrevocably lost. Further, her love for Vronsky and for her son have now been rendered irreconcilable by Karenin. But she now speaks from a vulnerable psyche that is alive, for the first time in her life, to her loving sexual voice, and she craves a responsive, consoling resonance to that voice from her lover. Vronsky, as an armored man of honor, is distracted by upholding his honor (the required duel with the aggrieved husband) and does not give Anna the responsive voice she needs. The lack of this responsive voice makes Anna doubt her own voice, which takes the form of doubting Vronsky's love, ultimately destroying her capacity to know, to feel. It is psychologically astute that Tolstoy links Anna's gnawing doubts about Vronsky's love with her passion for reunion with her son, which waxes as she supposes Vronsky's love to wane; correspondingly, she lacks feeling for the daughter she had by Vronsky.

Anna's emotional intelligence, on brilliant display at the novel's opening, had flourished within the patriarchal structure of Russian culture that she, like other Russian women of her station, had assumed to be in the nature of things. That structure crucially required the repression of any voice that might question its mythology of gender, including women's sexual voice—a way of life illustrated by Tolstoy's disastrous marriage to Sofya. Once Anna opens herself to her own sexual voice, she is psychologically vulnerable in a way she was not when she had stayed securely perched on the pedestal where women of her station were placed. The culture that surrounds her is, as Tolstoy shows, actively hostile to any such display of voice, which puts Anna in precisely the psychologically vulnerable position she is in: the authority of her voice requires the resonance of a lover before it can be believed, let alone acted on. What the novel shows us, in harrowing detail, is how the lack of resonance undermines resources of emotional intelligence, so that the brilliant reader of the human world under patriarchy, "with her subtle perceptiveness," is no longer able to read love or relationship after she places herself outside patriarchy and finds herself without any support for resisting it (530). Anna is terrifyingly alone. Her suicidal despair at the novel's end puts her in exactly the opposite place from the novel's beginning. There, her opening to sexual voice was so real that she could no longer live in the fiction she had been reading. But at the moment of her death, she is, as Tolstoy tells us, unable to release the grip of the fiction she is now calamitously living out unto her suicidal death under the wheels of the approaching train:

And at the same instant she was horrified at what she was doing. "Where am I? What am I doing? Why?" She wanted to rise, to throw herself back, but something huge and implacable pushed at her head and dragged over her. "Lord, forgive me for everything!" she said, feeling the impossibility of the struggle. A little muzhik, muttering to himself, was working over some iron. And the candle by the light of which she had been reading that book filled with anxieties, deceptions, grief and evil, flared up brighter than ever, lit up for her all that had once been in darkness, sputtered, grew dim, and went out for ever. (768)

Tolstoy shows us at every stage how Anna moves from brilliant human intelligence to irrational suicidal despair. The process starts with her intrapsychic doubts about Vronsky's love. But the silence of his lack of responsive voice is filled with the din of voices screaming in condemnation once her liaison with him becomes notorious. Conspicuously, the loudest such voices in *Anna Karenina* are those of women. At one point, Karenin's heart had opened in loving forgiveness of his wife's transgressions (a moment when he was engulfed for the first time in his life by humane feelings that he identified with "the Christian law . . . that he forgive and love his enemies" [413]), and he was willing to allow Anna to see her son. But his heart and mind are closed by the influence on him of the religious sectarian Countess Lydia Ivanovna who, on the basis of Karenin's "loftiness" and Anna's "baseness," persuades him that he must protect his son from the taint of seeing his mother (519). Anna is publicly insulted by other women when she goes to the theater (547, 549), and Vronsky's mother, who admired Anna before the liaison, now scorns her; indeed, even Vronsky's sister-in-law refuses to be hospitable to Anna because of the effect on her daughter. For the mother of Kitty and Dolly, Anna is "a vile, disgusting woman, quite heartless" (556). Kitty argues with her husband, Levin, that it was not right for him to visit, let alone pity, Anna (702–3), and she herself tries to avoid seeing her (758–60). Near the end of her life, when she most desperately needs a confidante, Anna goes to see Dolly, a woman who earlier, after Anna successfully negotiated the crisis in Dolly's marriage, had exclaimed, "Remember this, Anna: I will never forget what you did for me. And remember that I've loved and will always love you as my best friend!" (99). It is at this point near the end of her life that Anna's terrifying isolation, her solipsism, becomes evident as she keeps herself enclosed in her bitter illusions; she is alone, in a place where "not a single decent woman can receive me in my position" and where even Dolly must fail her: "Dolly won't understand anything either. And I have nothing to tell her" (758). Dolly and her sister Kitty are there in the same room with Anna but not there relationally. Dolly knows something is wrong ("I thought she was going to cry" [760]), but she, who once promised Anna love forever, does not act on her knowledge to respond to Anna's evident suffering. Anna is utterly, fatally alone in her irrational despair.

Vronsky, who loved Anna, is traumatized by her suicide. His initial response is to attempt suicide himself, but he finds a more honorable way to sanctify his self-destructiveness when he commits his life and fortune to leading troops in another of Russia's unjust imperialistic wars, the Serbian war (778–79, 780). For Tolstoy, it is evident that the war in question is unjust, as Levin makes quite clear (804–9). What is of interest is the sense Tolstoy makes here of a psychology of manhood that allows men like Vronsky to throw themselves into such unjust political violence even unto their deaths (one senses that Vronsky will certainly die in this war). Tolstoy is drawing out yet further psychological implications of the role that the code of honor plays in the psychology of men and women. We have already seen what Tolstoy makes of the impact of the code on sexual voice: Vronsky's sense of honor as a man, preoccupying him with the obligation to use violence (dueling) to protect his or Anna's honor, distracts him from feeling and responsively expressing his love for her in a way that would have given her a resonance for the authority of her loving sexual voice. The psychology of honor, to this extent, draws its power from breaking intimate relationship based on voice. Tolstoy carries his astute psychological analysis further in showing us how Vronsky's sense of honor, based on breaking intimate relationships, allows him to find redemptive meaning in political violence as a way of recovering his honor ("Yes, as a tool I may prove good for something. But as a human being I am a wreck" [780]). The psychology of male honor thus understood rationalizes unjust political violence in the same way it rationalizes the repression of sexual voice, by forging an armored psychology that directs violence at any voice that might reasonably contest it. Tolstoy underscores this point when Levin alludes to the psychology that allows men not to see how bad their arguments for war are: "They're wearing impenetrable armour, and I am naked" (809).

There is nothing inevitable in the narrative that ends with Anna's suicide. The story could have gone in a different way. Tolstoy wants us to see that suicidal despair may arise in excess or in despite of a life that could easily have gone much better. He carries us into the psyche of Anna's growing despair because it is a despair that he knew at Arzamas and that would recur thereafter in his life. Tolstoy identifies with Anna's despair because he had come to share it or something like it.[59] His marriage, as we have seen, enormously empowered his artistic voice, but it also calamitously confronted him with his limits as a man, in particular when he confronted Sofya. What Tolstoy ascribes to Anna, a growing sense of loving sexual voice, was something he had always valued as a man and now was trying to understand in himself and in his wife as he, for the first time in his life, combined intimate voice with his sex partner. What was disastrous in Tolstoy's marriage was his lack of respect for his wife's sexual voice, which is, unsurprisingly in such an autobiographical artist, the subject matter of *Anna Karenina*. When he decided that the narrative would end in Anna's suicidal despair and death, he was killing not only her but also a part of himself he had always valued—his sexuality (ultimately, he turns to celibacy as the required course). Tolstoy was plunged into a crisis of vocation.

Tolstoy on Nonviolence

Tolstoy records this crisis in *Confession,* which was probably begun in 1879.[60] *Anna Karenina* was finished in 1877, and Tolstoy was exhausted. Turgenev visited him in the summer of 1878 and found he was "in the grip of nearly suicidal melancholia."[61] Wilson argues that *Confession* is "a transparent piece of self-deception: transparent, that is, to everyone except the author."[62] Tolstoy simplifies and distorts his earlier history, which was always "troubled by a conflict between an unyielding, intellectual rationalism and a passionately religious temperament."[63] The most remarkable distortion is that he "regarded writing as a trivial endeavor" yielding to "the temptations of enormous monetary rewards and applause for worthless work."[64] Tolstoy forgets the creative energy with which he wrote and rewrote and recorrected Sofya's copies of *War and Peace.* He reveals what Wilson calls "his extraordinary, and surely psychotic, ability to find dissatisfaction precisely in the areas which should have given him the greatest and the noblest forms of pleasure"when he describes his state of mind on finishing *Anna Karenina*.[65] "Very well, you will be more famous than Gogol, Pushkin, Shakespeare, Moliere, more famous than all the writers in the world—so what?[66] Tolstoy thinks that by asking this question, he shows his indifference to literature. But, as Wilson notes, "in fact, it reveals quite the reverse. It shows that he had seen it all as a competition: a competition which, moreover, he had won."[67]

There was always a strong element of role-playing in Tolstoy's sense of himself as a young man, but his development and expression of artistic voice was his way of speaking truthfully about the problem of manhood in connection both to politics and war (*War and Peace*) and to personal life (*Anna Karenina*). He now falsely regards his art as a kind of role-playing, "not living my own life but the life of another that was carrying me along on its crest."[68] As the artist he is, Tolstoy offers a speaking image to capture his sense of terror about the place to which his art had brought him: a man in a well between a wild beast above and a dragon with open jaws below, suspended on the branch of a wild bush, tasting drops of honey falling from the bush that no longer satisfy, the branch being eaten by black and white mice.[69]

The way to understand the terror that he said "was leading me toward suicide" is to note what, for Tolstoy, dissipates it.[70] It is not art, but it is not his family either: he pointedly rejects both as the solution. Rather, the solution is God, but it is God understood in a very specific way: "the conviction that I could not be the fledgling fallen from a nest that I felt myself to be. If I lie on my back in the tall grass and cry out like a fallen fledgling, it is because my mother brought me into the world, kept me warm, fed me, and loved me. But where is my mother now? If I have been cast out, then who has cast me out? I cannot help but feel that someone who loved me gave birth to me. Who is this someone? Again, God."[71]

Tolstoy, of course, had never known his mother. The person he had known as a mother was Aunt Toinette, who had died in 1874 while he was working on *Anna Karenina*. If we take all the elements of maternal care that Sara Ruddick discusses (preservation, growth, acceptability), it was, for Tolstoy, Aunt Toinette who had shown this kind of loving care to him, precisely the kind of patient care of an often wayward boy and man that eventually brought that man, though nurturing his artistic voice, into some kind of maturity and ethical wholeness. Aunt Toinette

p 77

was now dead, and the person who stood in her supportive place (nurturing his art) was Sofya. But as *Anna Karenina* records and Tolstoy's life shows, the marriage was becoming increasingly problematic, precisely because Tolstoy had reached his limits as a patriarchal man and would not respect Sofya's sexual voice as a woman. He tried to conceal his tracks in *Anna Karenina* by offering in Levin a character that was so evidently Tolstoy, including his contradictions.[72] On this reading, Levin's marriage to Kitty offers us a normative model of redemptive family life, in contrast to Anna and Vronsky. But as John Bayley observes, Levin is a kind of self-consciously distracting subterfuge, which allows Tolstoy better to focus on the character with whom he really identified—Anna, a sexual woman.[73]

Here, Tolstoy is not using his art merely to play a role, as he claimed in *Confession*. He is, as an artist, confronting in Anna a suicidal despair he felt in himself, a despair that became public in the years after the completion of the novel. The despair was over what led to Anna's despair: the loss or the lack of a partner's loving voice as a resonance for one's own loving voice. The death of Aunt Toinette left a gaping hole in his emotional life, which his marriage to Sofya did not fill. Tolstoy had broken his passionate love affair with a "bad" peasant woman in order to marry a patriarchally conventional "good" woman he barely knew. Sofya and others had certainly nurtured and strengthed the creative voice of *War and Peace* and *Anna Karenina* in ways that enabled Tolstoy not only to create wonderfully real women as characters but also to create comparable men struggling increasingly with and against the terms of a manhood defined by codes of honor. But never having loved a free sexual woman as an equal, Tolstoy cannot go in his art where he has never been; he can go into Vronsky's sexual feeling for Anna but not Anna's for Vronsky. Tolstoy's imagination (extending to a woman the same respect for sexual voice he knew as a man) fails him precisely where he lacks any experience to draw on. His imagination crashes into the stone wall of his inexperience, as he, identifying with Anna, violently turns on her and thus on himself.

Tolstoy was now confronted with a crisis in his sense of manhood, a crisis reflected in the way he described his conflicted feelings for Sofya: "a 'man of integrity'—I mean what I say: both 'integrity' and 'man.'"[74] When Aunt Toinette expressed disagreement with Tolstoy, such expressions did not threaten her womanhood; on the contrary, he highly idealized both

77

his aunt and, a fortiori, his mother (his idealizations of these women appear in the character of Princess Mary in *War and Peace* as a kind of elevated ethical voice). But with Sofya, for the first time in his life, Tolstoy sought in one woman both a loving voice and a satisfying sex partner. As we know, his inflexible conception of legitimate sex was brutally insensitive to Sofya's desires and interests. Sofya's disagreements with him were now psychologically read by Tolstoy as threats to her womanhood and, by implication, to his manhood. The suicidal terror he experienced was a panic, I believe, over gender in general and his manhood in particular. Tolstoy's artistic imagination failed him as he faced his own acute sense of loss, which he could resolve only by turning to a moralistic idealization that expressed his disassociation from what he knew, as an artist, about women's sexuality. Tolstoy rationalized loss by a willful repudiation of sexual relationship. Tolstoy becomes, in effect, his idealized, asexual mother.[75]

What is remarkable in this development is that it arose out of the astonishing truthfulness of Tolstoy's artistic voice, for in his two great mature novels, he gave voice, as we have seen, to a humane ethical skepticism about the role codes of honor destructively played in the construction of aristocratic Russian manhood and womanhood. Tolstoy had carried his analysis as far as he had reached in his life, but his life, as a sexual man and husband, remained obdurately, obstinately patriarchal. The price he paid for his willfulness on this point was terrible, indeed, psychologically suicidal—the sacrifice of his artistic voice. That voice had confronted him with the impact of the Russian military man's patriarchal code of honor on a psychology unable to love and willing to lend itself to unjust violence, including unjust imperialistic wars. Such a truthful voice, the voice of Anna, ultimately accused Tolstoy himself.

Tatyana Tolstaya, a descendant of Tolstoy (he was her great-granduncle), has recently clarified his crisis of vocation as part of a larger pattern of Russian writers who, while inspired by Pushkin's astonishing artistic achievements, "didn't see the most important thing—his inner freedom." In a sense, they were afraid of it: "not one of them possessed that inner freedom, and none were able, or dared, to allow himself that inner freedom. . . . Pushkin alone, whom his contemporaries thought an empty, worldly, frivolous man, a philanderer and naughty child, dared to ask the question: 'Whether it depends on the tsar or depends on the People—isn't it all the same to you?'"[76] Tolstaya captures how these artists, as men, probably thought of Pushkin—as, in an important sense, not a Russian man but a "naughty child." (EOF) 0:46:04.20

Tolstoy had, of course, been a quite "naughty child" himself and an even more "naughty" young man. The truthfulness of his artistic voice, during the period when he trusted that voice, was his insight into that experience, his growing sense that manhood was an important part of the ethical problem of Russian politics, culture, and intimate life. To his credit as an artist, he carried that analysis quite far and cannot reasonably be accused during this period of a lack of free artistic voice. He was as free during this period as Pushkin and undoubtedly very much inspired by him as well, in particular in his treatment of women. It was only when Tolstoy lost confidence in his artistic voice that his vocation radically changed from artist to prophet of an ethical religion of nonviolence. He still produced some important fiction (short stories such as "The Death of Ivan Ilych," "The Kreutzer Sonata," "Father Sergius," and "Hadji Murad"),[77] but his major later novel, *Resurrection,* was overwhelmed by the denunciation of social injustice at the expense of psychological truth.[78] As one would expect, the fiction no longer featured complex real women like Natasha or Anna; indeed, the portrait of the wife in *The Kreutzer Sonata* was framed obsessionally through the misogyny of her homicidally jealous husband. Tolstoy could no longer depict real women because his artistic voice was no longer nurtured by loving relationships with real women. His truthful artistic voice had, speaking as Anna, accused Tolstoy as a man. His repudiation of his artistic voice was Tolstoy's way of silencing that accusing voice within, a voice he heard all too often in his life hereafter from his increasingly estranged wife, for whom Tolstoy's loss of artistic voice was the loss of the man she loved.[79]

Silencing that voice required Tolstoy to repudiate its truthfulness, as if, contrary to fact, he "was not living [his] own life but the life of another."[80] Denying the truthfulness of his artistic voice led, in turn, to the denial not only of his wife's sexual voice but also of his own. Since artistic voice was, for Tolstoy, grounded in his relationships to the caring love of real women, the repudiation of such voice required him to find reasons for breaking these relationships. His new voice also required a new vocation—no longer artist but prophet of an ethical religion of nonviolence. That sense of new vocation arose from an intensely felt relationship that would replace his relations with real women. His sense of it was put revealingly in words quoted earlier: "the conviction that I could not be the fledgling fallen from a nest that I felt myself to be ... because my mother brought me into the world, kept me warm, fed me, and loved me."[81] Tolstoy was drawing on an idealized relationship with his mother (whom he never knew) and with his deceased Aunt Toinette, which psychologically filled the gap left when he no longer valued either his artistic voice or his relationship with his wife. Tolstoy turned to such idealizations as a way of covering over his sense of aching loss of real relationship, first to the peasant woman he loved and second to Sofya, whom he may never have understood, let alone loved as a person. Tolstoy's new ethically prophetic voice reflected this shift, drawing on his real relationships not with sexual women but with the sexually idealized voice of his mother and aunt, a voice he associated with nonviolence because his aunt patiently endured and nurtured his own wayward ways in the modes of nonviolence that characterize maternal care. His new voice was formed in relationship to this person, God, made very much in the image of Tolstoy's conception of the idealized maternal care he had known, to which he now desperately turned to resolve his sense of desolating loss.[82]

This crisis of vocation was resolved in Tolstoy's intimate sense of relationship to, indeed identification with, Jesus of Nazareth. The movement here was not logical or even rational; it was intensely psychological in the highly personal developmental terms I have described, as Tolstoy broke relationship to real sexual women, a break marked by his loss of artistic voice, and adopted a voice based on the asexual idealization of maternal caretakers. Tolstoy read Jesus as the solution to his developmental crisis, as a person whose life and teaching, in the way suggested in chapter 1, embodied the ethical powers of maternal care, in particular a requirement of nonviolence—but a requirement understood as the injunction of a man.

Tolstoy was, to say the least, not a conventional religious believer, let alone a Christian believer. He accepted neither Christology (Jesus as the son of God) nor even the belief in God as usually understood; he excoriated Orthodox Christian teachings in his *Critique of Dogmatic Theology*.[83] We would think of him today as an atheist, albeit an atheist whose ethical views were endowed with an intense religiosity adapted from the Orthodox faith of his childhood (a person's realization of his or her ethical powers was, for Tolstoy, a kind of self-deification).[84] He was compelled by a conception of Jesus not as god or divine but as revelatory of ethics. Since he rejected the way traditional Christianity read Jesus, he had

p. 81

to explain the truth of his reading by redirecting his talents from art to a new vocation—ethical prophet—that he willfully undertook and for which he had, in fact, little talent. First, he had to learn the language of the Gospels (Greek) and then translate them and offer a commentary that extracted their true ethical meaning, which he did in *The Four Gospels Harmonized and Translated*. Second, he had to explain and defend his conception of religion arising from his interpretation of the Gospels, which he did in *My Religion*. Third and last, he had to philosophically explain his neo-Kantian conception of religious and ethical personality and how and why it found enduring rational meaning in his reading of the Gospels, which he did in *On Life*.[85]

What is remarkable about all these arguments is that, although Tolstoy offered them as compelling theses that appealed to the rationality, not to the faith, of all persons, none of them is compelling in such terms. In his influential compendium of his views, *The Gospel in Brief*, he summarized as follows the five commands he regarded as the core of ethics stated in the Sermon on the Mount: "I. Do not be angry, but be at peace with all men. II. Do not seek delight in sexual gratification. III. Do not swear anything to any one. IV. Do not oppose evil, do not judge, and do not go to law. V. Do not make any distinction among men as to nationality, and love strangers like your own people."[86]

The distinctive feature in Tolstoy's reading of the Gospels is his prohibition of all forms of sensual delight ("Do not think that love toward woman is good") and all forms of violence (including defensive forms).[87] Neither interpretation is a compelling interpretation of the Gospels and certainly not of ethics as such. The Sermon on the Mount in Matthew 5–7 is not a self-interpreting text. Matthew 5:39 commands: "That ye resist not evil: but whosoever shall smite thee on thy right cheek, turn to him the other also," but this text speaks not to defensive violence in general but to narrower issues of the civil law of damages regarding insults to honor (see chapter 1).[88] It is no more interpretively plausible to ascribe pacifism to Jesus than it is to ascribe Tolstoy's condemnation of sensual pleasure to him, freighted as it is with a misogyny quite foreign to Jesus's open-hearted life and teaching. (Jesus is said to have lived a "bon vivant existence with robbers and sinners . . . more scandalous and ominous than a mere matter of breaking purity rules dear to . . . the Pharisees."[89] His "scandal" is captured at Matthew 11:19: "For the Son of Man came eating and drinking, and you say: 'Behold an eater and drinker, a friend of toll collectors and sinners."[90] Tolstoy's austere dogmatist has nothing to do with the historical Jesus. It is even less reasonable to suppose either command Tolstoy ascribed to Jesus is rooted in ethical reasoning as such. Tolstoy made into rather implausible, rigidly doctrinaire ethical rules elements in the Sermon on the Mount that are better understood as "symptoms, signs, examples, of what it means when the kingdom of God breaks into the world which is still under sin, death, and the devil."[91]

Yet Tolstoy found his reading of the Gospels compelling, and there are certainly some other sexually conflicted men of genius, among them Ludwig Wittgenstein, who found in his *Gospel in Brief* a deeply moving and clarifying vision of ethics.[92] For the rest of us, however, what needs to be understood is not the quite bad arguments Tolstoy offered for his position but what it was in his background and psychology that made these highly controversial positions seem to him revelatory of apodictic truths of ethics. Keep in mind: nothing in Tolstoy's argument was based in a faith beyond reason. For Tolstoy, it had to be reason all the way down.

We can plausibly understand Tolstoy's reading in terms of the developmental crisis in his sense of manhood discussed earlier. What moved Tolstoy in his reading of Jesus was how it subverted the sense of Russian aristocratic manhood that he had come to regard as increasingly problematic:

> I have been taught since my childhood that Christ is God and his teaching divine, but, at the same time, I was taught to respect the institutions which through force secured my immunity from evil. . . . I was taught to judge and punish. Then I was taught to make war, that is, to resist evil men with murder, and the military caste, of which I was a member, was called the Christ-loving military, and their activity was sanctified by Christian blessing. Besides, from childhood up to my manly estate I had been taught to respect what directly opposed Christ's law. To resist the offender, to avenge by the use of violence a personal, family, national insult,— all this they not only did not deny, but impressed upon me as something beautiful and not contrary to Christ's law.[93]

Tolstoy was so gripped by a pacifist reading of "Do not resist an evildoer," as the essential core of Jesus's ethical revelation because it spoke directly to his sense of crisis as a man.[94] Manhood was, on this view, so ethically problematic because one's identity as a man was armored against ethical argument by the ways in which one's sense of honor as a man depended on the use of violence whenever that honor was put at threat. Tolstoy made his point in autobiographical terms: "As I recall my former life, I now see that I never permitted my hostile feeling to be fanned against those men whom I considered above myself, and that I never offended them; but, on the other hand, the slightest disagreeable action of a man whom I considered below me provoked my anger at him and my indignation, and the higher I considered myself above such a man, the more easily did I offend him; at times a mere imagined baseness of a man's position provoked my desire to offend him."[95] The interpretation of Jesus as condemning all violence enabled Tolstoy to see how much violence, keyed to insults to honor, "separate[d]" men from a sense of their common humanity.[96]

The condemnation of violence in the psychology of manhood hardly requires the condemnation of sexual pleasure as such; on the contrary, as *Anna Karenina* suggests, it is such manhood that makes loving voice for men so difficult. However, Tolstoy repudiated the truthfulness of his artistic voice, including what it had told him about the sexual voice of women as well as men. He refused to know what he knew, denigrating what he had learned from an artistic voice that had grown in relationship to sexual women. At the crucial point where Tolstoy lacked experience of the sexual voice of a woman as an equal, his imagination failed him, a loss covered over by a rigid idealizing moralism not based on experience. He now sought in Jesus, based on his idealized mother and Aunt Toinette, a condemnation of violence that condemned sexual pleasure as well, in terms of rather explicit misogyny: "The greatest evil is caused the world by the much lauded love of woman, of children, of friends."[97] The erotically charged Tolstoy decided that celibacy was the ethically required course, a decision Sofya condemned as hypocritical (they continued having sex, leading to pregnancies she did not want, long after his conversion).[98]

Tolstoy was so absorbed by Jesus, understood as condemning both violence and sex, because he thereby recovered and tapped his rather idealized conception of maternal care, which was, for him, always desexualized. The evil of the suppression of rational ethics was thus analogized to a woman's suppression of her interest in motherhood, and what Jesus meant by love was exemplified by a mother's love in having and nurturing children.[99] In this way, Tolstoy appealed to a psychology rooted in highly idealized maternal care, but as a patriarchal man, he rationalized it to himself in terms of something very like rigid obedience to the commands of one's patriarchal superior—a gentle, reasonable, and maternally loving Jesus interpreted as a willful Prussian autocrat. That he modeled Jesus's complex and nuanced ethical teaching in terms of five rather unreasonable rules shows the conflicted, contradictory psychology of a man who had come to question so much of traditional manhood but remained intractably patriarchal in core areas of sexuality.

As an artist, Tolstoy had explored his sexual voice through identification with Anna Karenina. Now, as the prophet of an ascetic ethical religion of nonviolence, he found his prophetic voice through an identification with Jesus, who was, for him, more idealized asexual mother than man.[100] Wilson offers a telling story about an English novel, *The Ground Ash,* that moved the prophetic Tolstoy deeply; it is about a boy, identifying with Jesus, who is killed by fellow boys because his serious Christianity leads him to be stigmatized as "a muff and mollycoddle and a spoony and a sop and everything else that is odious and abominable in the eyes of his schoolfellows."[101] Tolstoy's response to the incident in the novel shows how critical he had become of the conventional terms of a manhood held in place by the violent bullying of young boys into submission to the terms of their gender role.

There is a touching insight here into what motivated Tolstoy's ethical religion of nonviolence, namely, a pervasive culture of male violence that, from boyhood on, was unquestioned and unquestionable. Tolstoy understood this culture all too well. His concern with the problem of manhood in this later period evidently came at the expense of his more balanced concern for womanhood as well, as in *War and Peace* and *Anna Karenina.* His solution to the developmental crisis in his sense of manhood took the form of abandoning his artistic voice allegedly on ethical grounds, but in fact, his new prophetic view abandoned the ethical sensitivity to women's voice and the claims that had been such an important feature of his mature artistic works. Nothing in a fair attention to the life and teachings of Jesus required such misogyny; quite the opposite, Jesus's open and humane treatment of women is one of his more attractive and indeed compelling features. Tolstoy thus suicidally sacrificed his artistic voice for no good ethical reason but for bad sexist reasons, and his alleged Bible interpretation was no better and indeed arguably much worse (distorting, as it did, distinctive features of Jesus's generous, open-hearted, antipatriarchal ethical voice). But the rather extreme solution he adopted to his developmental crisis—disarming manhood of violence as a legitimate weapon—psychologically made possible Tolstoy's growing recognition of the problem of violence in the life of men, including violence against any voice of a man that might challenge dominant conceptions of manhood. The English novel about boyhood gripped him for this reason, and his political pacifism took the form it did in order to do justice to this insight. / o : z / : z |

Tolstoy's most developed statement of his political pacifism is *The Kingdom of God Is within You,*[102] a text that had an important influence on Gandhi.[103] Invoking the inspiration of William Lloyd Garrison, Tolstoy offered a general normative framework for understanding the ways in which what I earlier called patterns of structural injustice are held in place by the violent repression of a free ethical voice that would most reasonably contest such injustice.[104] Tolstoy discovered, from his own Russian perspective and experience, the good ethical sense of what he found in Garrison and the American radical abolitionists, in particular their ethical criticism of extreme religious intolerance (anti-Semitism), slavery, and racism (he ignored their criticism of sexism).[105] As one would expect in theocratic Russia, where the czar's political absolutism was based on religious orthodoxy, the core of Tolstoy's conception was the radical Protestant argument for toleration that questioned the legitimacy of any political enforcement of sectarian religious views that rested on the repression of the inalienable human right of conscience and other basic rights. Tolstoy powerfully objected on this ground to the idea of Russian religious nationality as the rationale for political repression within Russia and imperialist oppression internationally,[106] including the persecution of religious minorities such as the Dukhobors and the Molokans.[107] His voice was one of the most powerful ethically independent voices within Russia that consistently objected to the tyrannies of the Russian theocratic state.

Tolstoy always preferred the normative discourse of duties over rights,[108] but the normative structure of his political pacifism focused on the role that pervasive patterns of political violence unjustly play in the repression of the free exercise of ethical conviction, which is the rights-based argument for toleration.[109] What is distinctive in Tolstoy's use and

p.86

elaboration of this argument is threefold: his sensitivity to how men are bullied into submission to complicity with injustice, the universality of its scope (condemning general patterns of imperialism), and its application to pseudosciences such as social Darwinism.

Much of the argument of *The Kingdom of God Is within You* is about how men in particular are drawn into complicity with unjust forms of political violence, in particular fighting in largely unjust wars. At one point, Tolstoy conceded that state coercion might be justified if it protected citizens "from evil-disposed persons," but he denied that contemporary uses of this type of coercion could be justified on such grounds. Modern wars were, for Tolstoy, unjust, and the question for him was how the culture of manhood had made possible men's complicity with this injustice, supporting and fighting in such wars. He wrote with particular authority about this question because he himself had once enthusiastically fought and killed for Russia in the Caucasus and in the Crimean War. His picture of Russian aristocratic manhood was of a kind of brainwashing by the stupefying pomp, ceremonies, and regalia of a culture of manhood, based on a corrupt union of sectarian religion and autocratic political power, that formed its sense of honor in the violent defense of that corrupt union against all enemies, domestic and foreign. As Tolstoy put it, "The conscience is there, but it has been put to sleep—in those in command by what the psychologists call auto-suggestion; in the soldiers, by the direct conscious hypnotizing exerted by the higher classes." This is a devastating portrait, combining shrewd psychological and social observations (Tolstoy, *Kingdom of God*, 179, 328).

Tolstoy importantly saw these unjust patterns as universal, not just in Russian imperialism but also in American and European imperialism, "the will of those in power that Nice was incorporated into Austria, and that Poland was divided, and Ireland and India ruled by the English government, and that the Chinese are attacked and the Africans slaughtered, and the Chinese prevented from immigrating by the Americans, and the Jews persecuted by the Russians, and that landowners appropriate lands they do not cultivate and capitalists enjoy the fruits of the labor of others." Building on the insights of the American radical abolitionists, Tolstoy offered a pathbreaking analysis of the role of forms of structural injustice such as extreme religious intolerance (anti-Semitism) and ethnic and racial prejudice in rationalizing unjust forms of state power, including imperialistic wars, in America and Europe. He noted "the amazement of an Indian convert to Christianity" at the "complete contrast" between the unjust "reality and what he had expected to find among Christian nations" (190, 200).

Finally, Tolstoy acutely connected these injustices to a racist pseudo-science that he associated with Joseph de Maistre and social Darwinism (161–62). Such science enjoyed the same unjust support of the state that sectarian religion did because it naturalized injustice as a law of evolution (163–64). Making a point that anticipated the role of racist pseudoscience in the Holocaust, Tolstoy argued that it is such pseudoscience, as much as sectarian religion, that rationalizes political atrocity (346, 347–48).

Near the end of his life, Tolstoy took a particular interest in the Indian struggle for liberation from the British, defending such resistance in 1908 in his "Letter to a Hindu."[110] What is of interest in the letter is the case it makes for nonviolence as the form of resistance on the basis of a syncretic appeal to a range of ethical sources, including alleged Hindu sources. Tolstoy's view of Jesus was, as we have seen, that he was not divine but rather that he was a particularly profound ethical thinker who had discovered important truths implicit in all human ethical judgments. It is quite consistent with this view that there should be other ethical sources for such judgments, and in his most important philosophical work, *On Life,* Tolstoy had found support for his reading of Jesus in the Buddha, Confucius, and others.[111] "A Letter to a Hindu" offers its ethical argument on the basis of frequent reference to Hindu sources, with express reservations about what Tolstoy regarded as indefensible ideas such as karma and reincarnation.[112]

Gandhi was so impressed with "A Letter to a Hindu" that he wrote Tolstoy for permission to translate it and publish it in India with a preface that he himself would write, which would endorse its ethical argument but disavow its critique of Indian metaphysics.[113] There was a brief correspondence of mutual admiration between the two men, which lasted until Tolstoy's death in 1910; they agreed to disagree about karma and reincarnation.[114]

Tolstoy's Importance to Nonviolence

The great significance of Tolstoy in terms of our study of resistance to injustice involves not his political activism (Garrison, Gandhi, and King were much more important in this dimension) but what his life and work tell us about how the developmental psychology of manhood bears on the turn to resistance, a psychology we find as well in the other figures studied here. The great developmental struggle within his psyche was between his relationships with beloved maternal caretakers, who nurtured his artistic voice, and his passionate absorption in playing the roles of manhood that his culture valued, including sexual exploits with fallen women, military service, and marriage to a good woman. Tolstoy was a brilliant and aggressively competitive male role-player in all these dimensions, but he was also a great artist whose voice developed in relationship to maternal caretakers with very different views, including on the role of caring love in protection, growth, and acceptability. Tolstoy's psyche as an artist drew on this alternative perspective, which gave powerful artistic voice to an ethical criticism about the role codes of honor played in the lives of both men and women. It was such codes that rationalized and indeed heroized Napoleon's imperialistic atrocities; it was such codes that divided lovers, sometimes suicidally, from one another.

Tolstoy's crisis of vocation, in which he repudiated both his art and his family, was continuous with these developments. The fact that the Tolstoy who emerged from the crisis did not see the continuity, in particular the value placed on free ethical voice before and after, is indicative of the elements of irrationality in this crisis. It was Tolstoy's problem that he did not see his artistic voice as rooted in ethical voice and that he believed his new prophetic voice was always rooted in ethics when, in its crude misogyny, it certainly was not. What was continuous was Tolstoy's sense that ethical voice and traditional manhood were in fundamental conflict. His turn to nonviolence was his way of resolving this conflict. The psychology of this turn is more interesting than the often bad arguments he offered in defense of it.

For Tolstoy, violence was to traditional manhood what alcohol was to the alcoholic—a way of stupefying one's faculties of ethical choice and deliberation. What held structural injustice in place was precisely the ways in which political violence was unjustly inflicted on any conviction or voice that would reasonably question the injustice. Conventional manhood was, for Tolstoy, the psychological vehicle for such injustice because men's sense of honor was formed and rewarded in terms of a willingness to use violence whenever injustice was questioned. Once these features of conventional manhood were understood, the strategy of nonviolence was a way of breaking a cycle of violence that perpetuated injustice. The withdrawal of violence made possible what such violence repressed, the fostering of free ethical voice. For a man such as Tolstoy, who was looking for a way out of a conventional sense of manhood that was increasingly burdened with guilt and remorse, nonviolence was attractive because of its psychological appeal.

It does not, of course, follow that pacifist nonviolence in and of itself is the best way to resolve such conflicts. Tolstoy may have been quite wrong about this even in his own case; as Wilson acidly observes, "The more Tolstoy attempted to imitate Christ, the more violent the atmosphere [in his home] became."[115] As a nonviolent ethical prophet, Tolstoy gathered about him at Yasnaya Polyana a number of disciples—one of whom, Vladimir Chertkov, filled the yawning emotional gap between Tolstoy and his estranged wife with an intimacy that the marriage lacked,[116] an intimacy that the now unbalanced Sofya homophobically construed as sexual.[117] Sofya had read Tolstoy's diaries, in which he discussed his infatuation as a young man with other men, and his art had always dealt with remarkable frankness with homoerotic feeling among boys and men, often as soldiers. (Invariably, they are men who are otherwise aggressively heterosexual; there is no gay world in Tolstoy, though one presumably existed in Moscow and Petersburg.)[118] That Sofya had reached this point of wild accusation gives some idea of the emotional minefield that their marriage had become. Tolstoy did not help when, without her knowledge, he wrote a new will covering future royalties in favor of Chertkov, royalties that Sofya not unreasonably regarded as products of the support and help she had provided to her husband over the years of their marriage. The war between them now included their children on various sides of the dispute, raging arguments, and suicide attempts by Sofya. At the end, a pathetic Tolstoy escaped from the hell that had become his home only to die in a railway car, exhausted by the exertion.[119]

Tolstoy had been captivated by nonviolence as the solution to manhood because he believed it would release otherwise suppressed powers of ethical voice. But as his marriage shows, his obsessional concern for nonviolence from the perspective of manhood came at the expense of his own violent role in the suppression of women's voices, including the sexual voice of his wife (a theme we shall see as well in Gandhi and King). In fact, when he trusted his artistic voice (nurtured not only by Aunt Toinette but also by his relationship with Sofya and her family), Tolstoy

89

had also practiced nonviolence, for in repudiating his life as a soldier in Russia's wars, he had disarmed himself of the role violence once played in his conception of manhood and thus made possible a new kind of voice, his remarkable artistic voice and imagination. It is ultimately the sexual crisis in Tolstoy's marriage that was resolved by turning away from the sexual voice of his art (nurtured by Sofya) and aligning himself with the idealized voice of his dead maternal caretakers. Such idealization showed itself in Tolstoy's extreme denigration of sexuality as such, ending in an ascetic celibacy that rationalized misogynist hostility to his wife. But Tolstoy's artistic voice ultimately expressed itself in *Anna Karenina* in a truthful exploration of women's sexual voice that arose from his relationship with Sofya, a relationship that made possible a voice that resisted male violence. Thus understood, nonviolence in Tolstoy rested not on an ultimately pacifist position but on a more specific concern for the ways in which political violence had been aggressively targeted against any kind of free voice that would challenge the role structural injustice played in national and international politics. What Tolstoy was concerned with was what concerned Garrison as well: the protection of a robust right of conscience and speech that could think and speak thoughts that reasonably challenged the dehumanizing assumptions about classes of persons whose political force depended on the repression of their basic human rights.

Tolstoy's remarkable journey clarifies the developmental psychology of manhood that most fully realizes its ethical powers of free voice when it stays closest to its relational attachments both to certain kinds of maternal caretakers and to later relationships with women that nourish such voice. The free voice challenges the conventional terms of manhood, which rest on the violent repression of this voice. Rather, it calls for forms of nonviolence as a way of disarming conventional manhood and thus freeing voice. Nonviolence had been a feature of the maternal care that the men in our study had come to value: when they sometimes were wayward boys, such care brought them security, growth, and acceptability. Men like these gravitate to nonviolence, including the two kinds of nonviolence we have examined in Tolstoy's work—both his voice as an artist and his voice as an ethical prophet. In either case, nonviolence was linked to making certain kinds of voice possible. Whatever Tolstoy's view of the matter, both kinds of voice were, in him, forms of free ethical voice, and I have suggested that, of the two of them, his artistic voice rested on a more ethically defensible perspective because it did greater justice to the problem of voice in both men and women. Indeed, my argument suggests that Tolstoy's turn from the real sexual voice of his wife to the idealized, asexual voice of his maternal caretakers explains the conflicted psychology that motivated his move from a more ethical to a less ethical voice.

(EOF)

0: 41: 11.28

// CHAPTER THREE

Gandhi on Nonviolence

William Lloyd Garrison's nonviolence was an important organizing feature in the power and appeal of his voice to the small group of radical abolitionists whom he first attracted. In contrast, the nonviolence of Mohandas Gandhi and Martin Luther King was the basis of mass democratic social movements, and each of these men is best understood in terms of the movement he inspired. One of the most significant insights the psychoanalyst and historian Erik Erikson makes in his masterful psychobiography of Gandhi, *Gandhi's Truth,* is how fundamentally illuminating it would be to study Gandhi through the eyes of people still alive who were energized by him to participate in his social movement.[1] My discussion follows Erikson in exploring how and why Gandhi so profoundly moved the people he organized and influenced. Clearly, his appeal rested on his remarkable voice and the way in which it spoke across so many barriers to other persons, who in turn gave a resonance to his voice and for whom Gandhi was a resonance for a new kind of ethical voice. Since Gandhi's innovations in nonviolent voice occurred largely in South Africa, my discussion of this innovative period is more extended than that of his later elaboration of his method in India.[2]

Gandhi's Early Life and the Turn to Nonviolence

Two aspects of Gandhi's earlier background crucially bear on his invention of *satyagraha* (unwavering search for truth) in South Africa: first, his developmental psychology as an Indian boy brought up in close relationship to the loving voice of his mother and the trauma of his arranged child marriage, and second, his three-year residence in Great Britain to become a barrister, during which he was separated not only from his parents and siblings (his beloved mother died before his return) but also from his young wife.

Mohandas Gandhi was born in 1869, the youngest of six children, three sons and three daughters, born to Karamchand Gandhi, who married four times; his last marriage was to Mohandas's mother, Putlibai, who was only fifteen when they married, whereas her husband "was over forty."[3] (They would have one daughter and three sons.)[4] Although the Gandhis were merchants by caste (their name meant "grocers"), they had risen to important political positions.[5] In his autobiography (*An Autobiography: The Story of My Experiments with Truth,* 1993), Gandhi describes his father as "truthful, brave, and generous, but short-tempered" and "given to carnal pleasures" (3); "he had no education, save experience" (4). In contrast, he writes that "the outstanding impression my mother has left on my memory is that of saintliness. She was deeply religious," which showed itself in her taking "the hardest vows" of fasting and keeping them (4). Her children watched her fasting anxiously: "She vowed not to have food without seeing the sun. We children on those days would stand, staring at the sky, waiting to announce the appearance of the sun to our mother" (5). His mother also "had strong commonsense. She was well informed about all matters of state, and ladies of the court thought highly of her intelligence" (5).

Biographers often comment on the closeness of Gandhi to—indeed, his identification with—his mother[6] and on her highly personal religiosity centered in a syncretic Hindu sect, "the Vaishnavite religion and the Jain culture," a religiosity that included "vegetarianism and periodical fasting; cleanliness and purification; the making of confessions and the taking of vows; and above all, *ahimsa,* avoiding harm of living beings."[7] Erik Erikson sensitively captures the religion and its impact on Gandhi as a child: "[The] sect . . . prided itself on having unified the Koran with the Hindu scriptures and . . . abhorred any regression to the idolatry of either. . . . His mother's religion was of that pervasive and personalized kind which women convey to children, but it also prepared the boy for the refusal to take anybody's word for what anything meant."[8]

Gandhi subtitles his autobiography "My Experiments with Truth," a testing in terms of personal voice whose authority he first experienced in relationship to his mother's loving care and voice. This maternal care prominently included nonviolence (ahimsa) not only as a religious requirement but also as a way of life. In fact, the very anxiety children of

such a mother experience when she keeps her vows of self-imposed suffering imparted to Gandhi a concrete experience, within the microcosm
of family life, of the ways in which the ethical suffering of a beloved person engages the active concern and attention of others. Gandhi drew on
this experience in his most brilliant experiment with truth, satyagraha,
hypothesizing that such experience might have relevance to a certain kind
of ethical persuasion in politics.

There are striking analogies between the backgrounds of Tolstoy and
Gandhi: their families of origin involved political leaders (Tolstoy's grandfather, Gandhi's father and grandfather), and their sense of truthful voice
was nurtured by maternal caretakers. There is one further analogy as
well. Tolstoy's negative feelings about his sexuality can be traced to early
experiences with prostitutes and venereal diseases to which his brother,
as a kind of initiation ritual of Russian manhood, more or less coercively
introduced him in Kazan. Gandhi's similar negative feelings connect to
his marriage, at age thirteen, to the child bride Kasturbai, chosen for him
five years earlier by his parents, Vaishnava priests, and astrologers.[9] In his
autobiography, Gandhi writes of the marriage with a sense of shame
(10–11). He himself associates this shame with his aggressive sexual interest in Kasturbai at the expense of all other aims, including his obligations at age sixteen to nurse his dying father (the shame was over
having sex as his father died [28–31]) and his obligations to his wife as a
person with a mind. Gandhi pictures himself as an emotionally immature, patriarchal husband whose treatment of Kasturbai left her "simple,
independent, persevering and, with me at least, reticent" (12) and doggedly
illiterate (he perceptively blames her obdurate illiteracy on resistance to
his controlling conception of love [12]).

The analogy between the experiences of Tolstoy and Gandhi involves
the way in which both their families imposed on rather young men
forms of sexuality not freely chosen and not calling for any sexual responsiveness to their partners. It is no accident that Gandhi shared Tolstoy's
sexist view that all nonprocreational sex was evil and, ultimately, that
sex as such was evil;[10] in 1906, Gandhi finally took vows of celibacy
(*brahmacharya*), and he kept them after more than twenty years of marriage and having had four sons (strikingly, Kasturbai was informed only
after the vows were taken).[11] He was, like Tolstoy, almost as bad a father
as he was a husband.[12]

Gandhi left for England in 1888 to train as a lawyer after having
pledged to his mother that he would avoid wine, women, and meat; he

left Kasturbai in India with his first son. His three years in London were a time of intellectual, moral, and religious ferment for him. In addition to the academic opportunities he was seeking (he was a conscientious law student), he encountered a remarkable range of influences—cultural, religious, and intellectual. Freed from the constraining effects of his family, apart from the triple vow to his mother (which he rigorously observed), he had to work out what he was and what he was to become, what it meant to be an Indian in the capital whose influences had only recently reached the home he had left.[13] He writes of this painful period in his autobiography: "I would continually think of my home and country. My mother's love always haunted me. At night the tears would stream down my cheeks, and home memories of all sorts made sleep out of the question. It was impossible to share my misery with anyone. And even if I could have done so, where was the use? I knew of nothing that would soothe me. Everything was strange—the people, their ways, and even their dwellings" (45).

After a short period of playing at English gentleman, better sense prevailed. Gandhi turned to the more serious aspects of English life. Great Britain at this time was at the apogee of its imperialistic ambitions, ruling an empire that, of course, included India;[14] however, Britain's democratic constitutionalism included significant liberal values, among them the belief in universal human rights, and its religion was a form of Protestant Christianity that inspired Lockean liberalism.[15] Gandhi undoubtedly saw and closely studied the contradictions within British culture, including its religion, between its imperialism abroad and its democratic constitutionalism at home. Like many other colonial leaders, he discovered the West and the East at the same time and one by comparison to the other. He read widely about British and European law and politics, interacted with vegetarians and Theosophists, and, very importantly, studied Christianity, finding the Old Testament disagreeable but the New Testament arresting and deeply moving. He was later to say, "If then I had to face only the Sermon on the Mount and my own interpretation of it, I should not hesitate to say, 'Oh yes, I am a Christian.'" His interpretation was, however, much more along the lines of Tolstoy's reading of Jesus than that of conventional Christianity: "The meaning became clearer to me when I read Tolstoy's *Harmony of the Gospels* and his other kindred writings."[16] He also read about his own religious tradition, especially the Bhagavad Gita and Edwin Arnold's *Light of Asia,* which initiated him into the Hindu and Buddhist philosophies, respectively.[17] For the first time in his life, Gandhi began to take the Eastern tradition seriously, stimulated by the interest shown in it in London circles.

One of the important British works of this period that understandably influenced Gandhi was Edward Carpenter's *Civilisation: Its Cause and Cure,* first published in 1889.[18] Carpenter's socialist critique of British industrial capitalism pointed out the ethical and human price entailed in the "peculiar state of society, which we call Civilisation, but which even to the most optimistic among us does not seem altogether desirable," and he discussed alternative sources of ethical wisdom available in less industrially advanced societies—for example, Indian thought. That an industrially advanced society like Britain might be ethically backward and have much to learn from Indian thought was a concept Gandhi found enormously congenial and would later use prominently in his struggle against British imperialism. It was a concept Gandhi learned from both Tolstoy and Carpenter. Carpenter did not accept Tolstoy's pacifism, but he endorsed his view that Western "advanced" ideas might be inferior to Eastern ones.[19]

Carpenter, a gay man, was also an important feminist and early advocate of the rights of gay/lesbian persons, and his interest in India, like that of his friend the novelist E. M. Forster, was undoubedly both an erotically motivated, Orientalist sexual tourism and an ethically grounded, hungry quest for a contemporary high culture that was thought, like ancient Greece, to be more humanely open to diverse forms of sexuality.[20] Gandhi certainly took significant notice of the increasingly vocal feminist agitation in Britain (he several times cited it as a good example of courageous nonviolent resistance[21]), but his own views on sexuality could not have been less open to the kind of emancipatory interest in sexual voice (gay and straight, male and female) that Carpenter pioneered.

Gandhi was called to the bar in June 1891 and left for India two days later.[22] The Gandhi who set sail for home in mid-1891 had made immense strides in self-knowledge and in his sense of self-identity and worth since his naively eager departure from Bombay, unaware of the turmoil that lay before him. However, he was still quite shy, and he knew little of Indian law and even less about Indian courts and the ways of potential clients.[23]

The bitterest blow on his return was learning of his mother's death, which his family had kept from him. He had been longing to see her, and his grief was far deeper than that he felt at his father's death. In addition, he experienced professional setbacks in India. His low status haunted him; he was not treated with the respect that his time in Britain had convinced him was his due. Gandhi's experience in Britain had involved close relationships with British people, "a reminder that there was in late nineteenth-century England little of the racial prejudice and tensions which faced later Indian visitors to England." Now, however, back in India, he faced a more racist reality. His brother had asked him to intercede with a political agent for the Kathiawar states on his behalf, on the strength of Gandhi's having met the man in England. But when he approached the British official, he was curtly told that his brother was an intriguer who needed to pursue his case through the proper channels, and Gandhi was forcibly shown to the door. "His English experience had not prepared him for this sort of arrogance, and his initial reaction was to proceed legally against the official for insult and assault." He would encounter even more dramatic assaults in South Africa, experiences that would motivate the moral indignation that led to the invention of satyagraha.[24]

Reader's Note
went

The Invention of Satyagraha: South Africa

Gandhi want to South Africa for what he thought would be a short period to advise officials of a Porbandar trading firm about a court case in which they were involved; he was to stay for twenty years, from 1893 to 1914. These years in South Africa were crucial in Gandhi's development into a public man, both outwardly and inwardly. The most obvious developments involved the transformation of the shy, rather unsuccessful barrister into a skilled lawyer, political spokesman, and organizer, equipped at the end of his stay to play a public role in India.[25]

Gandhi arrived in South Africa expecting an appropriate respect for his legal education, his anglicized appearance, and his general comportment as an English-speaking Indian. His setbacks in India, including the incident with the political agent, had not affected his ethical sense of a complete equality with white subjects of the British Empire, "born largely of his experiences in London in training for the Bar and mixing easily in English society."[26] Such experiences led him to believe that ethical values of equal respect were fundamental not only to British institutions at home but also to the British Empire abroad. These experiences had

898

97

also led him to begin, while in London, his quest for the syncretic sources of the universal ethical values of equal respect that he believed could be supported by a proper Tolstoyan reading of Jesus of Nazareth, as well as Hindu religious works like the Bhagavad Gita.

Within a week of his arrival in South Africa, Gandhi was confronted by traumatic experiences that changed the course of his life. When traveling from Durban to Pretoria, he was thrown off the train in the middle of the night for daring to travel in first-class accommodations and spent the rest of the night shivering in the waiting room of the Petermaritzburg station. Gandhi was distraught and began to think about what to do. In his *Autobiography,* he writes: "It would be cowardice to run back to India without fulfilling my obligation. The hardship to which I was subjected was superficial—only a symptom of the deep disease of colour prejudice. I should try, if possible, to root out the disease and suffer hardships in the process" (112).

The next day, Gandhi traveled to Charlestown without difficulty, but the driver of the stagecoach that carried him to Johannesburg would not let him ride inside the vehicle and requested that he sit next to him instead. With reluctance, Gandhi agreed (113). Even at this early stage of his evolving sense of protest, he would not undertake a futile, self-destructive course. But when he was later asked to move and sit on a piece of "dirty" cloth on the floor to allow the white man in charge of the coach to sit and smoke, he bridled at the insult and refused (113–14). Thereupon the man came down from his seat and assaulted Gandhi (114). Gandhi pregnantly observes—for in the observation lies the political psychology of satyagraha—that white passengers intervened at the sight of the injustice:

> The passengers were witnessing the scene—the man swearing at me, dragging and belabouring me, and I remaining still. He was strong and I was weak. Some of the passengers were moved to pity and exclaimed: "Man, let him alone. Don't beat him. He is not to blame. He is right. If he can't stay there, let him come and sit with us." "No fear," cried the man, but he seemed somewhat crestfallen and stopped beating me. He let go my arm, swore at me a little more, and asking the Hottentot servant who was sitting on the other side of the coachbox to sit on the footboard, took the seat so vacated. (114)

Some months later, Gandhi was kicked into the gutter by a sentry for daring to walk past President Paul Kruger's house in Pretoria. A white friend passing by on horseback, shocked at the incident, offered to support a court case brought against the man and expressed his sorrow at the incident; Gandhi replied: "What does the poor man know? All coloured people are the same to him. He no doubt treats Negroes just as he has treated me" (130).

Gandhi had encountered a situation that he had not anticipated but that had existed in South Africa for some time. Indians had begun to migrate to South Africa in the 1860s as indentured laborers to work on sugar and coffee plantations, and they had suffered many kinds of indignities and discrimination, especially in Natal and Transvaal, where they were heavily concentrated. After his traumatic experiences and with the support of the most influential Indian in Pretoria, Gandhi called "a meeting of all the Indians in Pretoria ... to present to them a picture of their conditions in the Transvaal" (125). He spoke about the importance of truthfulness in business, calling for higher standards not only of business but also of personal hygiene, and about a sense of themselves as Indians sharing common grievances despite religious and other differences. In fact, most Indians there were Muslim (126). Further meetings of this type followed, in which Gandhi made "a deep study of the social, economic and political condition of the Indians in the Transvaal and the Orange Free State" (128).

In April 1894, Gandhi had successfully finished his work in Pretoria on the matter that had taken him to South Africa by arranging a settlement that was satisfactory to both parties. The experience there led to a considerable growth in his self-confidence, both in his capacity for humanely healing broken relationships and in his legal professionalism: "Here it was that the religious spirit within me became a living force, and here too I acquired a true knowledge of legal practice" (131).

Gandhi was about to return to India when the legislature of Natal began debating the Indian Franchise Bill, which would have taken away Indian voting rights. Gandhi told his Muslim employer that the bill "is the first nail into our coffin. It strikes at the root of our self-respect" (139). The employer urged him to stay on to lead the fight; Gandhi readily agreed as long as his remuneration would be raised from the Indian community at large "for public work," not paid as conventional legal fees by his employer (140). At this time, he was working as a public lawyer within the system of legal and political remedies available to him as a British-trained barrister representing the interests of the Indians of Natal. He founded the Natal Indian Congress, and his campaign succeeded in partially ameliorating the harshness of the bill. As a British lawyer who believed that invidious racial disqualifications such as those in the franchise measure were inconsistent with the British constitution, Gandhi organized a memorial that challenged the pending bill in the Legislative Assembly of Natal.

His most important and revealing discussion of the development of his theory and practice of nonviolent protest is *Satyagraha in South Africa* (Navajivan Publishing House, 1928).[27] In that work, he notes that the assembly was "startled" by the challenge but passed it anyway (27). A memorial bearing ten thousand Indian signatures (almost the whole population of free Indians in Natal) was then submitted to Lord Ripon, secretary of state for the colonies, who "disallowed the bill and declared that the British Empire could not agree to the establishment of a colour bar in legislation" (27). The Natal government brought forward another bill, removing racial distinctions but indirectly disqualifying Indians. The Indians protested this bill without success and did not choose to carry their argument to the Judicial Committee of the Privy Council. It was enough of a precedent, Gandhi thought, "that the colour bar was not allowed to be set up" (27).

His later campaigns against immigration restrictions and discriminatory licensing laws were much less successful. He increasingly acknowledged persuasive limits on the various strategies he had used in the past; "it is no new experience to find that arguments based on reason do not always appeal to men in authority" (78). He was looking for alternative approaches to ethical persuasion.

Gandhi's thought and life during this period were undergoing important changes: "Thought came to have no meaning for him unless it was lived out, and life was shallow unless it reflected a carefully thought-out vision of life."[28] There was a natural affinity between such extreme ethical pragmatism and Tolstoy's prophetic ethical religion, a religion that reduced the enduring meaning of the life and teaching of Jesus of Nazareth to several commands, the most important of which, for Tolstoy, was not to use violence even in resisting injustice. Gandhi wrote: "Tolstoy's *The Kingdom of God Is within You* overwhelmed me. It left an abiding impression on me"; through reading this and other Tolstoy books, he "began to realize more and more the infinite possibilities of universal love."[29] The walls of his ashrams were bare except for the cross, which he saw as an expression of suffering love and on which he meditated constantly.[30]

What may have "overwhelmed" him in *The Kingdom of God Is within You* was the way in which Tolstoy took seriously the unjust coercion directed at any free ethical voice that would challenge the terms of structural injustice. Gandhi's own traumatic experiences with racism violently directed against his protests of racist treatment had opened his mind to the ways in which whole groups of persons, such as people of color in South Africa, had been held in a kind of slavery involving the abridgment of their basic human rights, a servile status rationalized in terms of unjust racial stereotypes.[31] He certainly saw American racism as well as European anti-Semitism as examples of evil (he called the Jews the "untouchables of Christianity"),[32] and he came to view the treatment of untouchables under Hinduism as exemplifying the same evil. What held such evils in place was, as Tolstoy saw, forms of violence of the sort that Gandhi had himself experienced when he challenged injustice, a violence triggered by putative threats to a sense of manhood by any voice or action that protested the underlying injustice.

Gandhi certainly shared a form of the developmental psychology discussed earlier in regard to Tolstoy—an identification with the voice of a maternal caretaker for whom nonviolence was the means to nurture, growth, and ethical acceptability. For both these men, the relationship involved a highly idealized conception of loving care (Gandhi thus writes of his mother's "saintliness"[33]), drained of sexual and emotional complexity, that showed itself in a correlative problem the men shared in relating to women as sexual partners. If anything, Gandhi more openly acknowledged this identification. He had learned from his mother the importance of truthful voice in her highly personal religion, and he carried this voice in his psyche as he increasingly questioned his sense of Indian–British manhood, plunged into crisis by his personal experience of irrational ethnic hatred and violence while he was in South Africa. Such manhood expressed itself, as Tolstoy clearly saw, in the repression in oneself as a man (as well as in others) of a free ethical voice that would reasonably question the violence. Gandhi confronted the political consequences of this problem when, in his political activism on behalf of Indians in South Africa, he acknowledged "that arguments based on reason do not always appeal to men in authority."[34] Tolstoy's argument "overwhelmed" him

p. 102

because it explained why his South African struggle against a structural injustice like racism had become so difficult, namely, because an injustice of this type, resting on the violent repression of voice, showed itself by not hearing, let alone taking seriously, this voice.

How can this problem of callous, armored, indeed violent resistance to hearing any claim protesting injustice be circumvented? Tolstoy's view was that there is an ethical voice under the armor and that nonviolence is a way of disarming the armor of manhood so that this voice can be heard. During this period, Gandhi was also reading moral and religious literature, including Plato's *Apology* and William Salter's *Ethical Religion* (1889); he translated the first into his native Gujarati and published a summary of the second, also in Gujarati.[35] Salter's work argued for an ethical minimum as the core of any religion worth having (the ethical culture movement), a view that attracted Gandhi for the same reason Tolstoyan syncretism appealed to him.[36] During his stay in Africa, two other books influenced him deeply in addition to Tolstoy's *The Kingdom of God Is within You:* Henry David Thoreau's *On the Duty of Civil Disobedience* (1847) and John Ruskin's *Unto This Last* (1862). Thoreau, like Plato, spoke of the ethical voice of resistance to injustice, including, for him, refusing complicity with injustice. Ruskin's work suggested to Gandhi, consistent with Carpenter's *Civilisation* as well, that new forms of life involving manual labor were needed as an alternative to the excesses of industrial capitalism.[37] Inspired by Ruskin, Gandhi decided to live an austere life on a commune, at first on the Phoenix Farm in Natal and then on the Tolstoy Farm just outside Johannesburg. During this time, Gandhi began a range of experiments involving diet, child rearing, nature cure, and his professional and personal life, including his vow of celibacy in 1906. A surprisingly large part of his autobiography is absorbed by these personal experiments—what George Orwell trenchantly called "the commonplaceness of much of its material."[38]

But Gandhi was seeking as well a new kind of political voice that might be more ethically persuasive than the arguments he was making as a public lawyer; this was to be his most important experiment in truthful voice. The experiment came in response to a law the Transvaal proposed in 1906 and passed in 1907—the Black Act, which required the registration and fingerprinting of all Indians and gave the police the power to enter their houses to ensure that the inhabitants were registered.[39]

34:30.93

Gandhi's unconventional way of responding to the crisis posed by the proposed law had been prepared by his service, rooted in values of maternal care, during the Zulu rebellion shortly before. Considered a resident of Natal, he felt he must do his part, consistent with his beliefs. He made an offer to the government to raise a stretcher-bearer corps for service with the troops, and he joined the army with a small corps of twenty or so Indian men. In *Satyagraha in South Africa,* Gandhi described himself as acting as a nurse to wounded Zulus whose wounds Europeans would not dress (90–91). He acted and felt like a loving nurse to a group of people of color even more despised than the Indians—people whom Europeans would not help. It was while working for the corps that two ideas—celibacy and poverty—"floating in [his] mind became firmly fixed" as forms of self-denial that he had come to believe removed impediments to undertaking the kinds of duties he now saw as required of him as an ethical and political leader. Now, nothing, he believed, "would prevent him or make him shrink from undertaking the lowliest of duties or largest risk" (91). At this crucial period shortly before the first experiment with satyagraha, we see in Gandhi's caring relations with the despised Zulus a devotion to ideals of maternal care that, by virtue of the ideals' very demands for lowly or personally risky service, required surrendering what he interpreted as the distracting aims of sexuality and material prosperity.

On return from the war, Gandhi read the draft of the Black Act, which he translated into Gujarati for his newspaper, read in both South Africa and India. He became convinced that, even if the usual forms of political protest proved fruitless, "the community must not sit with folded hands. Better die than submit to such a law" (92). The next day, he discussed the issue of what to do with a small group of leading Indians, to whom he explained the ordinance: it required the registration of every Indian man, woman, and child, and failure to register would lead to forfeiture of the right to live in Transvaal. The proposed law "shocked them as it had shocked me. One of them said in a fit of passion: 'If any one came forward to demand a certificate from my wife, I would shoot him on that spot and take the consequences'" (94). Gandhi quieted the man and then addressed the meeting: "If we fully understand all the implications of this legislation, we shall find that India's honour is in our keeping. For the Ordinance seeks to humiliate not only ourselves but also the motherland. The humiliation consists in the degradation of innocent men. . . . It will not, therefore, do to be hasty, impatient, or angry. That cannot save us from this onslaught. But God will come to our help, if we calmly think out and carry out in time measures of resistance, presenting a united front and bearing the hardship, which such resistance brings in its train" (94).

What is so striking about Gandhi's way of thinking is how he interpreted the sense of injustice in terms of a conception of male honor likely to appeal to his male audience, a sense of manhood palpably put at threat by a law that would apply to wives as well. Manhood thus at threat usually leads to violence, as the angry husband's statement makes clear. Gandhi, however, was, as a political leader, improvising something quite remarkable, indeed pathbreaking—close in spirit to what Jesus may have meant by "Do not resist an evildoer. But if anyone strikes you on the right cheek, turn the other also" (Matt. 5:39). On the one hand, he was appealing to a sense of insulted male honor that had to act, but on the other hand, he was subverting the conventional connections of such insult to violence by calling for a nonviolent response. Gandhi's political genius was on display here as, under the pressure of circumstances and the development of both his psychology and his ethical convictions, he experimented with a new kind of response to such insults and waited to see if and how his proposal gave a resonance for a new kind of resisting voice in his audience. We can see this quite clearly in another meeting he held at a Jewish theater, which was rented because it was large enough to allow as many people as possible to attend.

The meeting occurred on September 11, 1906, and was attended by some three thousand persons. In *Satyagraha in South Africa,* Gandhi admits he was improvising (95). The most important of the resolutions he had drafted, which was passed by the meeting, was "the famous Fourth Resolution by which the Indians solemnly determined not to submit to the Ordinance in the event of its becoming law in the teeth of their opposition and to suffer all the penalties attaching to such non-submission" (95). One of the most venerable members of the Indian community suggested that they should "pass this resolution with God as witness and must never yield a cowardly submission to such degrading legislation" (95). Gandhi immediately sensed a new moral seriousness in both the proposal and the hardships to which it would lead. He seized the moment and moved the argument beyond the usual majoritarian processes of the politics of protest in the past (that is, passing by majority vote reso-

lutions that appealed to state officials to repeal or disallow a given measure or not take a certain step). (EOF)

In the meeting, Gandhi first pointed out that "there is a vast difference between this resolution and every other resolution we have passed
up to date [and] that there is a wide divergence also in the manner of
making it" (97). He marked the difference in terms of the ethical and religious foundations now urged for resistance: "We all believe in one and
the same God, the differences of nomenclature in Hinduism and Islam
notwithstanding. To pledge ourselves or to take an oath in the name of
that God or with him as witness is not to be trifled with. If having taken
such an oath we violate our pledge we are guilty before God and man.
Personally I hold that a man, who deliberately and intelligently takes a
pledge and then breaks it, forfeits his manhood" (97).

It followed that no one could be bound by another in such a matter,
as happens under normal majoritarian voting procedures, under which
losers are bound by the majority. The issue here was different and a matter of each individual's personal conscience (98).

Finally, Gandhi pointed to the grave consequences a person might
incur if he took and kept the pledge:

> He must be prepared for the worst. Therefore I want to give you
> an idea of the worst that might happen to us in the present
> struggle. Imagine that all of us present here numbering 3,000
> at the most pledge ourselves. Imagine again that the remaining
> 10,000 Indians take no such pledge. We will only provoke
> ridicule in the beginning. Again, it is quite possible that in spite
> of the present warning some or many of those who pledge
> themselves may weaken at the very first trial. We may have to go
> to jail, where we may be insulted. We may have to go hungry
> and suffer extreme heat or cold. Hard labour may be imposed.
> We may be flogged by rude warders. We may be fined heavily
> and our property may be attached and held up to auction if
> there are only a few resisters left. Opulent today we may be re-
> duced to abject poverty tomorrow. We may be deported. Suffer-
> ing from starvation and similar hardships in jail, some of us may
> fall ill and even die. In short, therefore, it is not at all impossible
> that we may have to endure every hardship ourselves on the un-
> derstanding that we shall have to suffer all that and worse. If

some one asks me when and how the struggle may end, I may say that if the entire community manfully stands the test, the end will be near. If many of us fall back under storm and stress, the struggle will be prolonged. But I can boldly declare, and with certainty, that so long as there is even a handful of men true to their pledge, there can only be one end to the struggle, and that is victory." (99)

Gandhi concluded by speaking of his own sense of ethical responsibility once having taken the pledge:

I am fully conscious of my own responsibility in the matter. . . . Even then there is only one course open to some one like me, to die but not to submit to the law. It is quite unlikely, but even if every one else flinched leaving me alone to face the music, I am confident that I would never violate my pledge. Please do not misunderstand me. I am not saying this out of vanity, but I wish to put you, especially the leaders upon the platform, on your guard. I wish respectfully to suggest it to you that if you have not the will or the ability to stand firm even when you are perfectly isolated, you must not only not take the pledge your-selves but you must declare your opposition." (99–100)

With this speech and the events that followed, Gandhi decisively moved beyond his identity as a British barrister and conventional pub-lic lawyer to a new self-conception as a religious and ethical leader of a mass movement calling for the recognition and remedy of structural in-justice. But it was a movement of a new kind. Varieties of nonviolent resistance had existed before Gandhi's South African experiments, as we have seen both in the resistance of antebellum radical abolitionists and in Tolstoy's support of the resistance of religious minorities perse-cuted in Russia. Gandhi certainly knew of many of them,[40] but under the pressure of circumstances, he improvised something that he sharply distinguished from those forms of resistance (which he termed "passive resistance"[41]). Such resistance was called by Europeans "a weapon of the weak who had no other recourse left to them."[42] Gandhi denied that the European view applied to his innovation of nonviolent resistance. In *Satyagraha in South Africa,* he states that Indians were using "soul force"

106

(103) and not merely, faute de mieux, in the absence of any more effective mode of resistance (suffragists, he notes, "did not eschew the use of physical force" when they thought it might be effective [104]). In contrast, Gandhi says, those participating in his new experiment "never used physical force, and that too although there were occasions when they were in a position to use it effectively" (104). Certainly, the Indians in South Africa were politically weak (they could not vote), and there would not have been any need for such resistance "if they had had the franchise," and if the Indians had arms, "the opposite party would have thought twice before antagonizing them" (105). But the power of soul force, as Gandhi explained it, was its ethical strength in conviction that revealed its transformative powers both for the agent and for the audience through nonviolent public mass action of a certain sort. For the agent, Gandhi underscored gains in self-respect: "The power of suggestion is such, that a man at last becomes what he believes himself to be" (105). Structural injustice rested on dehumanizing stereotypes that stripped whole classes of persons of the respect for the rights owed them, including rights of conscience and speech. Soul force rested on the ethical strength to speak and act in resistance to such injustice, and thus, it expressed and acknowledged the human dignity of those who were formerly dehumanized. "Believing ourselves to be strong, two clear consequences result from it. Fostering the idea of strength, we grow stronger and stronger every day. With the increase in our strength, our Satyagraha too becomes more effective" (105–6).

For the audience, such protest confronted them with the experience of "love" as opposed to "hatred," an experience that made possible a new kind of ethical persuasion (106). To acknowledge the distinctive features of his new experiment in protest, Gandhi organized a competition to give a name to what the Indian community was doing. The outcome was the name *satyagraha,* from the words for truth and firmness, which he employed thereafter; sometimes he used its English version, *truth force* or *soul force.*[43]

The decisive speech that Gandhi gave on September 11, 1906, was one any aggrieved Indian man of honor would find it impossible to resist; Gandhi challenged, almost competitively, his audience's sense of manhood; as he reports in *Satyagraha in South Africa,* "The community's enthusiasm knew no bounds."[44] The meeting's president joined him in taking the oath, and so did the whole gathering. But building on his own developing convictions of personal ethical voice, Gandhi gave priority in this new form of rather disciplined political protest to an appeal to ethical voice first in men and then in women that challenged dominant conceptions of gender, both manhood and womanhood. Men were to resolve insults to their honor not by violence but by strengthening their sense of voice through joining with others in nonviolent protest to that violence; they also had to be willing to undergo unjust suffering at the hands of those who would impose on them the terms of structural injustice. The appeal of this approach to women was, as we shall see, one of Gandhi's more remarkably successful experiments in truth.

The forms of satyagraha in South Africa were diverse, even at this early stage giving an idea of its flexibility and its capacity to "feel out the situation," so to speak, at least when Gandhi was in charge. Its main thrust was breaking a law deemed to be fundamentally unjust, exemplified by the Indians' refusal to register for the Black Act and their deliberate entry into Transvaal without permits. Jail was the penalty in these cases, and Gandhi argued at the time that being jailed was, in these circumstances, not a disgrace but a proud badge of self-respect: "They will at once be free of their shackles. The gaol will then be a palace to them. Instead of being a disgrace, going to gaol will enhance their prestige."[45] The attitude was to be elaborated further in India as satyagraha gathered force against the raj. Gandhi's defense of satyagraha was that it was a means for Indians to find strength in themselves in a new way—"in complete contrast to the Indian self-image of cowering before the mighty meat-eating Englishman in the schoolboy doggerel he had known so well."[46] To be jailed in this cause became a symbol of self-respect and indeed a qualification for office in India when the Indian National Congress (INC) came to power.

Satyagraha was, however, not just a matter of courageously breaking unjust laws that were targeted by the movement. It was also a political theater in which dramatic forms of symbolism would awaken and strengthen the aggrieved community's awareness of the injustice of its situation, increase its ability to work in unity in opposing such injustice, and bring opponents to a sense of shame and guilt. In South Africa, Gandhi showed his sense of political dramaturgy in creating political symbols—a sense that was, if anything, to be even more highly developed in India later on. One arresting example was the great bonfire of registration certificates in August 1908 after the government reneged, in the Indians' view, on its acceptance of their voluntary registration in the Transvaal. A large iron cauldron was set up in a mosque in Johannesburg, and some two thousand registration certificates were "all thrown into the cauldron, saturated with paraffin, and set ablaze"[47] as a kind of prelude to the renewal of the struggle.

Gandhi's initial experiments in satyagraha had been limited to the participation of men. "Some brave women had already offered to participate," but Gandhi at first resisted: "It would be derogatory to our manhood if we sacrificed our women in resisting a law which was directed only against men" (251). But his sense of the ethical powers of satyagraha soon embraced women as participants when Indians were confronted by a judicial decision that held that marriages outside the Christian faith were no longer legally recognized and the government declined to act on protests to the injustice of the decision (251–52). Gandhi perceived this as an "insult offered to our womanhood" (252), and he now was open to the participation of women in the movement: "With some hesitation he explained to the women of Tolstoy Farm and Phoenix the ordeal and dangers of appearing in court and going to gaol, not wanting them to break down at critical moments and thus damage the whole satyagraha movement. But their eagerness and fortitude proved remarkable. One was pregnant and several had babies in arms, but they responded enthusiastically to Gandhi's call. One almost died in gaol because of the poor food, and another died within days of release after contracting a fatal fever in prison."[48]

Gandhi arranged for participation by women in 1913 as part of a symbolic invasion of the Transvaal by a select group from Phoenix who did not have permits, quite deliberately courting imprisonment. They were followed by a group of women, including Gandhi's wife, who were also jailed.[49] Later the same year, Gandhi led a long march of over two thousand men, women, and children across the Transvaal border; all were deported to Natal, prosecuted, and jailed.[50]

Tolstoy had observed to Gandhi that "the Transvaal struggle was the first attempt at applying the principle of Satyagraha to masses or bodies of men."[51] What would have surprised Tolstoy even more was that, in Gandhi's hands, the experiment would energize masses of women as well. From the point of view of Gandhi's aims of ethical persuasion, participation by women was "deliberately chosen to arouse the moral sense of Indians in Africa and India, accustomed to the seclusion of women and their high valuation as symbols of purity and family life."[52] One Indian in the homeland had told Gandhi not to waste his life on South Africa and was quite unimpressed "with the satyagraha movement in its initial stages. But women in jail pleaded with him as nothing else could."[53] Of the marches of settlers from Phoenix, including women, Gandhi said, "That was to be my final offering to the God of Truth."[54] Truth was, for him, a deliverance of personal ethical voice. He had found his distinctive voice in the meeting of September 11, 1906, when he found resonance in an audience of men for a voice that challenged the traditional terms of insulted manhood; this voice was made psychologically possible for Gandhi by the role played in his sense of self and voice by his relationship to his mother's caring voice, which prominently featured nonviolence. If this subversive ethical voice had appeal to men, as Gandhi experimentally discovered it did, it might have appeal to women as well—indeed, as he eventually came to see in India, even more appeal.

Within satyagraha, Gandhi always gave a prominent place to discussion and compromise with antagonists, even at the height of the struggle. These were always important features of his style both in South Africa and India and were rooted in the ethical convictions that motivated his work. The Tolstoyan foundation of these convictions was Gandhi's abiding sense that personal ethical voice existed in all persons as persons and that this voice was, in some important way, alive in the psyche even of persons whose lives were founded on the terms of structural injustice that rested on denying that voice in themselves and in others.

It is significant that this ethical conviction had developed in Gandhi through his experiences both in Britain and in South Africa. He interpreted religions in general as rooted in a common ethical voice and for a period interpreted British constitutionalism, at home and imperially, in terms of such universal ethical values as well, as embodied in the 1858 proclamation that promised Queen Victoria's Indian subjects freedom from discrimination on grounds of religion, race, or color.[55] Gandhi had spent sufficient time in Britain to understand the contradictions within the British culture, including the tension between its tradition of democratic liberalism and its imperialism, grounded in a racism that was inconsistent with its liberal values. Satyagraha was invented not only to create a new kind of moral community of mutual respect among those subject to a structural injustice like racism but also, by virtue of its proponents' nonviolent mass resistance and willingness to suffer unjustly, to speak in a voice that would find a resonance in the otherwise suppressed ethical voice of British constitutionalism and religion. Gandhi's efforts to discuss and compromise with the officials he challenged arose from this dynamic, in one case leading a follower in South Africa to assault Gandhi physically for being too compromising with the authorities (the follower subsequently apologized).[56] Early in his stay in South Africa, Gandhi had spoken of the racist insults to which he was unjustly subjected in terms that suggested humane sympathy for the impact of racism on racists: "What does the poor man know? All coloured people are the same to him. He no doubt treats Negroes just as he has treated me."[57] What Gandhi meant by love in satyagraha was the caring attention to the suppressed voice of such men, including the officials who ran the British Empire. Thus, in 1908 and 1911, he met face to face with the official in charge of these matters in South Africa, J. C. Smuts, and worked out the basis for a settlement of the Indian community's outstanding grievances there, which in 1911 included the repeal of the Black Act and the legal equality of Indians under the new immigration law. Later grievances, some involving the invalidity of non-Christian marriages, were resolved by a commission of inquiry into Indian grievances in 1914.[58] Gandhi left for India that year, feeling his work in South Africa was done. Satyagraha, at least in the South African context, had proven its worth.

Satyagraha in India

Gandhi's first book, *Hind Swaraj* (*Indian Home Rule*), was written and published in 1909 before his return to India, for which it very much set the stage.[59] The work shows how far Gandhi had come from the Anglophile student of the late Victorian era. He had divested himself of the trappings of a successful lawyer, simplified his home and life by removing any traces of Westernization, and found his voice as the ethical leader of a mass movement. He was, in fact, in the midst of a total disillusionment with the values of Western civilization, a disillusionment arising from his experiences in Britain and South Africa interpreted in light of Tolstoy, Carpenter, and Ruskin.

Hind Swaraj is Gandhi's major work on Indo-British relations and Indian home rule. Of everything he wrote, it comes closest to a sustained political theory. Its form is a dialogue between editor and reader, with Gandhi speaking in the voice of editor. He makes quite clear that he differed from those in India who wanted to get rid of the British, whether by violence or not. His English preface opposes such "a suicidal policy" because the policy did not take seriously the Indian predicament, namely, the death grip of purely materialistic values imposed by the British raj (7). Such rule by Indians would not address the predicament, as the editor points out sharply to the reader: "[You] want English rule without the Englishman. You want the tiger's nature, but not the tiger; that is to say, you would make India English, and, when it becomes English, it will be called not Hindustan but Englistan. This is not the Swaraj I want" (28).

As far as Gandhi was concerned, the British, as their own internal critics like Carpenter and Ruskin argued, were uncritically wedded to values and a way of life that denied their basic spiritual identity, suffocating it under the weight of false values of wealth and gain. True swaraj would return India to its traditional spiritual values, as Gandhi perceived them. So swaraj could neither be imposed on nor given to India; rather, all Indians had to experience those values for themselves and learn to rule themselves—and only on such a new ethical foundation of transformed individuals would an India worth having arise. The sole road to the ethical independence Gandhi advocated was satyagraha, the force of truth. Only Indians educated by this kind of discipline and training would be able to stand up to their present rulers and to begin the indispensable process of reforming the country's polity and society by refusing to be a party to any program that was hostile to India's true values. The Indian people, having come to ethical maturity through satyagraha, might become the light of the world; even the English could "become indianised" (7) and thus redeem themselves.

There is something jarring in juxtaposing the improvisational intelligence and good sense of Gandhi's experiments with satyagraha in South Africa and the doctrinaire, anachronistic, polemically uncritical argument of *Hind Swaraj,* which is, after all, as close as Gandhi ever came to a systematic statement of his ambitions for India. As a political document for mainly Indian consumption, it may have made some polemical sense; as a serious analysis of the damage colonialism had done to both India and Britain, it made little analytical sense, papering over some of the problems Gandhi would encounter when the audience of his satyagrahas was no longer the British but Indians themselves. After all, what were his real links with the India of the twentieth century? He had been away from home for twenty years. ✎

But Gandhi's work in South Africa had prepared him remarkably well for his role in India. His experience in South Africa had been far greater in range than that of most politicians of the day in India. In South Africa, Gandhi had "encountered in microcosm many of the Indian subcontinent's diversities and the divisions among Indians."[60] He had thus had an opportunity to hone his political skills with a spectrum of Indians much more reflective of the diversities of India itself. His most successful experiment, satyagraha, had democratically empowered Indians in South Africa to unite across their divisions in politically effective ways that might have broader applicability in India. Satyagraha might prepare India's masses—otherwise divided by caste, gender, religion, and region—for the common responsibilities of democratic citizenship in a secular India.

Gandhi's work in India stretched from his return in 1914 to his death by assassination in 1948. His striking impact on Indian political life during that period grew out of his role in leading a number of satyagrahas.[61] These satyagrahas were by no means consistently successful in their avowed aims; some were notably disastrous. For example, the satyagraha against the Rowlatt antiterror bills led to arson, looting, and violence against some Englishmen, and on April 13, 1919, Brigadier General Reginald Dyer ordered his troops to fire on an unarmed crowd without warning, killing 379 people and wounding 1,137 (Gandhi called it a mistake of a "himalayan miscalculation" to encourage disobedience to law when the protesters were not properly disciplined in nonviolence).[62] However, the incident and the Hunter Commission's subsequent exoneration of Dyer discredited colonial rule in the eyes of most Indians.

Gandhi's brilliance in speaking to the ethical voice under the British colonial armor was conspicuously on display in his arrest and trial in March 1922 for leadership of the Non-cooperation Movement. He turned the trial to his own protesting ends by not adhering to its logic. He refused to defend himself against the legal charge and not only pleaded guilty but asked the judge to take into account some of the incriminating material he had ignored. The proceeding became, in Gandhi's hands, an ethical trial of British rule in which he explained his own trajectory "from a staunch loyalist and co-operator" to someone who had "become an uncompromising dis-affectionist and non-co-operator" and wondered at the morality of a legal system that required the imprisonment of people like him (Parekh, *Gandhi,* 17). He ended by presenting the judge with a moral dilemma: if he believed in the legal system, he had a duty to impose the "severest penalty" on Gandhi; if he felt there was something wrong with the system, he had to ethically condemn that system and resign (17).

Gandhi's voice deeply moved the British judge. Bowing to the defendant, he said Gandhi was in a "different category from any person I've ever tried or am likely to have to try" (17). Reluctantly, the judge sentenced Gandhi to six years of imprisonment but observed that, if the government were to release him earlier, no one would be "better pleased" than he (66). Gandhi's response was to express gratitude for the courteous way he had been treated and to thank the court for imposing a sentence that was "as light as any judge" could have imposed (18). This astonishing moment in British colonial history shows the intelligence and power of Gandhi's mode of operating, the raj's sometimes surprising decency in hearing his voice, and the respectful manner in which Gandhi and colonial officials sometimes conducted their relations, here undoubtedly under the influence of a sense of their common fraternity as British lawyers. Notably, the British government never tried him again, though he was incarcerated on several occasions (17–18). The ethical power of Gandhi's voice, accentuated by his arrest and imprisonment by the authorities he challenged, was not lost on Martin Luther King Jr., who wrote "A Letter from Birmingham City Jail" while he, like Gandhi, was imprisoned.

Gandhi's great moment came in 1930 after representative institutions established since 1919 had not yielded significant results. After much reflection, Gandhi decided to organize his own satyagraha against the government's decision to tax salt in 1930. The form of the protest called for breaking the law by making salt on the seashore. This was to be Gandhi's, not the INC's, satyagraha, expressly limited to himself and carefully chosen associates, and all participants were required to pledge that they would accept nonviolence not just pragmatically but would observe discipline and adhere to it even under the greatest provocation. Gandhi shrewdly chose the salt tax as the issue for several reasons: it connected to the life of all Indians and for this reason united Hindus and Muslims, it affected the poor especially heavily, and it publicly displayed the inhuman callousness of the raj. Also, since the revenue generated by the tax was small, it was likely that the protest would not lead to onerous reprisals.

Along with seventy-eight male companions representing various regions and religions, Gandhi, now sixty-one years of age, started his twenty-four-day march south toward the coastal village of Dandi, some 240 miles away. The effort was similar to his five-day march into Transvaal accompanied by a group of over two thousand people. He walked between ten and fifteen miles a day, applauded and sometimes joined by hundreds of people from the local villages carrying copies of the Bhagavad Gita, quoting from it and the Bible, and critically challenging the conscience of the Christian government by drawing a parallel between Gandhi's and Jesus's confrontations with authorities. In the bright light of world publicity as the whole of India cheered him on and the international press covered his progress day by day, Gandhi reached Dandi on April 5. There, with the brilliance of a great man and an artist of political theater, he picked up salt in defiance of the government's prohibition. Along India's seacoast and in its numerous inlets, thousands of people, mainly peasants, imitated his example. The government responded in some instances with brutal beatings and the imprisonment of protestors, including Gandhi, for various lengths of time. The salt satyagraha was momentous in convincing Indians that colonial rule was fragile and that they had the ability to end it if they had the moral will to do so. And because it displayed on the world stage the inhumanity of the raj, it internationalized the Indian struggle for independence and exposed the government of democratic Britain to the pressure of both domestic as well as world public opinion (20–21).

The impact of the 1930 satyagraha on British public opinion was shown when the effort led to negotiations in London, where Gandhi arrived in September 1931, seventeen years after his last visit. The British public embraced this remarkable figure:

> A popular and much sought-after figure, he met many leaders of opinion, Oxford academics, religious figures, and even George Bernard Shaw and Charlie Chaplin. He visited different parts of the country including Lancashire, where he apologized to the textile workers for the damage his boycott of British cloth had caused them and asked for their sympathetic understanding. He made a "never to be forgotten" visit to C. P. Scott of the *Manchester Guardian,* "the most impartial and the most honest paper in Great Britain." . . . He visited the King at Buckingham Palace

p. 116

dressed in his usual loincloth, which he had adopted in 1922 as a mark of his identification with the poor, throwing over his shoulders a shawl that he had worn in Britain to protect him against the cold. When a journalist commented on his sparse attire, he replied that "the King had enough on for both of us." When a year later Winston Churchill called him a "half-naked *fakir,*" Gandhi thanked him for the "compliment" and wrote that "he would love to be a naked *fakir* but was not one as yet." (21)

Gandhi attracted democratic affection and respect in Britain as he had in India and in South Africa through his relational humane skills as a person connecting with other persons, however divided by background and disagreements—skills of connection that flourished because of the unthreatening style and manner, indeed the wit and laughing grace, that he brought to his nonviolent activism. He was much less comfortable in the conference room where the meeting was held to negotiate with the government, in part because he was not yet treated as the supreme leader of the Indian people but as one of several leaders of various communities. As the meeting continued, he saw more clearly that if India was to win independence on Gandhian terms of swaraj, he had to win over minority communities, in particular Muslims and the untouchables. Both groups raised serious problems but, as it turned out, the former proved far more problematic than the latter (21–34). Notably, Gandhi won over women.

One of the most striking features of Gandhi's experiments in voice, both in the ashrams and in satyagraha, was their appeal to women, empowering an active sense of exercising their moral and political agency in ways that challenged dominant gender stereotypes of their role and place.[63] After some initial hesitation, Gandhi brought women into active participation in satyagrahas near the end of his South African campaigns, even to the extent of having them break the law and court imprisonment. Their participation proved more courageous, full-hearted, and effective than he had anticipated, an experience that provided "the foundation for his involvement of women in politics in India, so convinced had he become of their potential strength of character and will, as well as the publicity value of their sufferings in a satyagraha campaign."[64] Women actively participated not only in Gandhi's satyagrahas in India but also in other ways.[65] His experience with the courage of women, as demonstrated in satyagrahas and elsewhere, led him to speak repeatedly during this period of their comparative moral strengths, relative to men, for such protest and resistance and to argue that women were indeed better suited than men to certain kinds of resistance.[66] His very real concern for women's plight in India focused on evils such as child marriage, which had been so disastrous in his own life.[67] While his views were not feminist in the Western sense, he certainly saw clearly the impact of women's moral and political agency not only in advancing his own understanding of the aims of Indian regeneration but also in subverting the notion of the idealized pedestal, including purdah, that had isolated them for so long.[68] With his sense of the importance of experiments in voice whose outcomes one could not predict, he would have been the first to acknowledge that such an emancipation of voice might have consequences that would challenge and enlarge his own ethical vision.

There was, however, one group—the Muslims—that his Indian experiments had not successfully integrated into his sense of an Indian ethical identity that would be worthy of swaraj; this failure was the bitterest defeat for nonviolence in Gandhi's life, leading as it did to the partition of British India into India and Pakistan and bloody ethnic murders on both sides: "Possibly a million died in all, and nearly two million fled their homes and trekked to the 'right' religious side of the new international boundaries."[69] His mother's religion, so influential on Gandhi, had combined Hindu and Muslim elements, and he would have been the first to deny that there was anything in Hinduism or Islam or any religion intrinsically that rendered it inhospitable to the aims of satyagraha. His experience in South Africa clearly showed that Muslims (outnumbering Hindus there) could be energized with Hindus to participate in satyagraha. And in India itself, Gandhi inspired a Muslim movement, the Khudai Khidmatgar (Servants of God), among the Pukhtuns (Pathans) of the North West Frontier, usually regarded as a warrior people; the movement was dedicated to Gandhian nonviolence and to an Indian nationalism rather than the communal separatism that led to the creation of Pakistan (where the Pukhtuns still reside, although they are virtually erased from the national historiography of postpartition Pakistan).[70] If the notoriously violent Pukhtuns were converted to an ethics of nonviolence, Muslims elsewhere, with similar leadership, could have followed the same path.

But as V. S. Naipaul trenchantly observes, Gandhi "had no means, in India, of formulating the true racial lessons of South Africa."[71] British colonial authorities had long played the game of divide and rule in order to hold the raj together (for example, establishing separate electorates for Muslims). Moreoever, the situation of World War II gave the Muslim League and its spokesmen an open arena in which to cooperate with the British and entrench their positions during a period when the INC had disastrously withdrawn its cooperation and launched massive civil disobedience over British India at war. This only increased Muslim leverage over the British, who, not aware of the role they were playing in setting the stage for the tragedy that would follow, gave the Muslims a virtual blocking veto on all constitutional changes.[72]

In 1942, Gandhi seriously misread the political situation.[73] As an Indian leader, he refused to consider any concession or negotiation on the principle of Indian unity transcending religious barriers, insisting on his own position against the more realistic plea of others that the INC accept partition and the creation of Pakistan now as a basis for settlement with the league before the distrust and violence got out of hand, which it did.[74] Rather, Gandhi embarked on civil disobedience on the ground that the Muslim masses would thus reveal that they were aligned with the INC. Gandhi's judgment was "a naïve and tragic misreading of the communal situation."[75] Muslim fears were genuine. They had ruled over India for centuries and naturally feared vengeance or at least discrimination in an independent India.[76] Gandhi's now well-established ways of thinking and acting (grounding nonviolence in Hinduism) may have made it difficult for him to bridge the yawning gap between increasingly polarized Hindus and Muslims.[77]

By the time of the final negotiations for independence, INC leaders had, despite Gandhi's objections, accepted partition as the only way to face the reality of a deteriorating situation as violence sparked off more violence. Now a marginal figure, Gandhi was preoccupied at the end of his life with the escalating intercommunal violence, for which he blamed himself. The violence showed, he argued, that the earlier nonviolence of Indians had been the nonviolence of the weak, not the strong.[78] Along these lines, George Orwell cynically characterized Gandhi's nonviolence in India as successful because it was so consistent with British interests: "He could be regarded as 'our man.'"[79] According to this view, nonviolence was successful, when it *was* successful, because it allowed the British to continue and then end their colonial government of India on their own patronizing terms. Gandhi was, however, undoubtedly a potent, in-

118

dependently persuasive influence on both British public opinion and governments. What may have been correct in Orwell's skepticism was the implicit question of whether, once Britain was gone or going, Gandhi's techniques had much of an audience among Indians.

Gandhi apparently agreed with Orwell's skepticism. He regarded what happened in India at partition as an indictment of himself because the intercommunal violence showed how little satyagraha had done toward achieving the moral regeneration from the effects of colonialism that he regarded as the purpose and meaning of swaraj. He expiated his remorse by offering his own personal satyagrahas in the last years of his life, and these efforts may be the best testament to what he meant to leave as an enduring legacy to humankind. In stark disregard of his own safety, Gandhi began his pilgrimage of peace to the Noakhali district of Bengal, the scene of the worst Hindu-Muslim violence. His presence and force of personality succeeded in restoring peace in Bengal and elsewhere.

Gandhi did not go to Delhi on August 15, 1947, when India became independent. The terms of independence were so remote from his idea of swaraj that he saw nothing to celebrate. He remained busy at what he thought was an important job, combating the violence several hundred miles away. Shortly after independence, mass violence erupted in Calcutta, to which Gandhi immediately rushed. When all his appeals failed, he undertook one of his fasts to death on September 2, 1947, just as he had done a few months earlier. Almost miraculously, the violence stopped within three days (Brown, *Gandhi,* 378–79). Gandhi broke his fast on September 4. The press attaché of the viceroy, Lord Louis Mountbatten, observed: "Mountbatten's estimate is that he has achieved by moral persuasion what four Divisions would have been hard pressed to have accomplished by force" (379).

Having finished in Calcutta in early September 1947, Gandhi went to Delhi, meaning to proceed to the Punjab. But the capital of a now free India experienced such communal violence that he remained in Delhi in order to deal with it. On January 12, 1948, his sense of helplessness led to his decision to fast to death yet again until communal peace was restored. Gandhi broke his fast only after important leaders of communal bodies agreed to a joint plan that would make normal life in the city possible again. (E₀F) | 0 0:52:32.46

P. 120 The successes of Gandhi's fasts in Calcutta and Delhi demonstrated the moral force he still had. But in the rising enmities that accompanied partition, Hindus derided Gandhi's role "as weakness toward Muslim demands" (380). During his last months in Delhi, angry Hindus disturbed even his prayer meetings; people objected, for example, to the reading of the Koran and shouted "Death to Gandhi," and the prayers could not continue (381). On January 30, 1948, Gandhi was assassinated by a young Hindu who was deeply offended by his work for peace and unity (382).

Gandhi's Voice as Woman's Voice: Ethical Strengths and Perils

Gandhi had defended one of his fasts to death in terms of his sense of himself or part of himself as a woman—"I know you have not missed the woman in me"—and credited his "feminine" qualities of heart and soul with his resolve to choose a "way of life through suffering unto death. I must therefore find my courage in my weakness" (167). Indeed, his sense of the passion behind his motivation was put in terms that likened himself to a prophetess: "She who sees life in death and death in life is the real Poetess and Seeress" (167). There is a striking analogy between Gandhi's way of making this point and that of Hester Prynne in Hawthorne's *The Scarlet Letter,* who appeals to her sense of herself as "a prophetess" (227). Hester is, however, clear that such a person "must be a woman" (228).

Gandhi was a man, but one whose sense of ethical voice required both men and women to question gender: "My ideal is this: A man should remain man and yet should become woman; similarly a woman should remain woman and yet become man. This means that man should cultivate gentleness and the discrimination of woman; and woman should cast off her timidity and become brave and courageous."[80]

Many female associates of Gandhi, both Indian and European, remarked that they could relate to him as they would to other women and felt quite secure and relaxed in his presence.[81] and Gandhi told Manu Gandhi, his granddaughter, that while he had been a father to many, he had been a mother to her.[82] Manu observed that Gandhi, uniquely among men, had "been endowed by God with the mother's loving heart which a woman is blessed with."[83] Gandhi elsewhere spoke of his efforts to take seriously a woman's interests and feelings: "I have mentally become a woman in order to steal into her heart."[84]

Gandhi shared with Garrison and Tolstoy a close relationship to the loving voice of a maternal caretaker, namely, his mother—a relationship that gave a resonance to his own ethical and religious voice. His sense of his mother was, like Tolstoy's, highly idealized. He related to an early biographer an attachment to her that was revelatory of its quality: "I was my mother's pet child, first because I was the smallest of her children but also because there was nothing dearer to my heart than her service. My brothers were fond of play and frolic. I found not much in common with them. I had no close bond with my sister either. Play had absolutely no fascination for me in preference to my mother's service. Whenever she wanted me for anything, I ran to her."[85]

As Erikson, the psychoanalyst, pointedly observes, "Always when *she* needed *him!* Never an intimation that *he* may have needed a *mother.*"[86] What marks the way Gandhi spoke, here and elsewhere, about his mother was his idealization of her in terms of virtues to be followed and even worshiped, her "saintliness," her tolerant personal religion of disciplined fasts and nonviolence, ahimsa.[87] When Gandhi told his biographer that he "taught his mother a lesson in *ahimsa,* by telling her that she should keep the older brothers from beating him rather than encouraging him to beat them back,"[88] he put into his child's mouth the query to his mother, "Should you not, mother, prevent my brother from beating me instead of asking me to imitate him?"[89] Here we see in action a son's mythologizing not only of his mother but also of himself as the son of such a mother, showing "a competitive attempt at becoming more maternal than the most motherly of mothers."[90]

The great strength of Gandhi's forming his ethical voice as a resonance of the authority of his mother's voice showed itself in a creative ethical intelligence that was open to new ethical means and ends and that took seriously the moral experience of women usually silenced and marginalized. Truth was, for Gandhi, a deliverance of personal ethical voice. He had found his distinctive voice at the mass meeting of September 11, 1906, in South Africa when he found a resonance in an audience of men for a voice that challenged the traditional terms of insulted manhood; this voice was made psychologically possible for Gandhi by the role in his sense of self and voice of his relationship to his mother's caring voice, the hidden transcript of her highly personal religion that prominently featured nonviolence. Men were to resolve insults to their honor not by violence but by strengthening their sense of voice in protesting violence through joining with others in protest and showing their moral strength by their willingess to endure unjust suffering. Gandhi may have been as surprised as anyone that his proposal would enjoy broad support among men: "The community's enthusiasm knew no bounds."[91] Certainly, what he proposed was not part of the conventional culture of male honor, which it quite clearly challenged. It is precisely because Gandhi found his voice in the authority of a women's voice usually suppressed by that culture that he was able creatively to feel his way to a new moral politics and a supporting psychology. If such an ethical voice of nonviolence were a common feature of women's caretaking experience of nurture, protection, and ethical acceptability, why might not such a voice and experience be of broader applicability? Gandhi, who identified with the maternal role of nursing when he cared for his father and later the injured Zulus in South Africa, may have been thinking of satyagraha as a kind of nursing of a very difficult child, prone to fits of violence when he did not get his way; if that child was to be nurtured and protected and brought persuasively to some sense of ethically legitimate conduct, he needed loving care, including care when he was violent.

Gandhi was testing this kind of hypothesis when he proposed and led the first experiments in satyagraha in South Africa. He could not have even entertained, let alone proposed, such an unconventional hypothesis if he had not taken seriously the authority of an ethical voice he found in his mother. A more conventionally patriarchal upbringing, in which he identified completely with his father's patriarchal voice, would have ruled out any development along these lines. Gandhi had the ethical intelligence to see a possibly persuasive nonviolent alternative because he took seriously the notion that the voice and psychology he found in relationship to his mother might be much more common than the dominant patriarchal culture allowed or supposed, whether that culture was Indian or South African or British. Even the most patriarchal men may have had close relationships with their mothers, relationships whose impact on their developmental psychology lingers despite their attempts to cover it over with the armor of patriarchal manhood. Gandhi's hypothesis was that even patriarchal men have an inner voice that they can be brought to hear by an appropriate strategy of nonviolence such as satyagraha. Satyagraha, which expresses the ethical voice of resistance to structural injustice and appeals to the inner voice in the perpetrators of this injustice, may ethically and psychologically disarm the armor of conventional manhood and allow these men to hear and take seriously the free ethical voice within.

Gandhi, who had so closely studied and valued his mother's caretaking, developed a corresponding sensitive and responsive emotional and ethical intelligence to the ways in which intimate voice goes underground earlier in the developmental psychology of boys and girls.[92] He drew on what he had seen to develop in himself a kind of voice that would give a resonance to suppressed intimate voices, strengthening them and bringing them to bear on politics in new ways. Gandhi's enduring significance lies not in his writings but in the relational power of his personal voice and presence and leadership and the mass social movements he inspired. Because he stayed so powerfully in touch with a voice he had experienced and developed in early childhood, he read the human psychology of his audiences in terms of that voice and called on it in himself and others in ways that, in appropriate circumstances, enabled men to disarm the armor of patriarchal manhood and feel and act on an ethical voice that challenged the terms of such a manhood.

Gandhi sometimes spoke of this process of disarming others in rather tender mother–child terms, "as a child clings to its mother's breast,"[93] the image of a refractory, hungry child touched to the heart by a mother's unexpected goodness in feeding his hunger, the child responsively clinging to her breast; in the same way, "the knowledge that the Indians, forgetful of their wrongs, were out to help them in the hour of their need, had melted their hearts," acts of nonviolent civil disobedience that had the aim and effect of "soften[ing the] heart by self-suffering."[94] What Gandhi found in South Africa was that otherwise hard-bitten government officials (like Mr. Chamney, Registrar of Asiatics) were visibly shaken by satyagraha: "I then saw that tears stood in Mr. Chamney's eyes. I had often written bitterly against him, but this showed me how man's heart may be softened by events."[95]

This was a new conception of political courage—the willingness to suffer oneself to do good to others—but it was a courage Gandhi knew people had; he saw it clearly in the experience of women as mothers, and he self-consciously argued late in his life, in 1940, that it could and should be generalized to embrace humankind:

> My contribution to the great problem lies in my presenting for acceptance truth and *ahimsa* in every walk of life, whether for individuals or nations. I have hugged the hope that in this woman will be the unquestioned leader and, having thus

found her place in human evolution, will shed her inferiority complex.

//I have suggested that woman is the incarnation of *ahimsa*. *Ahimsa* means infinite love, which again means infinite capacity for suffering. Who but woman, the mother of man, shows this capacity in the largest measure? She shows it as she carries the infant and feeds it during nine months and derives joy in the suffering involved. What can beat the suffering caused by the pangs of labour? But she forgets them in the joy of creation. Who again suffers daily so that her babe may wax from day to day? Let her transfer that love to the whole of humanity, let her forget she ever was or can be the object of man's lust. And she will occupy her proud position by the side of man as his mother, maker and silent leader. It is given to her to teach the art of peace to the warring world thirsting for that nectar.[96]

Here, there is something quite ethically and psychologically radical in Gandhi's taking quotidian virtues of women's experience, as mothers, and giving them a moral and psychological significance and importance they were not previously supposed to have, namely, as a model for the virtue of courage that the self-suffering in satyagraha calls for. Women's experience shows, Gandhi argued, that we are humanly capable of such self-suffering for the good of others, indeed, that such loving care affords the nurture, growth, and ethical legitimacy of human development.

Gandhi had originally invented and practiced satyagraha as an appeal to a new kind of ethical voice in men, but late in his stay in South Africa, he experimented with the participation of women, including his own wife, in satyagrahas protesting laws invalidating their marriages, which affected them directly. The ethical impulse to satyagraha was a questioning of the role gender had unjustly played in the violent suppression of voice; if the point applied to men, it should, Gandhi reasoned, apply to women as well. The experiment was brilliantly successful, and he elaborated its successes in India, drawing women into participation. The very terms of his conception of Indian resistance took the form of an egalitarian metric for understanding resistance that equally embraced Hindus and Muslims, untouchables, and, of course, women as well as men. Nonviolence itself as a political strategy intrinsically downplayed gender differences because it ruled out the forms of militaristic violence that

traditionally have been supposed to be justified on the ground of gender differences like physical strength and aggressiveness.[97] And Gandhi's
development of political symbols of resistance, among them the spinning
of cloth at home, appealed to women as well as men.

In his 1940 discussion of women's moral powers in satyagraha, Gandhi
came very close to Hester Prynne's appeal for a new prophetic voice,
which had to be a woman's voice. But of course, it was Gandhi's patriarchal voice that claimed prophetic voice, albeit a voice that drew strength
and authority from women's experience and from women's relationships
to him. There is a problem here involving the residual patriarchal control of voice (like Tolstoy's) that suggests perils in the kind of relationship
Gandhi had to his mother's voice, in particular when the relationship is
disassociated from later relationships to women on equal terms. The
problem arises from a dynamic of voice when it is based, as it was in the
case of both Tolstoy and Gandhi, on an idealization of a maternal caretaker that, as idealization, fails to take into account the full intellectual
and emotional complexity of women, including their sexual voice. An
idealized voice is not, to put the point bluntly, a real voice; indeed, it
may suppress free voice. When Hawthorne (drawing on the abolitionist
feminists) has Hester Prynne imagine a new ethical voice, it is a woman
speaking in her own voice, not a man imagining what an ideal woman
might say. Gandhi, following Tolstoy, confused the ideal with the real.
Tolstoy thus developed a conception of prophetic ethical voice that questioned the role unjust political violence played in many forms of structural injustice, but he never questioned the role this violence played in
the repression of women's sexual voice; indeed, his own life and marriage exemplified the consequences of this failure, as he callously disre-
garded the voice, including the sexual voice, of his own wife. Ultimately,
Tolstoy condemned sexuality itself.

Gandhi shared this psychological and ethical problem with Tolstoy.
Its psychology was rooted in the same kind of mythologically desexualized idealization of his mother, and its ethical difficulty was its failure to
take seriously the notion that real women have or may have sexual
voices that require attention and respect; this psychology of desexualized
idealization explains Gandhi's sharp separation, in his otherwise remarkable 1940 appeal to women's experience of their self-suffering, from any
question of pleasure they may have taken in sexual relations. Tolstoy and
Gandhi each had a sexual history (for Tolstoy, sex with prostitutes and

VD; for Gandhi, an arranged child marriage and premature sexual relations) that explains how sexual relations became for them so disassociated from anything remotely resembling a loving interest in a partner's sexual pleasure and voice. Like Tolstoy, Gandhi ultimately gave this unhappy sexual history the imprimatur of ethics and religion when he adopted celibacy (brahmarcharya) as the required course in 1906.

George Orwell found Gandhi's rationale of brahmarcharya, as well as its associated practices, to be one of his most questionable commitments because it called for a detachment from all personal relationships that was ultimately "inhuman."[98] This may have had consequences that were disastrous not only for Gandhi's wife and children but also for his larger ethical ambitions.

Erik Erikson, who enormously admired Gandhi's achievement, puts this point in terms of a discussion, "a personal word," that interrupts his fascinating analysis of Gandhi's developmental psychology and role in history. Erikson writes a letter to Gandhi, with whom he feels on intimate terms, putting into words a critique that he feels he must raise in order to come to terms truthfully with Gandhi as a person and a leader. Erikson questions several incidents in Gandhi's life involving forms of sadistic cruelty to women—in one case, the callousness to his wife that his celibacy reflected, and in another case, his shaving of young girls' hair as a response to the sexual excitement young boys at Tolstoy Farm felt on bathing with the girls. Erikson sees these and other similar incidents as all too conventional "patriarchal bad manners": "How much you [Gandhi] were inclined to treat those closest to you as possessions and whipping-posts." If Erikson is correct about the ways in which Gandhi's insight was blinded by his own violence, it may also illuminate something Gandhi never understood but for which he felt personally responsible, namely, the violence to which nonviolence apparently led at the time of India's partition.[99]

Gandhi had invented satyagraha in the circumstances of the racist degradation of the Indian community in South Africa as a way of giving expression to the free ethical voice of a community unjustly burdened by structural injustice. He believed the protesting voice of such nonviolent resistance might ethically persuade South African and British public opinion to hear, attend, and act on its claims of justice. Gandhi cut the link between insults to manhood and violence, calling instead for a nonviolent resistance that expressed and appealed to ethical voice, including that of individuals who inflicted and perpetuated structural injustice. In developing and elaborating satyagraha, Gandhi always had an exquisite relational sense of audience, encompassing both the people who would undergo the discipline of satyagraha and the leadership and public in the community being protested. His three-year period of study in Great Britain imparted to him an invaluable understanding of the tensions and contradictions within British political and ethical life, including its Christianity, its constitutional democracy, and its racist imperialism. Gandhi found an adoring audience in Britain in 1931 because he appealed to an ethical voice already very much alive in its political, ethical, and religious culture.

Gandhi's intelligence and relational sensitivity certainly explain the successes his satyagrahas had in South Africa against racist laws and in India as a way of securing ultimate independence from Britain. But Gandhi, who had been callously insensitive to his own wife, displayed in his public life a similar self-righteous rigidity that, as independence approached, was neither politically intelligent nor relationally sensitive to the growing religious polarization of Indian life. There had been early warning signs that he could misjudge the capacity of Indians to sustain nonviolence, as in the "himalayan miscalculation" of his 1919 satyagraha against the Rowlatt bills.[100] Then, as independence neared, Gandhi insisted on satyagrahas as the answer to all problems in a formulaic way that Edward Carpenter had warned (against Tolstoy's prohibition of all violence, including self-defense) might lead to worse evils: "All the while to cleave to a formula only means to admit the evil in some other shape which the formula does not meet—to forswear the stick only means to resort to rebuke and sarcasm in self-defence, which may inflict more pain and a deeper scar, and in some cases more injury, than the stick; if self-defence in any shape is quite forsworn then that only means to resign and abandon one's place in the world completely."[101]

Carpenter's warning against Tolstoy had an eerie force against his devoted follower, Gandhi. Though he read the contradictions and tensions within British political and ethical life so astutely, Gandhi could not read the tensions among Indians. We need to keep in mind that his sense of his own tradition was crucially formed in the process of his discovery of Western culture (in particular its constitutionalism and its Christianity), his interest aroused at the same time both by Western culture and the interest Westerners took in Eastern religious cultures. There is no doubt

an important strand of nonviolence in Eastern religious cultures (for example, in Buddhism, Jainism, and Taoism), but Gandhi's feeling for nonviolence came not from mainstream Hinduism but from his mother's
highly personal devotion to "a small sect that prided itself on having unified the Koran with the Hindu scriptures, and which abhorred any regression to the idolatry of either."[102] Gandhi brought to Hinduism an ethical
commitment to nonviolence that he had formed on the basis of his
mother's religiosity and his interest in the Jesus of Nazareth of Leo Tolstoy.

There can be no doubt that Gandhi believed with complete sincerity
and deep conviction that Hinduism was the religion of nonviolence he
supposed it to be, but even a quite cursory reading of the Bhagavad Gita
would suggest that it does not call for nonviolence. Its narrative starts
with the warrior Arjuna doubting whether it can be correct for him, as
a warrior, to fight to the death against blood relatives who are on the
other side of a conflict; to this plea for the ethics of nonviolence, Lord
Krishna responds in terms of the male code of honor, "The coward is ig-
noble, shameful."[103] Krishna condemns Arjuna's nonviolence in terms of
the moral duties incumbent on a warrior and the metaphysical system
(including reincarnation, in which there is no final death) that holds
such duties in place as the structure of a life worth living.

Gandhi's commentary on and translation of the Bhagavad Gita attempted to square the text with nonviolence.[104] Bal Gangadhae Tilak, a
leader of the Indian independence movement and an expert on the Gita,
had pointed to texts like those quoted earlier to show that, rather than
supporting nonviolence, the poem actually requires violence as one's
duty in certain circumstances.[105] Not unreasonably, many Hindus, Tilak
among them, never read the Bhagavad Gita in the way Gandhi did.
Bhikhu Parekh's important study concludes that Gandhi's interpretation
of the Hindu tradition is not, to say the least, compelling: "There is no
evidence that, with isolated exceptions, any major Hindu thinker or
ruler was deeply perturbed by political violence and interested in exploring an alternative to it."[106]

Gandhi accepted the ethical principle of nonviolence because of the
authority of his mother's voice in his life and because of his Tolstoyan
reading of Jesus of Nazareth. Thus, his reading of the Hindu tradition in
general and the Bhagavad Gita in particular may have been found quite
implausible by many Hindus. In *Hind Swaraj,* Gandhi had implausibly
argued that Western culture was irredeemably corrupt and that Eastern

culture, properly reformed, would morally redeem humankind. Through this ideology, he blinded himself not only to the deeper ethical problems in his own culture but also to how much his distinctive ethical views were based in the religion of the culture he had come to dismiss— Christianity. In this connection, it is certainly striking that his satyagrahas were most successful when Christian Britain was his audience.

How then did Gandhi successfully use satyagraha in India at all? It succeeded, when it did succeed, as a strategy against the British, and many Indians may have regarded it as a useful way to secure independence on grounds quite independent of any ultimate ethical belief in nonviolence as such. Even Indians to whom Gandhi's ethical vision genuinely appealed (and there were undoubtedly many) were moved more by his remarkable personality, his relational sensitivities to human feeling and suffering in all its forms, his astonishing personal courage, and his record of solid achievement in bringing ordinary Indians, otherwise so divided by caste and religion and gender, into a sense of common democratic participation for humane goals larger than themselves, including a better life for themselves and their children. Gandhi's enduring legacy to India may be not independence or his reform of Hinduism but rather nonviolent secular democratization, whereby masses of Indians experienced for the first time a practical sense of empowering political and moral agency in terms of common goals; this is a legacy of networks and a civic culture based on mutual cooperation among different groups that, where it exists in India today, is much less likely to be subverted by intercommunal violence.[107]

Like Tolstoy, Gandhi was more radically cut off from human relationships at the end of his life than he ever had been. What comes to mind in both cases is the tragedy of King Lear, an old man blind to the folly of giving up all human possessions and attachments howls in despair at the emptiness within, longing for the attachments he willfully cannot even acknowledge as a human need.[108] I earlier suggested that Gandhi, who thought celibacy was required for ethics, paid a price for his failure to take seriously women's sexual voices: his own search for and experiments in truthful ethical voice were flawed and distorted by the deep untruth of repressing his own sexual and sensual voice. Such untruth shows itself, Erikson argues, in self-righteous impulses to sadistic cruelties that are rationalized as moral, thus corrupting the very aim of nonviolence—respect for free and equal voice—by forms of violence that are invisible to the person flawed by this untruth. Gandhi's rigid insistence on nonviolence as the only response to combat evil (including Jewish nonviolence as a response to the Holocaust[109]) blinded him to the violence of his nonviolence. He did not see his own morally responsible, acquiescent complicity with evil when he successfully insisted in 1942 on his own position despite the more realistic plea of others who argued that the INC should agree to the creation of Pakistan as a means of settling with the Muslim League before the distrust and violence got out of hand (as, of course, it did).[110]

The relational moralist had, in the end, withdrawn into a kind of self-righteous solipsism. "Hitherto, Gandhi had talked about becoming half a woman; it would seem that he now wanted to become a complete woman."[111] He had become totally absorbed by his idealization of his mother, an idealization that, in his case, precluded any sexual voice or sensual relationship. It was during this period that Gandhi experimented with sleeping with naked young women, principally his ward, Manu, on the ground that this would show his now total repression of sexual feeling.[112] In fact, it showed a desperate need for loving human connection that Gandhi could not accept in himself. He rationalized as ethical what was actually sadistic exploitation of his inexperienced ward.

Remarkably but all too humanly, Gandhi found ethical strength in his despair in the two great fasts to death near the end of his life in Calcutta and Delhi. These were his last, highly personal satyagrahas, a genre of satyagraha that no longer required the participation of anyone else. Gandhi had written about how, as a child, he had anxiously attended to his mother during her fasts.[113] Now, he again found his truthful ethical voice in being the motherly nurse to a bleeding India in his last two fasts, each of which moved Indians to stop their slaughter of one another. The elderly Gandhi, who as a boy had found in his mother's fasts such speaking moral power, discovered yet again through such fasts one last sublime experience of hearing other ethical voices awakened in resonance to his own. Can there be any greater tribute to the psychological powers of his ethical voice? For Hindu patriarchal conservatives, however, this was the last straw in Gandhi's betrayal of Hindu manhood. And in the end, he fell victim to a religiously inspired violence enraged by his unmanly nonviolence.

CHAPTER FOUR

King on Nonviolence

00:40:26.27

Martin Luther King, like Gandhi, must be understood not only as a person in and of himself but also as the leader of the nonviolent mass movement of protest that he inspired; the brilliance of the historiography of Taylor Branch's *Parting the Waters* is that it studies King in this way, on the analogy of Jesus of Nazareth, whom we know entirely through the words of the people in the movement he inspired.[1] We, of course, know much more about the exact words (spoken and written) of both Gandhi and King; Jesus wrote nothing. But there is something deeply true in regarding all three men—Jesus, Gandhi, and King—as speaking in a voice of moral authority that lives in history because it found a resonance in the voices of persons who were empowered to join social movements that would give expression to their newly discovered voices. Gandhi and King were leaders of mass movements of political protest, and Jesus as well led a movement of protest and reform. Further, all three were the victims of homicidal political violence directed at their teachings, which prominently featured nonviolence. These are not accidental analogies. Gandhi was deeply moved by a Tolstoyan reading of the life and teaching of Jesus of Nazareth, and King in turn drew inspiration from Gandhi as well as, of course, from Jesus.

Martin Luther King draws together all the strands of my study. First, he was a Baptist minister who came to regard the social movement he led as yet another reformation and great awakening within Christianity that challenged the traditional religious, ethical, and political authority of the Christian churches in terms of a certain reading of Jesus of Nazareth. Second, he was a major twentieth-century leader of the struggle within the United States against the structural injustice of racism, a struggle that reasonably can and should be traced to the antebellum radical abolitionist movement that denounced both American slavery and racism. Third,

King self-consciously thought about and shaped his social movement as part of a worldwide struggle against patterns of Western imperialism motored by racism, an understanding of social protest clearly stated by Tolstoy and acted on by Gandhi. Fourth and last, when King addressed the mechanics of leading a nonviolent mass social movement, he drew on the close study of Gandhi's satyagrahas as a disciplined model for how such a movement should be conducted.

To understand King and the distinctive features of his nonviolent movement of civil disobedience, we must place him and his period in the larger historical context of African American protest and dissent. The conditions were right for the emergence of both a leader and a movement in the middle of the twentieth century, but why was nonviolence the predominant feature of that movement?

African American Protest as a Tradition

Our earlier study of Garrison and the radical abolitionists sets the stage for understanding the first period of African American protest, for these individuals were remarkable among abolitionists not only for their criticisms of American slavery (an institution that held African Americans in bondage) but also for their indictment of the racism it reflected. The general radical abolitionist conceptions of justice were constitutionalized by the terms of the Reconstruction Amendments, including the constitutional condemnation of state-supported cultural racism.[2] However, in 1896, in *Plessy v. Ferguson*, the Supreme Court of the United States held state-sponsored racial discrimination to be consistent with the equal protection clause of the Fourteenth Amendment, one of the more egregious examples of grave interpretive mistake in the Court's checkered history.[3] In this opinion, the Supreme Court itself powerfully advanced the cultural construction of American racism.

The long road to the overturning of *Plessy* by *Brown v. Board of Education* in 1954 was marked by the critical testing and recasting of the assumptions that had made *Plessy* possible.[4] The great change in these background assumptions was in part achieved through the mobilization of a constitutional movement led by the National Association for the Advancement of Colored People (NAACP), founded in 1910 by a coalition of African Americans (among them W. E. B. DuBois) and white liberals.[5] Black Americans in the South and elsewhere asserted their First Amendment rights of protest, criticism, and advocacy, and they were finally accorded some measure of national protection by the Supreme Court (reversing early decisions to the contrary) in the exercise of these rights.[6] The consequences were those to be expected by the liberation of free moral voice,[7] including the increasingly important black creative voice in American literature and other arts that confronted Americans with a sense of the human voice burdened with irrational hatred.[8]

In his argument to the Supreme Court on behalf of the NAACP, Thurgood Marshall dramatized the force of this moral voice in terms of blue-eyed, innocent African American children indistinguishable in all reasonable respects from other children playing with them and living near them except for the role the Supreme Court would play in legitimating a constructed difference (segregated education) that enforced, in fact, an irrationalist prejudice with a long history of unjust subjugation.[9] The Supreme Court was compelled to face a stark moral choice: either to give effect to a culture of dehumanization or to refuse to remain complicit in such rights-denying evil. Moral responsibility for one's complicity with evil could not be evaded. In effect, Marshall, as an African American, stood before the Court in the full voice of his moral personality as a free person and asked the justices either to accept responsibility for degrading him as subhuman or to refuse any longer to degrade any person. State-sponsored racial segregation, once uncritically accepted as a reasonable expression of natural race differences, now was construed as itself an unjust construction of an irrationalist dehumanization that excluded citizens from their equal rights as members of the political community and was, as such, deemed unconstitutional. In 1954, in *Brown v. Board of Education,* the Supreme Court of the United States articulated this deliberative interpretive judgment for the nation by unanimously striking down state-sponsored racial segregation as a violation of the equal protection clause of the Fourteenth Amendment.

In 1967, in *Loving v. Virginia,* a similarly unanimous Supreme Court struck down as unconstitutional state antimiscegenation laws.[10] The Court rejected, as it had in *Brown,* the view that the dominant interpretive judgments of the Reconstruction Congress left no room for its own independent interpretive responsibilities. For this reason, the Court rejected the equal application theory of *Pace v. Alabama* on the same grounds it had rejected it in 1964 in a decision invalidating a state criminal statute prohibiting cohabitation by interracial married couples.[11] The equal protection clause condemned all state-sponsored sources of invidious racial discrimination, and the Court held that antimiscegenation laws were one such source.

In these and other cases, the Supreme Court of the United States, under the impact of the NAACP, reinterpreted the equal protection clause in ways much closer to the normative views of the radical abolitionist movement that inspired it (its language of equal protection came out of abolitionist criticisms of slavery and racism). It was the radical abolitionists who interpreted both racial segregation and laws forbidding miscegenation as racist violations of equal treatment, a view that the Supreme Court finally adopted in *Brown* and *Loving*. And it was a group of radical abolitionists—the abolitionist feminists—who argued that equality condemned as well all forms of structural injustice, such as sexism, that had the same structure as racism; this abolitionist view has now been endorsed by the Supreme Court, which condemns sexism on the same basis it condemns racism (the condemnation includes forms of homophobia as well).[12] Our story here, however, starts at the moment when this constitutional development was expressed in one of the greatest successes of African American constitutional protest, namely, *Brown v. Board of Education* in 1954—a moment that saw the entry of Martin Luther King onto the stage of American history in ways and with consequences we must now explore.

King's Early Life

Martin Luther King Jr. was born in 1929 in Atlanta, Georgia, to a family of Baptist preachers. His mother, Alberta Williams, was the only child of Rev. A. D. Williams, a slave preacher's son and a graduate of Morehouse College in Atlanta, and Jennie C. Parks, a graduate of Spelman College (which had been financially supported by John D. Rockefeller and bore the name of his abolitionist wife, Laura Spelman). Williams had built the Ebenezer Baptist Church into a prosperous, important congregation after having moved it and his family to a better part of town. The area had been abandoned by whites after the 1906 race riots that killed over fifty blacks; a similar racist riot erupted two years later in Springfield, Illinois. In response to these riots, the NAACP was founded by DuBois and others in 1910 (Branch, *Parting the Waters,* 27–49).

(EOF)

(F) p. 135

Alberta Williams had gone to Spelman like her mother; she was "always known for her sweet shyness and humility," lacking the assertiveness of her father and "her mother's stature as the 'First Lady of Ebenezer.' But she became an astute observer of church politics, as taught to her by both parents, and she developed an enormous strength—passive, absorptive, sure of herself—on her own ground, which was always church and family" (32–33).

Michael King ("Daddy King"), later known as Martin Luther King Sr. and the father of Martin Jr., was the second of ten children born on 00:57.47 a sharecropper's farm. After saving his mother from a beating by his drunken father, he fled for his life to Atlanta "to pursue the most coveted profession open to unschooled Negroes, the ministry" (34). He was interested in marrying Alberta before he met her because of her father's eminence at Ebenezer (where he was "the highest-paid Negro minister in Atlanta at the end of his first year" and national treasurer of the National Baptist Convention) (43, 34). King and Alberta were married in 1926 and lived with her parents. The Reverend Williams died suddenly in 1931, and at the insistence of his widow, Mike King was appointed his successor at Ebenezer (40).

Martin Luther King Jr. was the second of three children and had a special closeness to his maternal grandmother (49). The depth of Martin's attachment to her is suggested by his two suicide attempts as a boy, both over shock at harm that befell her. The first occurred after his younger brother, A. D., slid down a banister at high speed and ran into Grandmother Williams, knocking her to the floor. Martin, terrified, ran upstairs to his room at the back of the house and threw himself out of the window (48–49). The second attempt occurred when Martin was a seventh grader and was told his beloved grandmother had died of a heart attack: "Young King discovered unforgettable feelings of anguish that went to the very bottom of him. . . , so overwhelming him that once again he threw himself out of the upstairs window" (57). King identified his feelings for religion in his life from this time, arising from the loss "of the one person in the household who seemed to combine pure love with natural, unforced authority" (57–58).

Andrew Young, who worked closely with King, observed that "Martin's mother, quiet as she was, was really a strong, domineering force in the family."[13] When the young Martin, who had played with white boys until he went to school, was told by their mothers that he could no

p. 136

135

longer play with them, it was his grandmother and mother who explained slavery and segregation to him, and it was his mother who told him, "Don't let this thing make you feel you're not as good as white people. . . . You're as good as anyone else, and don't you forget it."[14]

It was one of DuBois's more astute observations about African American cultural life that black churches were "for the most part, curiously composite institutions, which combine[d] the work of churches, theaters, newspapers, homes, schools, and lodges";[15] further, appearances notwithstanding, women were major players in these churches.[16] Black churches have historically been a sanctuary of moral strength for African Americans against the ravages and indignities of slavery and, after slavery ended, against vicious racism, exemplifying a striking form of the hidden transcripts (an interpretation of religion at war with the interpretation of the dominant white culture) through which subordinated groups nourish an ethical voice of resistance.[17] Even in the formally patriarchal Baptist Church, women played a powerful role not only as audiences but also in forms of organization and participation in which they were important participants, for example, in the National Baptist Convention, the largest religious movement among African Americans.[18] The theology that expressed this experience "identified the church and Christ himself with feminine attributes—representing Christ, that is, as soft, gentle, emotional, and passive," and it derived its "conception of a triumphant feminine ideal from the Beatitudes of Christ's Sermon on the Mount."[19] Black women in particular found in Jesus "the divine co-sufferer, who empower[ed] them in situations of oppression. For Christian Black women in the past, Jesus was their central frame of reference. They identified with Jesus because they believed Jesus identified with them. As Jesus was persecuted and made to suffer undeservedly, so were they. His suffering culminated in the crucifixion. Their crucifixion included rape, and babies being sold."[20] The slave woman thus identified her pain and struggles with those of Jesus: "Come to we, dear Massa Jesus. De sun, he hot too much, de road am dat long and boggy (sandy) and we ain't got no buggy for send and fetch Ooner. But Massa, you 'member how you walked date hard walk up Calvary and ain't weary but tink about we all dat way. We know you ain't weary for to come to we. We pick out de torns, de prickles, de brier, de backslidin' and de quarrel and de sin out of you path so dey shan't hurt Ooner pierce feet no more."[21] Sojourner Truth found in her personal encounter with Jesus a tough, active love that could embrace even whites:"There cam another rush of love through my soul, an' I cried out loud—'Lord, I can love *even de white folks!*'"[22]

Martin Luther King Jr. came from a family of strong and pious Baptist women, with his grandmother the wife of a preacher and his mother the daughter and the wife of preachers; both had, as noted, attended Spelman.[23] These intelligent and educated women brought to their relationship with the young Martin a powerful sense of their distinctive religious and ethical voice as maternal caretakers, linked to the personal experience of Jesus as a loving, caring presence to which their caretaking witnessed; this hidden transcript of black women's religion nourished Martin's distinctive public ethical voice. We know that his antipathy to violence started at an early age, when the influence of these women was undoubtedly strongest.[24] Such women identified intensely with the Jesus of the Sermon on the Mount, as we see in Sojourner Truth's love of whites clearly modeled on Jesus's command to love our enemies. It is revelatory, in this connection, that King's insistence on a course of nonviolence during the Montgomery bus boycott was a decision that conflicted with the will of Daddy King on at least two important occasions. First, both King and his wife, Coretta, refused to leave Montgomery after their house had been bombed, as both their fathers demanded.[25] And second, King decided, contrary to his father's advice, that he had to disobey a state court order not to demonstrate, leading to his imprisonment in Birmingham City Jail. His father commented: "Well, you didn't get this nonviolence from me. You must have got it from your Mama."[26]

But the patriarchal character of authority in Baptist churches in that period carried with it as well, as it did elsewhere in American patriarchal culture and institutions of the era, the familiar division of women into two dichotomously exclusive categories: idealized, asexual, good women (one's idealized mother) and fallen, sexual, bad women. It is important to be clear about what the form of this patriarchal authority involved in the Baptist black ministry, as it was one of the conventional assumptions of manhood that the young Martin (the son and grandson of Baptist ministers) had to take seriously. King absorbed from the women in his family a voice that was to challenge the gender roles of both black men and women; but once he decided to be a minister, these patriarchal conventions established parameters within which he, as a black man and minister, had to work. We can get some idea of the conflicts he faced if we introduce some context for the choices he made, namely, the perspective

of a great black artist of this period who knew and hated black ministers and knew and deeply admired King.

There is no more brilliant investigation into the impact that the notion of the idealized pedestal had on men and women in the black
churches during this period than James Baldwin's remarkable first novel,
Go Tell It on the Mountain.[27] The novel is a thinly disguised autobiographical study of Baldwin's relationship with his mother and his stepfather, a
black preacher, and his stepfather's sister. All three had been born in the
South, and in the course of the novel, they move north to Harlem, where
Baldwin was born and brought up as the eldest child in a large family
born to his beloved mother and her increasingly cruel and ultimately
mentally ill husband. As his biographer David Leeming observes, "For
Baldwin the love that he learned in part from his mother was to emerge
as the central idea in a personal ideology that was to inform his later
life."[28] Baldwin always remembered his mother in something she said to
him in his teens: "I don't know what will happen to you in life. I do
know that you have brothers and sisters. You must treat everyone the way
I hope others will treat you when you are away from me, the way you
hope others will treat your brothers and sisters when you are far from
them."[29] The question explored in *Go Tell It on the Mountain* is why his
preacher father not only did not love as his mother did but also why he
was indeed consumed and ultimately destroyed by hatred.

Baldwin seeks the answer to his question in the effects of the patriarchal pedestal (good, asexual women versus bad, sexual women) on the
psychology and ethics of black men and women of the South in the particular form, the racialized pedestal, that, as we earlier saw, American
racism unjustly imposed on them. The very role of the black churches as
an institution that, as DuBois noted, helped maintain the dignity of
blacks against the indignities of racism led to enforcement of a form of
the pedestal. Since the racialized pedestal unjustly ascribed to all blacks
a degraded sexuality, resistance to such unjust images led to an insistence
on an idealization of good black women's sexuality that rested on the repression of sexual voice and a corresponding devaluation of any women
who had a free sexual voice and lived accordingly. Baldwin is mainly
concerned with the impact of this form of the pedestal on men like his
stepfather, which was first urged on him by his devout mother and, after
a history of sexual dalliance, later adopted by him at her death when he
becomes a minister.

In *Go Tell It on the Mountain* (New York, 1998), Gabriel's devotion to her ideals is expressed in his marrying Deborah, a woman scorned by other black men as tainted because she had been raped by white men. Before deciding to marry her, Gabriel (based on Baldwin's stepfather) first dreams of having armored himself in chastity, about to be stoned, and then battling (he wakes with a nocturnal emission); he then dreams of being on a cold mountaintop and being asked by a voice to go higher, finally coming to the sun and to peace (105–7). As his dreams show, he marries Deborah not from love but from a sense of better meeting his religious ideals, which disfavor any sexual feeling for the woman he marries; she is childless. Gabriel is attracted to and has an affair with a young woman, Esther, who gets pregnant by him. He refuses to consider her proposition that he leave his wife and run off with her because he regards her as a fallen women (127). Esther is repelled by his dishonesty, his fear, and his shame, which shames her "before my *God*—to make me cheap, like you done done . . . I guess it takes a holy man to make a girl a real whore" (128). Gabriel steals money from Deborah to help Esther leave for Chicago; she dies in childbirth, leaving a son, Royal, whom Gabriel never acknowledges as his own and who is killed as a young man. After the boy's death and soon before her own, Deborah confronts Gabriel with the truth, questioning his judgment about not going with the women he evidently sexually loved but regarded as a "harlot" ("Esther weren't no harlot" [143], Deborah states); he has, she says, done the wrong thing both ethically and before God (142–44). Both Esther and Deborah identify Gabriel's sense of the pedestal as the root of what cuts him off from any real relationship with them or with any person or with God.

Baldwin elsewhere describes the boundaries that the racialized pedestal, when absorbed into the minds and lives of blacks, imposes on any possibility of real relationships among them, a traumatic break in relationship "like one of those floods that devastate counties, tearing everything down, tearing children from their parents and lovers from each other, and making everything an unrecognizable waste."[30] As a consequence, "you very soon, without knowing it, give up all hope of communion. Black people, mainly, look down or look up but do not look at each other, not at you, and white people, mainly, look away. And the universe is simply a sounding drum; there is no way, no way whatever, so it seemed then and has sometimes seemed since, to get through a life, to love your wife and children, or your friends, or your mother and father, or to be loved."[31] The pedestal kills real sensual relationships of mutual voice and thus kills relationships: "To be sensual, I think, is to respect and rejoice in the force of life, of life itself, and to be *present* in all that one does, from the effort of loving to the breaking of bread. . . . The person who distrusts himself has no touchstone for reality—for this touchstone can be only oneself. Such a person interposes between himself and reality nothing less than a labyrinth of attitudes."[32] The pedestal is one of this "labyrinth of attitudes," a stereotypical assumption that cuts one off not only from the voice of others but also from one's own personal emotional voice. It thus stultifies emotional intelligence, without which love is narcissism. Baldwin had seen this in his father and other preachers and had come, for that reason, to be skeptical about the Christianity of the black churches in particular and of established religion in general.

When Baldwin met Martin Luther King Jr., he commented, "Reverend King is not like any preacher I have ever met before. For one thing, to state it baldly, I liked him."[33] He was thinking, of course, of his stepfather and other ministers like him that he had known. King was clearly a counterexample to Baldwin's highly negative view of black preachers; "what he says to Negroes he will say to whites; and what he says to whites he will say to Negroes. He is the first Negro leader in my experience, or the first in many generations, of whom this can be said."[34] But for all his admiration of and active support for King and his movement, Baldwin did take critical note of a problem in black leaders, including King: "One of the greatest vices of the white bourgeoisie on which they have modeled themselves is its reluctance to think, its distrust of the independent mind."[35] Even King had uncritically absorbed a conventionality that mirrored white conventionality, acquiescing, for example, in pressure brought "to force the resignation of his (King's) extremely able organizer and lieutenant, Bayard Rustin."[36] The resignation had been forced by Rustin's homosexuality. For Baldwin (a gay man), yielding to such pressures reflected a hypocritical public face of sexual conventionality, compromising the central aim of the civil rights leadership—the recognition of the human rights of all on equal terms, which "necessarily carries with it the idea of sexual freedom: the freedom to meet, sleep with, and marry whom one chooses."[37] Here, Baldwin is making reference to the racist obsession with miscegenation; the response of such conventionality is, "I am afraid we must postpone it [the right to sexual freedom] for the moment, to consider just why so many people appear to be convinced that Negroes would then immediately meet, sleep with, and marry white women; who, remarkably enough, are only protected from such undesirable alliances by the majesty and vigilance of the law."[38] The issue of sexual freedom is not, Baldwin argues, peripheral to the civil rights movement but central, as the Supreme Court itself recognized in 1967 when it struck down antimiscegenation laws in *Loving v. Virginia*.

Baldwin found in Martin Luther King Jr. a preacher who was, in many respects, quite different from his stepfather, but in some areas, he sensed in King the same kind of dishonest sexual voice, required by patriarchal conventionality, that he found in his stepfather. The problem, of course, arose from the ways in which the black churches, in resisting the racialized pedestal, adopted a form of the pedestal to accentuate their own sexual virtue and, correlatively, to condemn any blacks who deviated from it (for example, Bayard Rustin). The problem was, if anything, aggravated when some black churches under King's leadership became active in the civil rights movement. To be credible critics of dominant racist opinion (with its racialized pedestal), protesters had to be, if anything, hyperrespectable in the terms of southern white respectability, including the pedestal.[39] King had been prepared for this role by the ways in which, as a black man, he had accommodated himself to its public requirements of respectable manhood once he decided that he would, like his father and maternal grandfather, become a Baptist minister.

There was, of course, a problem of black manhood under racism that correlated to the problem of black womanhood, the consequences of which Orlando Patterson has argued are still very much with us.[40] The racialized pedestal defines the problem, a pedestal that allowed white southern men to indulge their sexuality on black women while rigidly controlling the sexuality of white women; the sexual desire of white women for anyone, let alone for black men, was such a threat to this ideology (rationalizing lynching) because it threatened the idealized pedestal itself (a point Ida Wells-Barnett had powerfully made).[41] Black men were correlatively trapped in a kind of sexual cage. Any sexual interest in white women called for lynching, and their ability to protect their own black women was compromised by the terms of white racism, which rationalized its sexual exploitation of black women on the basis of dehumanizing stereotypes of black sexuality as that of animals, not of humans. The more sexually promiscuous the blacks were, the more they accommodated themselves to the racist stereotype. Black men like King had sexual interests as strong as white men's, but their manhood as Baptist preachers required that they keep those interests under cover, so to speak, conforming in their public personae to the idealized roles of husband and father, and also that they hold their wives under comparable idealizing controls, all to make the appropriate public statement in rebuttal of the racialized pedestal. It was a role at which black men like King played, much as Tolstoy did when he decided that, as a man, he had to play to the hilt the roles of husband and father. James Baldwin, a gay man and an outsider to this conception of manhood, showed us the price black men and women paid in terms of real relationships when they took this line, and he apparently intuited, with the sensitivity and psychological insight of an artist, that King had paid and was continuing to pay such a price as well.

Martin Luther King Jr. attended Morehouse College in Atlanta, as his grandfather had. Most of his friends there were rebelling against the ministry, regarding the law, on the model of Thurgood Marshall, as a better means by which to serve humanity: "Idealists must look to the law, breadwinners to the church." This attitude was a stark cultural reversal of white views at that time, as was "the fact that some two-thirds of Negro college students always had been female." King first intended to be a doctor, then a lawyer. "At Morehouse, King worked hard to develop the accouterments of urbanity. . . . To friends, King was an affable personality resting on a foundation of decency, moving politely but steadily away from the religious straitjacket of his youth toward the Morehouse ideal of the successful, fun-loving gentleman." In 1946, when King was a junior at Morehouse, racism in the South became inflamed after colonized peoples in Asia and Africa denounced the racist hypocrisy of the nations that exercised dominion over them and when, in a similar spirit, black soldiers returning from World War II began to demand to be treated as equals; mobs in Monroe, Georgia, lynched no fewer that six Negro war veterans in a single three-week period during the summer (Branch, *Parting the Waters*, 61, 63).

King and his friends began to wonder if the ministry could be designed to fit their ambitions, which certainly did not endorse fundamentalism (King wrote that Morehouse freed him from "the shackles of fundamentalism" [62]). To this end, they attended the services and studied the preaching of Rev. William Holmes Borders, in particular "the high-toned sermons in which he arouses his congregation without merely repeating the homilies of eternal life" (64). By the end of his junior year, King gave up talking about becoming a lawyer, and in the fall, under considerable pressure from his father, he told Martin Sr. that he would follow him into the ministry. King gave his first sermon in his father's pulpit and was quickly ordained a minister and made assistant pastor of Ebenezer (65–66).

The last year at Morehouse "was a heady one for King" (66), and he and friends began to do work as ministers (preaching, marrying, burying), basking in the admiration of local females; by then, they (King among them) had "reputations as ladies' men" (73). The big news during King's last year was President Harry Truman's decision to be the first U.S. president to address an NAACP convention; subsequently, he would also support civil rights legislation. There was also the shocking assassination of Mohandas Gandhi in early 1948.

King had agreed to be a minister, as his father wanted, but he would be one on his own terms, going to a seminary as had the preachers he admired—Borders, Vernon Johns, and Harry Emerson Fosdick of the Riverside Church in New York (indeed, King used a Fosdick sermon as his first sermon at Ebenezer). He decided he would apply to Crozer Theological Seminary in Pennsylvania and told his mother and sister and brother before he told his father, who was suspicious but acceded. Crozer was a white seminary known for its liberal leanings in theology, and it was located far from his father (67–68).

King's Graduate Education, Religion, and Marriage

We can powerfully see the force and contours of King's struggle to find his own religious and ethical voice as a minister independent of his patriarchal father in his insistence, usually with the support of his mother, on seeking graduate education first in three years at Crozer Theological Seminary and then in doctoral work at Boston University. During this period, King forged both his own views on religion as ethical social gospel against entrenched evils such as racism and his remarkable preaching style, which was a main subject of self-conscious study at Crozer. As his years as a student drew to a close, just as he knew he had to finish his studies and adopt a working vocation as a Baptist minister in some form, he knew as a man that he must finally marry. This led to a remarkable process of negotiation with his parents, who were as much a part of his decision, for good or ill, as was the woman he married, Coretta Scott.

King arrived at Crozer Theological Seminary in Chester, Pennsylvania, a town outside Philadelphia, in 1948. There, he embarked on what was to be the most important educational experience in his life, one that turned the mediocre student of the Morehouse years into a scholar utterly absorbed by his education and earning grades that would make him valedictorian of his class (72). The intensity of the transition was due in part to King's desire to distinguish himself in a white culture, but it was a culture of a quite extraordinary kind at that time and place. At Crozer, students encountered "an atmosphere of unorthodox freethinking that went far beyond the rebellions of youth in that taut era" (69). The Negro students in the entering class enrolled there because it was a white school of very high reputation. Most of them had thus far had racially segregated educations, and they expected that at Crozer, they would enter an alien environment. They found, to their surprise, there were ten of them in a class of thirty-two, and there were, in addition, three Chinese students, several Indians, a Japanese student, and assorted other foreigners. They were all stirred together among the white students in classes, dormitories, and the cafeteria. No major seminary of any denomination had achieved such a racial mix before, and none would do so again in the twentieth century (70).

The Crozer administration was making a valiant effort at this time to inculcate egalitarianism among the students and also maintain rigorous intellectual traditions of liberal religious inquiry against the rising tide of more conservative religious thought that was "perfecting simpler messages of great popular appeal in a troubled, complex age." King welcomed the skeptical required courses he first took that raised and sorted out the best historical work then being done on both the Old and New Testaments; "the standing joke among the Crozer students who survived these courses was that [Professor] Prichard destroyed the biblical image of Moses in the first term and [Professor] Enslin finished off Jesus in the second" (71–72).

Crozer's approach was to tear down the belief systems of students through the skeptical study of the texts on which they based their beliefs and then to start over, building a belief system of religious knowledge that was as reasonable as possible. The approach corresponded exactly to King's own psychic situation and his deepest needs: "Having muscled his way into a state of religious skepticism some years earlier against the combined weight of his heritage and his father's authority, he found Crozer's idea of religion no less liberating than the racially mixed classes, the unlocked dorms, and the white maids. . . . He became suddenly and permanently fascinated. The floor of his room was soon piled high with books, and he would sometimes read all night" (73).

Among the philosophers and theologians King studied during his first year at Crozer was Walter Rauschenbusch and his *Christianity and the Social Crisis,*[42] a book usually regarded as the beginning of the Social Gospel movement in the United States and one of the few works King acknowledged as an influence on his religious beliefs.[43] Rauschenbusch was a German Lutheran turned Baptist whose experiences in the Hell's Kitchen area of New York City led him to reject the usual religious emphasis on matters of ritual, theology, metaphysics, and the supernatural to make room for what he took to be central—a spirit of brotherhood among humanity that is expressed through socially responsible ethical relationships. Rauschenbusch thus defined the proper role of Christian ministers as an elaboration of the Old Testament prophets, and he conceived Jesus of Nazareth, "the greatest of all prophets," as building on and elaborating this tradition.[44] The task of a Christian minister, he believed, was to give prophetic ethical voice to protest against the social injustices that pride, selfishness, and oppression inflicted on innocent people, transgressing the divine historical plan that should culminate in the Christian ideal of the kingdom of God on earth. For many of his followers, including King, Rauschenbusch gave an alternative reading of religion from a distracting otherworldliness to an ongoing work of social justice as the closest way we can come, as persons made in God's image, to participating in God's love.

King was introduced to Rauschenbusch at Crozer by George W. Davis, a professor who was the son of a union activist, the only pacifist on the Crozer faculty, and the strongest admirer of the life and work of Gandhi. It was Davis's copy of a book on Gandhi that King first read in the seminary library, and it gave him a positive sense of how Christianity as social gospel might be translated into action in a context that, in Gandhi's case, clearly involved resistance to racism both in South Africa and in India. King did not accept pacifism at Crozer—indeed, he criticized the pacifist work of A. J. Muste—but he took a third of his courses from Davis, whom he found warm and accessible.[45]

A major feature of his Crozer education were the classes in preaching. King's oratory "was among his chief distinctions at Crozer," and fellow students who remembered little else about him "would remember the text, theme, and impact of specific King practice sermons."[46] At Crozer, practice preaching courses brought him some of his highest grades and his greatest approval.[47] He and his black friends would often hilariously compare the elevated sermons their professors encouraged with their own homemade preaching formulas; King, a wonderful mimic, would offer parodies of sermons fellow students gave in local churches, delivering "the 'correct' versions in . . . exaggerated spiels of Enslin's rational historicism, speaking of Jesus as a gifted Jewish prophet with a lot of personal problems."[48]

Near the end of this study at Crozer, after he had decided to go on to doctoral work, King read Reinhold Niebuhr's *Moral Man and Immoral Society*.[49] "The experience did not change his plans, but it appears to have changed everything else, including his fundamental outlook on religion" (Branch, 81). Before he read Niebuhr, King had decided to pursue his doctorate "for reasons of pleasure, inertia, and prestige" (85), building on the personal fulfillment and recognition beyond his dreams that he had experienced at Crozer. His life would be one of study and would enable him to find his own way, perhaps in teaching at a seminary or university in the North; he thus circumvented his doubts about the ambitions and way of life of a black Baptist preacher of the South, for example, "Daddy King's unabashed pursuit of success" (85). After reading Niebuhr, "King experienced for the first time a loss of confidence in his own chosen ideas rather than inherited ones" (81).

King never really gave up what he had learned from Rauschenbusch, but neither had Niebuhr. Niebuhr had been a prominent advocate of the Social Gospel movement, as reflected in his background prior to becoming a teacher at Union Theological Seminary in New York in 1928 by way of Yale Divinity School. He had spent thirteen years before then as a Social Gospel minister in Detroit, achieving fame for his defense of autoworkers and Negro migrants trying to survive in Henry Ford's town in the wake of World War I; he was also a nationally known pacifist who had served several terms as president of the Fellowship of Reconciliation, which was headed by Muste during King's public career. The 1932 publication of *Moral Man and Immoral Society* was such a shock to nonfundamentalists interested in religion because it attacked the premise of

Social Gospel's picture that the steady advance of reason led by Enlightenment leaders, whether Social Gospel religionists or secular philosophers like John Dewey, could be depended on to secure justice. There was no good reason to think that better education in itself made people less selfish or cruel. Injustice survived because, as Augustinian Christianity had noticed, people were flawed by original sin. A religious liberalism that did not take this seriously was fundamentally flawed as well (82–83).

Niebuhr's internal criticism of Social Gospel religion was in part directed not only at its alliance with secular thinkers such as Dewey but also at its doctrine of progress; that doctrine was false in itself and too much in tune with the false science of Marxism, which suppressed the role of moral judgment in politics (81–87). Niebuhr interpreted original sin as a feature of human group psychology very similar to the secularized version of original sin of David Hume's political science of faction that James Madison prominently used as a realistic psychology of politics under democracy in justifying the design of American constitutionalism.[50] Madison, like Niebuhr, assumed that such facts of group psychology are permanent features of our human nature. But like Niebuhr, he also believed that we, as individuals, have ethical values expressive of conscience and that we must assess forms of government and politics in terms of whether they permit us to structure and limit such facts of group psychology so that they better meet reflective ethical aims of justice and the public good.

What may have particularly captured King's attention in Niebuhr's argument in *Moral Man and Immoral Society* (Louisville, KY, 2001) was the way he focuses on the group psychology of racism, whether in the British colonial domination of India or in the American South, as a problem that remains intractably intact (xxvii, 119–20) and that will be so as long as Tolstoyan pacifists fail to take seriously the need for legitimate forms of force to combat such evils (20, 269–70). In contrast, Niebuhr regards Gandhi's satyagraha in India as a much more effective way of combating this racism precisely because it is a nonviolence, rooted in the expression of ethical conviction in politics, that "does coerce and destroy" (241)—for example, the coercive effects of the Indian boycott of British-manufactured cloth on the "cotton spinners of Lancashire" (241). To the extent Gandhi's praxis is nonviolent, Niebuhr argues that its political advantage is its way of expressing ethical values of resistance, namely, "that it protects the agent against the resentments which violent conflict always creates in both parties to a conflict" (247). Such a politics gives very vivid proofs of moral goodwill whose effects are "tremendous. In every social conflict each party is so obsessed with the wrongs which the other party commits against it, that it is unable to see its own wrongdoing. A non-violent temper reduces these animosities to a minimum and therefore preserves a certain objectivity in analysing the issues of the dispute" (248). Niebuhr endorses Gandhi's satyagraha because it is "a type of coercion which offers the largest opportunities for a harmonious relationship with the moral and rational faculties in social life" (250–51). In particular, he gives a general view of Gandhi's strategic judgments of ethics and effectiveness, and he directly points out their relevance to African Americans' resistance to American racism:

> Non-violence is a particularly strategic instrument for an oppressed group which is hopelessly in the minority and has no possibility of developing sufficient power to set against its oppressors.
>
> The emancipation of the Negro race in America probably waits upon the adequate developments of this kind of social and political strategy. It is hopeless for the Negro to expect complete emancipation from the menial social and economic position into which the white man has forced him, merely by trusting in the moral sense of the white race. It is equally hopeless to attempt emancipation through violent rebellion." (252)

One can see what must have moved and unsettled King when he read Niebuhr. On the one hand, Niebuhr accords an indispensable role to prophetic religion in expressing ethical judgments in politics in the Social Gospel tradition, but on the other, he denies that education or progress or more reasonable argument will alone suffice against such evils as racism, which, as forms of group psychology, are so deeply entrenched in human nature and culture. Niebuhr's views of racism very much fit what King knew about the American South, and they resonated as well with a developing constitutional tradition that, under the impact of the NAACP, was coming to see state support of racism as a form of faction condemned by the equal protection clause of the Fourteenth Amendment. Ethically rooted resistance to the force of racism in American politics was, in light of these constitutional developments, now very much aligned with the principles of American constitutional law. Nothing could have more effectively jolted King from the trajectory he was on to join the faculty of some seminary or university in the North than Niebuhr's sharp antiassimilationist critique of such a trajectory: "The progress of the Negro race . . . is retarded by the inclination of many able and educated Negroes to strive for identification and assimilation with the more privileged white race and to minimise their relation to a subject race as much as possible" (274). Being a Baptist minister in the South might now make a new kind of vocational sense to King if it could, for example, be put in service to a prophetic religion of ethical resistance on the model of Gandhi's satyagraha.[51] King would devote much of his remaining graduate school career to the study of Niebuhr.

In 1951, King decided to pursue a doctorate at Boston University, especially because of the presence there of Edgar S. Brightman, a leading exponent of a school of theology called personalism.[52] In contrast to the metaphysical abstractness of the theology of Karl Barth and Paul Tillich, personalism "harked back to the intensely personal God of the Jewish scriptures and to early Christian theologians such as Augustine, who sometimes describes God using only a long list of human emotions, modified to remove any objectionable qualities and raised to infinite strength."[53] Martin Buber, whom King later cited frequently, captured the personalist point when he modeled man's relationship to God on personal ethical relationships of loving care and concern for the individuality of one another.[54] King liked Brightman and would take ten of his fifteen PhD courses from him or his personalist protégé, L. Harold De-Wolf (Branch, 92). King's dissertation would use personalism as a tool for criticizing the theology of Tillich and Henry Nelson Wieman as "too arid, speculative, and cerebral to answer human yearnings in the province of religion" (102).

King was now nearing the moment when he had to choose what kind of Baptist minister he would be, and in view of the patriarchal conception of manhood the ministry involved, he was also under considerable pressure from his parents to marry; indeed, he was now "doing his best to marry" (94). There is reason to believe that there was a psychic strain in King between his sense of his personal needs as a man and the kind of wife required of a Baptist minister. In his first year at Crozer, he had dated Juanita Sellars, a friend of his sister Christine who, like her, was a graduate of Spelman doing graduate work at Columbia University. She was very much the kind of woman Daddy King wanted his son to marry, but to his father's frustration, nothing came of the relationship (78). Later at Crozer, King evidently fell in love with Betty, the white daughter of a German immigrant woman who served as the cook for the Crozer cafeteria; in fact, King resolved to marry her. He was, however, cautioned by friends about the problems an interracial marriage would cause when it came to getting a ministry. While he was evidently willing to take whatever Daddy King would say of such a marriage, "he could not face the pain it would cause his mother" (89). King told friends both he and Betty were in love; he broke off the relationship. The breakup of any such love must be traumatic, and it is certainly worth noting, in light of King's later sexual infidelities and marital misery, that he made such a painful choice on the basis of an idealized image of his mother, an image that, for King, rationalized the suppression of his own loving sexual voice.

While doing graduate work at Boston University, King was aggressively dating with a view to marriage (94). Early in 1952, he called a woman he had never met on the recommendation of a friend. The woman, Coretta Scott, came from one of the few elite black families among poor farmers in rural Alabama. All the daughters in this family acquired enough of its courage and drive to seek education at a private school nearby, and Coretta followed her older sister north to Antioch College; after graduation, she had gone on to Boston's New England Conservatory of Music on a small scholarship. Her ambition was to be a singer of classical music. When King first met Scott, "he shocked her . . . by declaring that she would make him a good wife. 'The four things that I look for in a wife are character, intelligence, personality, and beauty. . . . And you have them all. I want to see you again'" (95–96). That he had a menu of idealized traits in "a good wife" immediately strikes one now, as it must have struck Scott then, as a highly impersonal way to frame a personal relationship. King put Scott through various tests to judge her eligibility to be a minister's wife, asking, among other things, that she agree to visit with his family in Atlanta. Like Juanita Sellars, she initially refused, but unlike Sellars, she eventually complied with King's angry demand. Daddy King regarded Scott as a country girl, not the kind of well-connected society woman he wanted his son to marry, and King's mother was also cool to the prospect. When his parents visited Boston in the fall, the father brought the issue to an emotional boil by asking Scott bluntly whether she took his son seriously and insisting that there were much better choices for Martin Jr. in Atlanta. Martin Jr. said nothing, but his father's outrageous intervention may have decided him; he told his mother, in the next room, "that he planned to marry the woman his father had just blistered unmercifully" (98). *(EoF) +7, 47, 81*

A few weeks later, King composed an outline for a sermon entitled "How a Christian Overcomes Evil" that included the following steps: first, to honestly identify the evil within—"the hidden fault must be called by its right name, otherwise we miss seeing our pride under fear of an inferiority complex" (99)—and second, to cultivate a virtue that crowds out the evil. The evil is later identified as "sensuality," something King claimed our pride rooted in an inferiority fear makes it difficult for us to acknowledge (99). Taylor Branch suggests that such pride may arise in reaction to a racism that ascribes an inferiority in black manhood— "warning that such a handicap in a Negro could make him blind to his own racial pride, or to the pride that lies beneath all considerations of race" (99). King never developed the outline into a complete sermon, which is understandable in light of the questions the outline raised about his own conflicted sexuality at this crucial period in his life. If a certain pride in one's manhood takes the form of living in a way that defies the sexual mythology of racism, that pride could suppress one's sexual voice in the name of an assertion of the idealizing pedestal of one's relations to a good wife or good woman. The outline of King's sermon suggests this conflicted psychology of suppressed sensuality and idealization at the time he decided to marry Coretta Scott.

Coretta and Martin were wed on June 18, 1953. Years ahead of her time, she insisted that the injunction to obey her husband be removed from the ceremony, which it was (101). However, when King was offered the position of pastor for the Dexter Avenue Baptist Church in Montgomery, Alabama (which had previously been occupied by Vernon Johns, whom King enormously admired) (1–26), Coretta's plea that they instead settle in the North went unheeded. King asserted "what he called his authority as head of the household" (112). His assertion of patriarchal authority in his marriage required Coretta to live in a part of the country she had been trying to escape and to give up any hope of the career in music that was her ambition. King would be a very different kind of Baptist minister than his father, but his marriage was just as patriarchal— as it turned out, for such an otherwise unconventional black man, disastrously so.

Nonviolence in Montgomery

King arrived in Montgomery to become pastor of Dexter in 1954, the year of the *Brown v. Board of Education* decision. The condemnation of American cultural racism in that opinion had once been the view of only the radical abolitionists within the larger abolitionist movement. Now, however, such a view was not limited to a political minority within a minority but was sponsored by the unanimous authority of the Supreme Court of the United States, which found racist practices in blatant contradiction to the normative premises that actuate the Reconstruction Amendments as fundamental constitutional law. Much work still remained to be done, and while developments in constitutional law would do some of that work, it was not clear that arguments to a countermajoritarian judiciary could do all the work alone. Building on and extending judicially enforced constitutional principles, there was a need to forge a democratic political consensus both in the South and in the entire nation supportive of the just claims of African Americans. Martin Luther King Jr. was a pivotal figure in helping to develop such a democratic consensus through a movement much less elitist than the NAACP had required—indeed, much more democratically inclusive. It was Thurgood Marshall himself who once dismissed King's views that his movement would aid desegregation because "school desegregation was men's work" (190), which suggests the difficulty black elites had in understanding the importance of the movement King was forging, a movement that prominently included women and even children and that helped shape the democratic consensus that passed the Civil Rights Act of 1964 and the Voting Rights Act of 1965. Nonetheless, King's movement would not have had the authority and appeal it commanded without *Brown* and related decisions.

King frequently spoke and wrote about the connections of principle between the antiracist struggle in the United States and the worldwide struggle against the role racism had played in Western colonialism in Africa and Asia.[55] Gandhi became important to him not only because of the disciplined strategies of satyagraha's nonviolence but also because of the great truth to which Gandhi gave voice regarding the unjust role racism played in South African prejudice against Indians, in the British raj over Indians, and in the other forms of prejudice Gandhi identified and condemned (including prejudice against the untouchables in India,

European anti-Semitism, and American racism). By placing American civil disobedience in this larger context, King found and appealed to an international audience for his movement, which, after he received the Nobel Peace Prize in 1964, enormously enhanced his authority within the United States.

But King was not a constitutional lawyer (though, as noted, he had thought about studying law); nor was he a religious prophet, inventing a new kind of ethical religion of pacifism, like Tolstoy and Tolstoy's follower, Gandhi. King always accepted the right of self-defense,[56] which pacifists do not, and his study of Niebuhr made him a lifelong skeptic of pacifism. He was a Baptist preacher very much within the Protestant Christian tradition and, after much struggle over vocation, a Baptist preacher of a black church in the deep and racist South. His originality was the prophetic ethical voice he found within this role, a voice that, to his initial surprise, energized a remarkably disciplined social movement and a voice that spoke to the conscience of the nation as no black voice ever had. The key was nonviolence.

In the long history of African American protest, nonviolence had its advocates only occasionally. Bayard Rustin, of Quaker background, was a pacifist and was imprisoned as a conscientious objector during World War II, and as a disciple of Gandhi, he was to give invaluable advice to King during the Montgomery boycott.[57] But the path of Frederick Douglass from nonviolent to violent resistance was much more typical. Douglass, as an ex-slave, initially gravitated to the nonviolence of Garrison, the man who had given him a forum to speak. But as the South proved increasingly intransigent to abolitionist arguments, Douglass claimed as his birthright the right to revolution as granted in the Declaration of Independence, and he argued persuasively that African Americans had a more legitimate claim to invoke that right against slavery and racism than white Americans had had when they invoked it against the British in 1776.[58]

King was clearly not a pacifist, so why did he choose nonviolence? He came to nonviolence both through the developmental psychology that gave rise to his sense of religion and through his strenuous theological studies of what made religion valuable. Almost certainly, his developmental psychology found its sense of religious voice not in his father's patriarchal voice but in the voices and loving care of his grandmother and mother, reflecting, as we earlier saw, a long tradition of the intense identification of Baptist black women with Jesus of Nazareth. His theological studies had brought him to personalism, the view, like Buber's, that what is valuable in religion is the sense of persons made in God's image and finding themselves in loving, caring relationships to the individuality of other persons. This psychology and ethics of religion were, like those of Gandhi, highly relational and attuned to the impact of one's voice on the audience, whether those in a movement one leads or in the audience the movement addresses. The model for what is authentic and valuable in religious experience is maternal caretaking, with the aims, usually nonviolent, of achieving protection, nurture, and ethical acceptability. As a boy, King had certainly experienced such care and love from his grandmother and mother, and he drew on that experience as a form of psychological and ethical intelligence that he could use, as Gandhi had, for broader ethical and political ends. King came to nonviolence, as Gandhi had, as an experiment in voice that shocked and disturbed him, for it carried him into a role he had not anticipated and burdened him with responsibilities he had never imagined himself bearing.

It was pivotally important, in this connection, not only that the Montgomery bus boycott began in the 1955 refusal of a woman, Rosa Parks,[59] to obey the laws governing segregation on buses but also that its initial groundswell of support came spontaneously from women and that women were disproportionately involved in the boycott itself.[60] The ethical leadership of women had become so conspicuous that when Montgomery's black male leaders first met to discuss tactics and some urged keeping their names secret, E. D. Nixon, a railroad porter and admirer of A. Philip Randolph, exploded in rage at their timorousness in comparison to the courage of women: "Let me tell you gentlemen one thing. You ministers have lived off their wash-women for the last hundred years and ain't never doing anything for them. . . . We've worn aprons all our lives. . . . It's time to take the aprons off. . . . If we're gonna be mens, now's the time to be mens."[61] Nixon's trenchant, salty observations questioned a black manhood that was apparently less ready, willing, and able than womanhood to resist injustice effectively. Constance Baker Mottley, an NAACP lawyer during that period, notes in this connection that, as regards nonviolence, "[King] sometimes had problems with young men who believed that violence was the answer, but . . . when he preached nonviolence to the largely elderly females in those Birmingham churches at night, King was preaching to the converted. . . . They were always there, night after night. Strong black women had always set the tone in Southern black communities."[62]

King arrived late at the meeting of the black male leaders, hearing the last of Nixon's taunts. He replied, "I don't want anyone to call me a coward" (Branch, 136–37), and stated that all the leaders should act openly under their own names. His remarks led to his being elected president of the Montgomery Improvement Association, which would coordinate the boycott and engage in negotiations over the demands of blacks. There would be a mass meeting at a Holt Street church that night, at which the leaders would see what kind of support they had.

When King was driven to the mass rally that evening, he was caught in a traffic jam, which he realized was caused by a huge crowd of some ten thousand people; they had overflowed from the church into the streets, where loudspeakers had been set up. King began:

> We are here in a general sense, because first and foremost—we are American citizens—and we are determined to apply citizenship—to the fullness of its means . . . But we are here in a specific sense—because of the bus situation in Montgomery. The situation is not at all new. The problem has existed over endless years. Just the other day—just last Thursday to be exact—one of the finest citizens in Montgomery—not one of the finest Negro citizens—but one of the finest citizens in Montgomery—was taken from a bus—and carried to jail and arrested—because she refused to give up—to give her seat to a white person (138–39).

The people in the crowd punctuated his speech with enthusiastic responses—"Yes" and "Amen," they called out repeatedly. They were stirring now, following King's argument: "And you know, my friends, there comes a time, when you get tired of being trampled over by the iron feet of oppression" (139). The individual responses now joined "into a rising cheer and applause exploded beneath the cheer. . . . Thunder seemed to be added to the lower register—the sound of feet stomping on the wooden floor. . . . The giant cloud of noise shook the building and refused to go away. One sentence had set it loose somehow, pushing the call-and-response of the Negro church service past the din of a political rally and on to something else that King had never known before" (139–40). Perhaps daunted by the force of what he had unleashed, King

p. 156

turned (as Gandhi had in his speech at the Jewish theater) to the pitfalls of using force in their boycott: "Now let us say that we are not here advocating violence. We have overcome that" (140). A voice from the audience demanded, "Repeat that! Repeat that!" King went on: "I want it to be known throughout Montgomery and throughout this nation that we are Christian people. The only weapon that we have in our hands this evening is the weapon of protest. If we were incarcerated behind the iron curtains of a communistic nation—we couldn't do this. But the great glory of American democracy is the right to protest for right" (140). When the shouts of approval subsided, King offered his final reason for nonviolence, namely, so that the protestors would distinguish themselves from the violence of the Ku Klux Klan (KKK): "There will be no crosses burned at any bus stops in Montgomery. There will be no white persons pulled out of their homes and taken out on some distant road and murdered. There will be nobody among us who will stand up and defy the Constitution of this nation. My friends, I want it to be known—that we are going to work with grim and bold determination—to gain justice on the buses in this city. And we are not wrong. We are not wrong in what we are doing. If we are wrong—the Supreme Court of this nation is wrong. If we are wrong—God almighty is wrong" (140). The crowd exploded a second time. Wave after wave of noise broke out as King fused the cutting edge of his ethical faith to their hearts: "If we are wrong—Jesus of Nazareth was merely a utopian dreamer and never came down to earth! If we are wrong, justice is a lie" (141). He had to wait until the responsive storm subsided, and then he delivered his soaring, indignant, inspired conclusion: "And we are determined here in Montgomery—to work and fight until justice runs down like water, and righteousness like a mighty stream!" (141). He used a passage from the prophet Amos, "the lowly herdsman prophet of Israel who, along with the priestly Isaiah, was King's favorite biblical authority on justice" (141). The applause continued as King walked out, and members of his congregation at Dexter marveled, never having heard him speak like that. King had achieved a power of ethical communion with his audiences that was to last for the next twelve years, until his death by assassination in 1968.

In the Holt Street speech, King found his prophetic ethical voice in relationship to the voices of his audience, in the process discovering the enormous power and appeal of nonviolence for that audience. He came rather accidentally to his leadership position through his response to a challenge to the manhood of the ministers of the black churches, a challenge that asked men to measure up to the example of women. The women in question already lived nonviolence, as Rosa Parks had done when she disobeyed the law knowing she might be arrested and punished and as other women had done when they began a boycott of the segregated buses in protest. Nonviolence was already very much in black women's religious culture, expressing their identification with Jesus of Nazareth and their intuitive sense, as maternal caretakers of both black and white children, of the place that loving care should have in the protection, nurture, and ethical acceptability of waywardly immature persons (black and white). When King, as a man and Baptist preacher, brought nonviolence into the center of a movement of mass social protest, he aligned himself with an experience women already found intuitive, as Constance Baker Mottley observes. He thus spoke to women about the moral authority of their own experience, empowering them to act on that experience in new ways and new contexts that challenged conventional gender roles. No small part of the appeal of the prophetic ethical voice discovered at the Holt Street meeting was attributable to the fact that black women in the audience recognized what they believed already, only now it was understood by them to have a wider scope, applicability, and resonance. In contrast, however, as Andrew Young, an important figure in King's movement, observed, getting black men to accept nonviolence was always more of a struggle: "Throughout the movement, the men were usually the last to become involved, always using the reason that they didn't believe in a nonviolent response to violent provocations. This was more an excuse than anything else. I began challenging the men as they went into the pool halls and bars, attempting to shame them for letting the women and children carry the movement. . . . Finally the men realized that their presence was essential. . . . Women and the elderly had borne the brunt of our demonstrations for far too long."[63]

But King was also speaking in a voice that challenged traditional manhood, including black manhood. His challenge appealed to two kinds of arguments, constitutional and religious. On the legal front, he built upon the remarkable successes of the NAACP's constitutional strategy, which had secured judicial acceptance of the principle that African American protest rested on a more reasonable understanding of American constitutionalism than did the strategies of its racist opponents;

African Americans grounded their protest on a constitutional right to protest, whereas Southern racists resorted to unjust and illegal forms of violence in response. By centering his movement for justice in nonviolence, King underscored the movement's grounds in voice, supported by fundamental constitutional principles of free speech. Indeed, under the impact of King's movement, such principles were held by the Supreme Court to include conscientious dissent of the sort the movement made: on grounds of free speech, conscientious dissenters were to be protected by the state (including police authorities) against the hostility and offense of audiences who disagreed with their message and tried to silence them by violence.[64] It was because the police in Birmingham and Selma, Alabama, were themselves often conspicuous agents of state violence against such claims that Americans during this period increasingly came to see that King's movement rested on constitutional principles. Its claims of voice were grounded in basic constitutional principles of free speech. And its protest of state-supported racism rested on constitutional principles of equal protection. Racist prejudices had, as King's movement showed, no other support but the irrationalist violence aggressively aimed by bigoted thugs against any voice that would challenge such racism.

And religiously, King appealed to the prophetic ethical voice within America's dominant religion, Christianity—specifically, the ethical voice of Jesus himself as a prophet in the tradition of the Jewish prophets. King was striking a chord he was to repeat throughout his career, stressing that the racist persecution of African American protest was, in principle, the same atrocity as religious persecution (for example, the religious persecution of Christians under the Roman Empire).[65] King's social movement was thus as much an ethical reformation of the true meaning of Christianity against its corruptions as it was a movement of justice under American constitutional law.

The appeal of both the constitutional and the religious argument lies in the fact that when a mass movement of resistance to injustice is centered in nonviolence, the irrationalism of the male code of honor (which expresses itself in violence against any insult to manhood) is challenged, exposed, and rebutted as the dominant and distorting force in struggles over competing views of justice and injustice. We earlier saw that a plausible interpretation of Jesus's injunction "If anyone strikes you on the right cheek, turn the other also" (Matt. 5:39) is its ethical skepticism about the ways in which insults to male honor triggered endless cycles of violence. King rediscovered or reinvented this interpretation, an interpretation that would have great appeal to black men of the South who had suffered for centuries under a racist regime of white male violence directed at imagined black threats to their honor, including lynchings. It also appealed to African American constitutionalism, which had come so far, under the leadership of the NAACP, by an insistence on pressing for constitutional rights of free speech and protest. By centering a mass social movement in nonviolence, King made central to the democratic experience of African Americans in general the exercise of their constitutional rights to protest, rights that had theretofore been invoked largely by black elites, including lawyers and intellectuals.

King had come across nonviolence, like the boycott, almost by accident. The function of boycott leaders, himself included, had been to inspire and to persevere, despite arrests and bombings of their homes. The boycott was lasting and effective, and the issue was ultimately resolved when the Supreme Court affirmed the ruling of a three-judge federal court that Montgomery's bus segregation ordinance was unconstitutional.[66] King had become a national figure, but his idea of leadership had not yet conceived the deliberate creation of new struggles and strategies. That would take place at Birmingham, Alabama, six years later.[67]

Nonviolence in Birmingham and the March on Washington

King had stumbled on nonviolence in the Montgomery bus boycott, but at that point, he was not experienced in either its theory or its practice. His interest in Gandhi at Crozer and Boston University was that of a scholar, though Niebuhr's favorable discussion of Gandhi as a model for African American protest undoubtedly impressed King enormously. As the events in Montgomery got under way, Bayard Rustin, long committed to pacifism and Gandhian nonviolence, went to Montgomery to advise and assist King. Rustin had worked for Muste at the pacifist Fellowship of Reconciliation and for a new organization the fellowship developed during World War II, the Congress of Racial Equality (CORE), as did James Farmer, a young Negro aristocrat. Together, they sat at the foot of a traveling Gandhi disciple named Krishnalal Shridharani, author of *War without Violence*; they studied the book as a kind of bible of CORE.[68] Other close studies of Gandhi's movements were also available

p. 160

during this period, and African Americans, including King, studied Gandhi as a possible model.[69] Rustin was impressed by the intuitive Gandhian method at work in the Montgomery boycott, and he worked happily in the background. King told him he was trying to practice nonviolence, but "he did not subscribe to Muste-style pacifism because he believed no just society could exist without at least a police power."[70] When the press discovered Rustin's background (including his gay sex life), he knew his advisory connection would be used to discredit the boycott, and he quietly left Montgomery. But he told Muste that someone qualified to teach nonviolence had to be sent to Montgomery. Glenn Smiley replaced Rustin.[71]

In 1959 King traveled to India with Coretta and his biographer, L. D. Reddick. Rustin had encouraged him to go, and King himself wanted time to absorb Gandhi's satyagraha as a discipline that he might find useful in his work in the United States. He talked at length about Gandhi not only with Prime Minister Jawaharlal Nehru but also with a range of Gandhi's disciples in India. He returned to the United States determined to make a fresh start on the basis of what he had learned in India. He was thinking of organizing the American equivalent of Gandhi's salt satyagraha and arranged for a conference in Atlanta, Georgia, at which there would be sustained discussion about how Gandhism could be implemented and adapted to American culture; workshops were led by Bayard Rustin, James Lawson, and Glenn Smiley, as well as by King and his close associate and fellow minister Ralph Abernathy. Rustin, Smiley, and others talked of some of the disarming nonviolent techniques they had discovered in the preceding twenty years. Lawson had been a Methodist missionary in India and was a Gandhian pacifist; King had persuaded him to move from Ohio to Nashville, Tennessee, where he had been running nonviolence workshops whose techniques would be tested at segregated stores there. Lawson and the other American Gandhians developed a discipline that could be taught and that would inspire young black men such as John Lewis and James Bevel to play important, courageous roles in nonviolent civil disobedience. When student sit-ins began in North Carolina cities and spread to Nashville, Lawson found himself giving crash courses in nonviolence late into the night. King embraced what the students were doing, as it represented what he had been thinking about for years—namely, identifying and pursuing new ways of nonviolent confrontation with segregation laws.[72]

In 1963 King was to develop and lead such a strategy in Birmingham, Alabama, followed by the March on Washington. The largest industrial city in the South, Birmingham was strongly segregationist. If protests were successful there, the symbolic significance would be enormous both regionally and nationally. King decided that the city might be an appropriate site for nonviolent mass civil disobedience because there were no crippling divisions in black leadership there as there had been elsewhere; in fact, there was only one indigenous black leader, the Reverend Fred Shuttlesworth, who was allied with King's Southern Christian Leadership Conference (SCLC).[73]

The other dimension of King's thinking was, of course, the audiences that his social movement would reach. In this case, there were three audiences, all of which might help the overall success of nonviolent mass resistance in Birmingham. First, there were the city's business leaders, at whom the resistance was to be targeted (rather than the government). Second, there was Public Safety Commissioner Bull Connor. The city's defense of segregation would be led, until the upcoming municipal election in March, by Connor, who was notorious for his temper and virulent advocacy of segregation. Connor's conspicuous violence might make exactly the right public statement about the basis of racism that the protest movement wanted to project. And third, there was the Kennedy administration in Washington, D.C. If prodded in the right way, this administration might be more responsive to a movement of mass protest than previous administrations had been.[74]

There was no guarantee that things would turn out better in Birmingham than they had anywhere else, and they could turn out much worse. Stanley Levison, one of King's closest advisers, attended the planning meeting for the protests in Birmingham, and he reported that there were discussions about Bull Connor's history of violence against demonstrations by the labor movement.[75] King then spoke: "'I have to tell you that in my judgment, some of the people sitting here today will not come back alive from this campaign. And I want you to think about it.'"[76]

When the Birmingham campaign finally began, its opening was not auspicious. In a recent city election, Connor had been defeated by a more moderate candidate, and some black activists were not inclined to rock the boat by participating in the projected protests (until the Alabama Supreme Court resolved Connor's challenge to the election, however, he would remain in day-to-day control of the police).[77] There was a mass

161

meeting to announce the protest, and seventy-five members of the audience volunteered to join future demonstrations; these volunteers were then trained in the discipline of nonviolence (by James Lawson, among others).[78] King called for a boycott of the segregated stores, and there were sit-ins as well, but he did not have the number of volunteers he had expected.

King made a major step toward surmounting the obstacle of insufficient volunteers by speaking to a large group of black ministers. He persuaded the black leadership to take his side, and at the more well-attended mass meetings, he declared that he intended to be arrested himself. King said he and Abernathy would make their protest, leading to jail, on the symbolically significant day of Good Friday. At virtually the same time, city attorneys secured an injunction from a state judge barring all marches or other protests.[79] By this point, the number of sit-in protesters in jail reached 160.

As the time for the Friday march approached, King met with his advisers. The movement's bail funds were depleted, so the protesters could not be assured that, on arrest, they would not have to spend weeks or even months in jail. There were protesters currently in jail who had been promised they would be bailed out within a week and for whom there were now no bail moneys available. King felt a responsibility to them, but he felt an overriding obligation to keep his promise to be imprisoned himself; he hoped his arrest might inspire greater participation in the movement. Everyone agreed that the movement had reached a crisis point.

Deeply disturbed, King left the meeting to go to another room to pray alone. Thirty minutes later, he reappeared, wearing a new pair of blue-denim overalls. The first sight of him made clear he had decided to go to jail. "I have to make a faith act," he stated.[80] He spoke with great firmness: "The path is clear to me. I've got to march. I've got so many people depending on me. I've got to march."[81] As for the injunction, it had to be disobeyed: "If we obey it, then we are out of business."[82] Daddy King was one of the first to speak, urging his son not to disobey the injunction. King Jr. let his father finish and then said there were more important things than the injunction. He and Abernathy began their Good Friday protest march later that day in defiance of the injunction. Connor's officers blocked the march, and a paddy wagon pulled up as the marchers, including King, were placed under arrest. Earlier that day, just hours before

p.163

the arrest, some of Birmingham's most liberal white ministers condemned the protests as "unwise and untimely" and had urged "our own Negro community to withdraw support from these demonstrations."[83]

At the city jail, King was placed in solitary confinement, cutting him off even from contact with Abernathy. No news reached him. He had no mattress or linen and was sleeping on metal slats. Being in jail had always been difficult for King, even when Abernathy was with him, but the sense of abandonment that came with his solitary confinement and the absence of any outside contact made it especially painful for him on this occasion. He said later that his first night alone in the Birmingham jail was among "the longest, most frustrating and bewildering hours I have lived. . . . I was besieged with worry."[84]

Unknown to King, movement lawyers had tried to meet with him on Friday evening, but they only made contact with him late on Saturday afternoon; questions of further access, including any phone call by King to the outside, were unresolved. Wyatt Walker, who had helped King plan the Birmingham campaign, knew a good issue when he saw one, and he got Coretta King to call the White House; an operator finally connected her with the presidential press secretary, Pierre Salinger, who was in Florida with the president. Salinger promised to pass on Coretta's message, and forty-five minutes later, Robert Kennedy, the attorney general, called her to express his concern and said he would make inquiries in Birmingham about the terms of her husband's imprisonment. Movement lawyers were again allowed to see King at the end of the day on Sunday, and they told him that Clarence Jones, a well-connected California entertainment lawyer, would be coming in from New York on Monday. Jones arrived at the jail to relieve King's anxieties about the bond money by announcing that Harry Belafonte and others had obtained sufficient funds to cover the bail costs. On Monday afternoon, without warning, President Kennedy called Coretta King to express his concern about her husband's imprisonment and to tell her that the Federal Bureau of Investigation (FBI) had informed him that King was safe. Thirty minutes later, a puzzled King was allowed to receive a phone call from his wife, telling him about the president's call.[85] (EOF)

Press reactions to the Birmingham campaign were largely negative, and King was dismayed when he read the newspapers Clarence Jones smuggled into his cell. He was infuriated, however, when he saw a report in a Birmingham paper about the white clergymen attacking the Birmingham campaign. The statement cut King to the quick. He was being criticized on his own turf by liberal clergymen, most of whom had incurred risk by publicly criticizing Governor George Wallace's "Segregation Forever" inaugural speech in January but none of whom had ever taken the kinds of risks for a humane morality that black ministers were taking, including being arrested, bombed, stabbed, and murdered. Now these white liberals stood behind the injunction and the jailers to attack King's voice and message. He began scribbling a response on the margins of the newspaper, which he passed to Clarence Jones when he visited, with instructions on how to follow the arrows to connect various sections. He borrowed additional paper from Jones, on which he kept working, draft after draft. By the time he had finished, he had written twenty pages of his most important statement of the role of nonviolence in civil disobedience, "The Letter from Birmingham City Jail" (San Francisco, 1986).[86]

This letter displayed the extraordinary range and versatility of prophetic ethical voice that King commanded as he himself employed a number of different voices in speaking to white liberals and in speaking for the full range of African Americans now moved to protest injustice. At no point in the argument was there an appeal to anything that would conventionally be understood as religious dogma or ritual or theology. Rather, King spoke of an ethical voice that craved and demanded just recognition by other persons of moral personality, and he spoke in a way (on nonviolent resistance to unjust laws and accepting legal punishment) that displayed what held such injustice in place—the traumatic breaking of ethical relationship by a structural injustice that repressed voice by violence and terror.

The terrifying impact of this culture on the psyche of African Americans had, of course, been described by brilliant black artists such as Richard Wright—for example, in his autobiographical novel, *Black Boy,* about what it was like to grow up black in the South under apartheid.[87] Wright provided a striking insight into how southerners controlled the lives and aspirations of African Americans. Various patterns of control— physical intimidation and the pervasive fear it engendered (including lynching as a mode of terror), economic domination, the psychological power of whites both to define and circumscribe the aspirations of blacks—were devastatingly effective in limiting the life options of young blacks to two alternatives, either conformity to the white system or exile. Even modes of resistance were, Wright argued, shaped by the need to accommodate dominant white culture.[88] He gave a searing insight into the experience of structural injustice and the kind of moral independence, often forged (as it was by the Grimke sisters) in self-conscious exile from the South, that was often required to combat it. It is surely significant, in this connection, that two of America's best black writers and critics of American racism—Richard Wright and James Baldwin— would live much of their lives as expatriates in Europe.[89] King had as profound an analytic understanding of the irrationality of racism as Wright and Baldwin, but he spoke about it in a voice that had a resonance for the people of the South, which such writers did not always have.[90]

Richard Wright identified blacks' religion as one of the tools of black oppression in the South, and a great force in his struggle, like the similar struggle of Baldwin against his stepfather, was his attempt to criticize the role religion had played in the life of his southern family, in particular in the religion of his grandmother. King had had a very different developmental psychology, involving a quite different kind of grandmother, and he came to a sense of ethical voice in religion (after a long period of exile and study in the North) that enabled him to offer an analysis of structural injustice that was similar to Wright's, but he did this as a minister of a black church in the South on the basis of the sense of voice that empowered him and moved others.

One prominent feature of this new kind of ethical voice was that it did not simply dismiss religion, as Wright did, but instead made its case to religious leaders, taking them and their arguments quite seriously and showing why their arguments were, on religious grounds, wrong.

In "Letter from Birmingham City Jail," King wrote several passages addressing the clergymen's criticism that his demonstrations were "untimely" (289, 292). But he noted that no demonstration was regarded as well timed "according to the timetable of those who have not suffered unduly from the disease of segregation. . . . I guess it is easy for those who have never felt the stinging darts of segregation to say, 'Wait'" (292). Then, in a sentence of some three hundred words, King confronted the ministers relationally, person to person, with the psyche of a people subject to a structural injustice like racism:

> But when you have seen vicious mobs lynch your mothers and fathers at will and drown your sisters and brothers at whim; when you have seen hate-filled policemen curse, kick, brutalize

and even kill your black brothers and sisters with impunity; when you see the vast majority of your twenty million Negro brothers smothering in an airtight cage of poverty in the midst of an affluent society; when you suddenly find your tongue twisted and your speech stammering as you seek to explain to your six-year-old daughter why she can't go to the public amusement park that has just been advertised on television, and see tears welling up in her little eyes when she is told that Funtown is closed to colored children, and see the depressing clouds of inferiority begin to form in her little mental sky, and see her begin to distort her little personality by unconsciously developing a bitterness toward white people; when you have to concoct an answer for a five-year-old son asking in agonizing pathos: "Daddy, why do white people treat colored people so mean?"; when you take a cross-country drive and find it necessary to sleep night after night in the uncomfortable corners of your automobile because no motel will accept you; when you are humiliated day in and day out by nagging signs reading "white" and "colored"; when your first name becomes "nigger" and your middle name becomes "boy" (however old you are) and your last name becomes "John," and when your wife and mother are never given the respected title "Mrs."; when you are harried by day and haunted by night by the fact that you are a Negro, living constantly at tiptoe stance never quite knowing what to expect next, and plagued with inner fears and outer resentments; when you are forever fighting a degenerating sense of "nobodiness"; then you will understand why we find it difficult to wait. (292–93)

King took on a number of different perspectives and voices, often changing from one phrase to another. He expressed sympathy with the lives of a people waiting "for more than 340 years for our constitutional and God-given rights" (292) and with the life of a child at a particular moment. He looked at the white clergymen through the eyes of Negroes and even tried to look at look at Negroes through their eyes ("The Negro has many pent-up resentments and latent frustrations. He has to get them out. So let him march sometime" [297]). He represented himself in a range of voices: as a suffering servant ("What else is there to do when you are alone for days in the dull monotony of a narrow jail cell other than write long letters, think strange thoughts, and pray long prayers?" [302]); as a father, husband, and son (292–93); as a modern-day Paul of Tarsus (290); as a fellow man of affairs ("If I sought to answer all the criticisms that cross my desk" [289]); and as a political leader (289–90). But he also spoke as a teacher and scholar, invoking Saint Thomas and Martin Buber:

> How does one determine when a law is just or unjust? . . . To put it in the terms of Saint Thomas Aquinas, an unjust law is a human law that is not rooted in eternal and natural law. Any law that uplifts human personality is just. Any law that degrades human personality is unjust. All segregation statutes are unjust because segregation distorts the soul and damages the personality. It gives the segregator a false sense of superiority, and the segregated a false sense of inferiority. To use the words of Martin Buber, the great Jewish philosopher, segregation substitutes an "I-it" relationship for the "I-thou" relationship, and ends up relegating persons to the status of things. (293)

And he wrote as a fellow student seeking common ground ("a fellow clergyman and a Christian brother" [302]).

King achieved here, by degrees, a universal ethical voice, timeless and beyond race. It was speaking in that ethical voice, he argued, that elicited such violence from bigots and such dismissal from white liberals (living "in monologue rather than dialogue" [292]), both wedded to a structural injustice that rested on the dehumanizing repression of the voice. What nonviolent civil disobedience did was to so "dramatize the issue that it can no longer be ignored," producing the "creative tension" over ethical contradiction that Socrates cultivated (291) (as he later commented, "Academic freedom is a reality today because Socrates practiced civil disobedience" [294]). White liberals, in particular, self-critically failed to understand their own complicity with racism: "Reinhold Niebuhr has reminded us, groups are more immoral than individuals" (292).

The universal ethical appeal of the argument derived from the way King put it in terms of the relational web of interdependent relations among persons, "an inescapable network of mutuality, tied in a single garment of destiny" (290), which a structural injustice such as racism traumatically disrupted, separating persons from any sense of their common relational humanity. Thurgood Marshall had made reference to this unjust breaking of relationship in his oral argument for *Brown v. Board of Education* when he observed that white and black children played together as children only to be violently separated by segregation laws requiring separate education. The violence in question was all too real and undeniable, especially when targeted against the protesting voice of African Americans: as King stated, "There have been more unsolved bombings of Negro homes and churches in Birmingham than any city in this nation. These are the hard, brutal and unbelievable facts" (290). What the nonviolence of civil disobedience showed so clearly was the political violence that held such injustice in place, a violence targeted at protesting ethical voice. The argument ended poignantly with King taking up the position of black women subject to such injustice when they protest—"if you would watch them push and curse old Negro women and young Negro girls" (301)—and, with his mention of Rosa Parks and the "old, oppressed, battered Negro women, symbolized in a seventy-two-year-old woman of Montgomery, Alabama, who rose up with a sense of dignity and with her people decided not to ride the segregated buses, and responded to one who inquired about her tiredness with ungrammatical profundity: 'My feet is tired, but my soul is rested'" (302). King turned at the conclusion to women's ethical voice, as well as to the role of "young high school and college students" (302), because they embodied and expressed a kind of courageous maternal care for healing a culture wounded by such traumatic breaks in ethical relationship.

King gave a universal ethical significance to such courage, which he associated with the willingness to die expressed by both Socrates and Jesus (295–96). Both, of course, were ethical teachers, and King's example of women and young students, as protesters, invested such protests with the same ethical significance. Women and students were at points of transmission of a racist culture that broke ethical relationships. As agents of King's movement, they imparted a new teaching that subjected that culture to protest and to remedy in terms of the ethical reintegration of all persons on equal terms. Elsewhere, he put this point in terms of Jesus's injunction in the Sermon on the Mount, "Love your enemies,"[91] calling for a response to insult not by violence, as traditional codes of honor required, but by protesting voice, which showed the degree to which a structural injustice such as racism was oppressive and stultifying to whites as well as to blacks. This voice could speak to the suppressed voice in whites, which showed itself in a sense of shame and guilt when confronted with nonviolence.[92] If King's sense of this ethical voice was first experienced in maternal caretakers with their nonviolent aims of protection, nurture, and acceptability, his universalization of this voice empowered the voices of women and children, among others, to bring a culture through nonviolence to some sense of the protection, nurture, and acceptability of ethical maturity of all in the interest of all.

We have already seen the resonance for women's protesting ethical voices that King's ethical voice offered them. In Birmingham, quite consistent with the argument he made in "The Letter from Birmingham City Jail," his voice remarkably energized protests there called "the children's miracle."[93] When he and Abernathy bonded out after nearly nine days in jail, King found that James Bevel's nonviolence workshops had drawn enormous numbers of students from high schools and even grammar schools; Bevel and his wife, Diane Nash, had had experience with recruiting students in their work on voting rights in Mississippi, and Bevel drew on that experience in Birmingham.[94] At a mass meeting with the young people, King thanked them for their support and hoped they would inspire their parents, but he was, at least initially, skeptical that Birmingham's jail was the right place for children.[95] The students did not agree. Bevel persuaded King to use a simple formula: any child old enough to belong to a church should be eligible to march to jail. On this understanding, King committed himself to the role of schoolchildren in protest.[96]

More than a thousand young people marched. Fire hoses were turned on them, some were beaten by Connor's police, and a thousand were jailed. American public opinion was shocked. In later marches, older people joined in significant numbers, comprising more than half the demonstrators. Some parents went to jail with their children. Under pressure from the Kennedy administration and feeling the effects of the economic boycott, the business leaders entered into serious negotiations with the protesters about their claims. A tentative settlement, calling for the phased integration of businesses, was announced.[97] Extremists then bombed the Gaston Motel, where King was staying, and the home of King's brother. Federal troops were introduced to make sure the settlement was observed.

Only after the success in Birmingham did King and his allies consider how they might use the national impact of the campaign to support new federal initiatives to protect civil rights. The Kennedy administration had decided to propose federal desegregation of all public accommodations; President Kennedy spoke on national television, and for the first time in his presidency, he gave a clear moral call for the American people to banish segregation and racism from the land.[98] The March on Washington, which had been proposed by A. Philip Randolph and Bayard Rustin, might now usefully be aimed at Congress rather than the president. The march, which was also planned by Rustin, took place on August 28, 1963, culminating in King's eloquent "I have a dream" speech. National public opinion had been moved toward support of the new civil rights bill, which was strengthened by the national shock over the September 15, 1963, dynamite blast that killed four young black girls in Sunday school at Birmingham's Sixteenth Street Baptist Church. After the assassination of President Kennedy, President Lyndon B. Johnson secured passage of the federal open-accommodations statute, the Civil Rights Act of 1964.

Nonviolence in Selma

In the wake of receiving the Nobel Peace Prize and after the landslide victory of President Johnson, King convened an SCLC staff retreat in Birmingham to chart the future course of the nonviolent movement. The primary issue on the agenda was voting rights in the Deep South. The group talked in depth about Selma, Alabama, as the site for a nonviolent protest. After the bombing murder of the four young black girls in Birmingham, Diane Nash had presented to King the germ of what became the Selma voting rights campaign in 1965.[99] King had now decided that the time was ripe for such an action. Selma might be an effective testing ground because an attitude of defiance had been strongly demonstrated there in the past. Selma activists were interested in mobilizing the community to protest the discriminatory registration practices that had kept all but several hundred Dallas County blacks from becoming registered voters. Also, analogous to Connor in Birmingham, Dallas County Sheriff James G. Clark Jr. was infamous for his bad temper and violent racism (Garrow, *Bearing the Cross,* 357–60). For the local leaders, the campaign would be a way to change voting practices in Selma, but for King and James Bevel (who planned the campaign), it was a way to challenge the entire structure of racial exclusion in the politics of the

South and to force Lyndon Johnson's hand on an effective voting rights statute. If Sheriff Clark's responses to nonviolent demonstrations were violent, it seemed probable that Selma might become the national symbol that the movement needed (380–81).

Selma's white leadership was able to keep Sheriff Clark under wraps in some circumstances, but in others, he met the movement's expectations. In one march when the demonstrators refused to move off the courthouse sidewalk as Clark ordered, he publicly beat Amelia Boynton, a Selma activist, an incident that received national publicity (379). In late January 1965, King marched and refused to split his group into smaller groups to comply with Selma's parade ordinance. As a result, he was arrested with 260 others; the leaders of the march refused to accept release on bail and were led away to a cell (King gave detailed instructions about future marches from the jail). National concern about these events led to growing presidential interest. On his release from jail, King, in fact, met briefly with President Johnson and was told a voting rights proposal would go to Congress soon (388). After King's return to Alabama, Sheriff Clark and his men provided another violent spectacle for the nation when they used nightsticks and cattle prods to drive a group of 165 protesters out in the countryside on a forced march at a runner's pace (388). At another demonstration in Marion, Alabama, state troopers unleashed a violent onslaught, shooting and killing a demonstrator, Jimmie Lee Jackson. These events brought renewed press coverage and calls for national legislation (391–92). King flew to Washington, D.C., and had a longer conversation with President Johnson about voting rights legislation under consideration (395).

Over the month of March 1965, police responses to demonstrations became increasingly violent. On March 7, voting rights marchers were beaten at Edmund Pettus Bridge, which spanned the Alabama River on Selma's east flank. Four days later, Rev. James Reeb died after a beating by white racists. On March 25, a Selma-to-Montgomery protest march concluded with an address by King. A few hours afterward, Klan night riders killed Viola Gregg Liuzzo while she transported marchers back to Selma. The national shock at these and other events finally led to the president's proposal of and congressional action on the Voting Rights Act of 1965, which suspended literacy tests in the South (they had been manipulatively used to disenfranchise African Americans), introduced federal examiners who would monitor elections to ensure that qualified blacks were allowed to vote, and required the Justice Department's consent for any change in voting laws in order to make sure such laws did not reflect racist disempowerment (411). The legislation was the most successful voting rights legislation in U.S. history in terms of securing constitutionally guaranteed rights to African Americans.[100]

The Scope and Limits of Nonviolent Voice in King

I have examined three of King's most successful experiments in voice— in Montgomery with the bus boycott, in Birmingham (leading to the Civil Rights Act of 1964), and in Selma (leading to the Voting Rights Act of 1965). But not all of the movements King led even in the South were successful in such ways, and the movements in the North against slums and poverty (for example, in Chicago) had even less success.[101] And in 1968, King was, of course, like Gandhi, assassinated by a racist bigot who was inflamed by his voice and success. Finally, there was increasing evidence in the last years of King's life of the deep emotional price he paid in depression and marital unhappiness for the role he had undertaken.

I now turn to a closer analysis of three dimensions of the role of nonviolence in King's voice—first, its impact in forming and sustaining a mass social movement (prominently including women); second, its impact on its audience in the South and then nationally and internationally; and third, its impact on King's increasingly conflicted psychology as a man.

The appeal of King's nonviolent voice for the movement he led drew importantly on both the achievements of African American constitutionalism (the Montgomery bus boycott occurred one year after *Brown v. Board of Education*) and the role of the black churches in the South. On the one hand, his insistence on nonviolent voice, protesting the structural injustice of racism, brought him into the very center of developing principles of American constitutionalism, including not only the constitutional recognition of the evil of racism as a violation of the equal protection clause of the Fourteenth Amendment but also a muscular, speech-protective interpretation of the First Amendment, which King's movement used, tested, and extended in significant ways.[102] On the other hand, the authority of his voice drew on an interpretation of nonviolence in the life and teachings of Jesus of Nazareth, in particular the

Sermon on the Mount (Matt. 5–7),[103] that justified participation in nonviolent civil disobedience as an ethical and religious duty of protesting prophetic voice. King's voice gave an ethically compelling sense to Jesus's injunction "Love your enemies" (Matt. 5:44), to which he appealed as early as 1957 as the proof text for the demands of his movement. As he put the point: "So this morning, as I look into your eyes, and into the eyes of all my brothers in Alabama and all over America and over the world, I say to you, 'I love you. I would rather die than hate you.' And I'm foolish enough to believe that through the power of this love somewhere, men of the most recalcitrant bent will be transformed. And then we will be in God's kingdom."[104]

"I look into your eyes" was a remarkably intimate thing for a preacher to say, but it captured both the style and substance of King's prophetic ethical voice. Much of the audience for that voice was composed of black women of the South. King connected with these women because his developmental psychology and his sense of God drew on loving maternal care, person to person, as a model for the very heart of religion. As Constance Baker Mottley puts it, when King "preached nonviolence to the largely elderly females in those Birmingham churches at night, [he] was preaching to the converted."[105] Nonviolent resistance by women began in the Montgomery bus boycott before he arrived on the scene, but King gave a new significance and sense of possibility to the resistance to injustice that had become an imperative of action for those women. He was the right man in the right place at the right time; his own original voice drew on experience in place and showed how it might be used as the basis for a mass movement based in religious conscience. His view of religion was very much his own, so different from that of the black churches in the past that it was questioned not only by the white clergymen who criticized the Birmingham campaign but by black ministers as well.[106] He certainly worked within the patriarchal assumptions of the Baptist Church, but his voice connected to black women not in terms of the patriarchal preachers familiar to them (thus, James Baldwin's remark that King was not like any preacher he had ever met) but in a way that spoke to them with a moral authority, grounded in nonviolence, that they recognized and responded to in ways that challenged dominant patriarchal assumptions. Under the impact of King's voice, these women moved out of their homes and out of their traditional sanctuaries in black colleges into the moral and political agency of mass protests with all of its risks and challenges, not least to their sense of themselves as women.[107] The feeling of black women for King was re-markable:

> One "sister" said that when King spoke she felt that God him-self was near; another testified that when she heard King's voice she could also hear the rustle of angels that she could see dimly, hovering over him.
>
> To many a mother, here was her symbolic son: neat, clean, well-spoken, smart, good-looking, manly. To many a childless woman here too was her son. At the same time, King was to the predominantly female audience the father symbol: strong, wise, protective. When it was suggested that King represented the father-son complex, one woman who may not have under-stood the term said, "Oh yes, Father, Son—*and* Holy Ghost."[108]

The intimacy of King's voice ("I look into your eyes") may have been, for these women, a new experience of a black man able to relate to them as persons, suggesting a new kind of humane relationship between men and women that empowered them as collaborative moral and political agents in remarkable ways.

Only now, in the light of the feminist project to recover women's roles in history, are we coming to some understanding of the part women played in mass demonstrations throughout the South and also in impor-tant leadership positions.[109] These women included, among many others, Ella Baker, Septima Clark, Diane Nash, and Fannie Lou Hamer.[110] King was enough of a patriarchal man to maintain the Baptist tradition that top leadership was kept in the hands of men, and some of these women, notably Baker, resisted him on this and other points. But these and other women were drawn into such active participation, including leadership roles (for example, the role Nash played in proposing the Selma cam-paign), by something that moved them, as women, in King's prophetic ethical voice and in his actions. The patriarchal problem was not just King's, of course; it was endemic in the civil rights movement. One of the important motives to feminism was the ethical empowerment some women attained by participating in a civil rights movement that led them to question its sexism and sexism generally, both as an aspect of racism and as an independent evil.[111]

The same ethical voice that, through nonviolence, energized a movement of mass political protest also gave a growing, strengthening resonance to the previously feeble voices of the white South that protested the role racism had played in its political and economic backwardness. King always emphasized how much blacks and whites shared in the South, referring to the "network of mutuality" that often made them part of one another's life[112]—sometimes as children on playgrounds, sometimes as black caretakers in white homes, sometimes in easy social and even sexual relationships, or in clandestine visits of whites to experience black dance or music. The dominant racist ideology required that such relationships not be recognized or accorded any significance that would challenge the ideology. King's nonviolent ethical voice, when it had energized a mass movement of often remarkably disciplined nonviolent civil disobedience, raised exactly the questions that, when heard, destabilized the hegemonic power the ideology had enjoyed for so long. What the nonviolence of the movement brought out with such clarity when its moral dramaturgy was most successful was that it was violence, including the violence of public officials such as Bull Connor in Birmingham and James Clark in Selma, that held this ideology in place. Voices raised in nonviolent protest, questioning racist ideology and practices, were the targets of public and private acts of merciless, brutal, and all too conspicuous violence.

What gave King's nonviolent voice increasing appeal to its audiences, in both the North and the South, was the way it drew on two things that American whites and blacks deeply shared: constitutionalism and a religion that was broadly Judeo-Christian. On the one hand, King appealed to a value of voice and free speech that was among the most broadly respected of all constitutional values, and the use of violence in response revealed an unconstitutionally racist culture at war with such values. On the other hand, King spoke with an authority grounded in the life and teaching of Jesus of Nazareth, understood, as King certainly thought of him, as the greatest of the Jewish prophets.[113] His view of Jesus was remarkably in line with the best work on the historical Jesus up to his time, and beyond that, it gave expression to a sense of religion as grounded in respect for persons that transcended sectarian religion or irreligion and that relentlessly criticized the role established religions had played in repressing prophetic ethical voice (a point powerfully made in "The Letter from Birmingham City Jail").

King's voice was rooted in a naturalistic sense of ethical values, what the abolitionist preacher Theodore Parker referred to in stating, "The arc of the moral universe is long, but it bends toward justice,"[114] a passage King loved and frequently repeated.[115] Ethical argument does not have this kind of appeal unless it touches something in our human developmental psychology, helping us recognize and resolve contradictions in our psyches. King called its effects "disarming the opponent,"[116] and he attributed these effects to an underlying sense of shame or guilt in the opponent that nonviolence elicited.[117] What made his voice psychologically possible was the value he placed on his relationships to the voices of maternal caretakers, relationships that he held on to despite his induction into patriarchal black manhood. What gave this voice such authority for African Americans and Americans generally was the way in which it showed that this ethical protesting voice was not peripheral or marginal but decisively central to the most reasonable interpretation in contemporary circumstances both of American constitutionalism and of Judeo-Christian religion. King's sense that nonviolence was a way of working through racism's psychic injuries of hatred, fear, and anger was a matter of strategic disarmament: by disarming themselves of the usual violence by which men act out their hatred, fear, and anger, African Americans found their ethical voice and feelings as deeply, centrally American and connected to fellow Americans by what King unashamedly called love: "I love you. I would rather die than hate you."[118] Is it really surprising that black women, who played so powerful a role in his movement, found in King's voice a maternal voice of caring love for sometimes wayward, difficult, or even violent children that they already knew themselves?

King evidently paid a devastating personal price for his voice and the leadership role it thrust on him, an issue powerfully explored in a recent book by a black Baptist minister, Michael Eric Dyson.[119] King had found his ethical voice through relationships to the personal religions of his mother and grandmother, but these relationships were sufficiently idealized that he had accepted the patriarchal conventions of good and bad women that had led him traumatically to break a relationship with a white woman he had loved at Crozer; instead, he entered into a more patriarchally acceptable marriage to a black woman who would advance his career. Dyson shows us a man increasingly subject to crippling depression, living in contradiction between his public views on marital fidelity and sexual liaisons that started as early as his time in Montgomery,[120] trapped

in a marriage increasingly bitter and acrimonious, and longing for intimate voice and connection, a longing that was never satisfied.[121] The
public man whose prophetic voice was so intimately appealing was deeply
alone.

King had long been subject to intrusive surveillance by the FBI's di-
rector, J. Edgar Hoover, which had first been permitted by Attorney
General Robert Kennedy and continued under President Lyndon Johnson. It is a rather sickening spectacle of politically motivated officials who,
concerned about King's growing importance in American and world
public opinion, wanted to be kept apprised of his plans so that that they
could minimize any political risks to themselves. Hoover's animus was
more personally vindictive, centering on three accusations: King's alleged
communist links, his alleged wealth derived from corrupt deals, and his
sexual liaisons. There was nothing in either of the first two accusations;
King was himself deeply anticommunist, and the few advisers who once
were linked to the Communist Party no longer were. Further, King had
always scrupulously segregated the money he raised for his movement
from money for his personal use; he was, in truth, not well off at all, a
fact that caused conflict with his wife and may reflect his ambition not
to be the kind of worldly minister Daddy King had been. The allegations
about sexual liaisons were true, and Hoover had indeed made tapes of a
number of them, tapes that, appallingly, he even sent to Coretta King at
one point. That King agonized over the damage the disclosures of his
sexual life would make to his reputation suggests his sense of conflict,
but he refused to stop having the liaisons even when pressed by his close
friend and sexual coparticipant Rev. Ralph Abernathy.[122]

Abernathy may have given us a way into understanding King's conflicts when he observed that King "was not a man the public knew
fully," pointing to "his humanity, warmth, and, above all, his unflagging
capacity to have fun and to make everybody else join in."[123] King was
"fun-loving, and when he was offstage you could usually find him
telling a joke or teasing somebody."[124] Any sharp division of public from
private life is always highly gendered, and King was no exception. He
aligned his public life with the love he called agape, his private life as
a fun-loving, sensual man with the lesser loves philia and eros.[125] Agape
was "creative, redemptive goodwill for all men,"[126] whereas philia was
friendship and eros romantic love. The difference, he argued at one
point, is that there is something "mundane, even debased"[127] about eros

and philia, whereas agape calls for concern even for people you do not like. (E OF)   32:39, 66

If King's public and private lives were as sharply distinguished as this dichotomy reveals, it suggests the burden that was placed on his psyche when he found his prophetic ethical voice in a nonviolence that was specifically directed against the role violence played in a manhood formed by codes of honor, namely, responding to insults to manhood by violence. From the time he found his voice in nonviolence, he heard the criticism from black men that it was unmanly not to use violence in combating injustice, or, as boys in the black slums of Chicago put it to him, "The expression of his manhood is . . . the ability to defend himself physically."[128] It was one of Malcolm X's familiar taunts against King that nonviolence was unmanly not only for men but also for women and children who were doing men's work of resistance,[129] and King's later criticisms of the growing appeal of the violence of black power acknowledged the basis of its appeal—manhood.[130] The whole originality of King's prophetic ethical voice was his questioning of this conception of manhood, whether it showed itself in white violence directed against nonviolent civil disobedience or in the violence of black power (both public and private).[131]

King's developmental history as a boy and then at Morehouse and Crozer and Boston University clearly shows a person playing at manhood, imposing on himself the kinds of patriarchal perquisites appropriate to a man about to become a Baptist minister. On the one hand, he assumed that a certain kind of marriage was appropriate to that role, but on the other, he obviously wanted to be a different kind of minister from his father, one rooted in a developmental psychology in which relationships with maternal caretakers played a pivotal role in his sense of the authority of religious voice. King found his voice in nonviolence, a move that sharply questioned the code of honor in traditional manhood with all the consequences we have now examined, and he spoke to his audiences, as we have seen, with a remarkable intimacy of voice, as if his voice as a minister may have been an unusually intimate kind of public voice. Paradoxically, once King discovered his public voice, it may have been the most intimate thing he had, something that reached out for a kind of connection he had denied himself in others areas of his life, public and private. We know this intimate voice touched and empowered many black women and men. But for King, it was a voice very much

p. 179

divided from a sensual, loving voice of the sort he craved in his personal life. The very fact that he thus exposed his manhood to criticism may have led him, defensively and perhaps competitively, to hold on more tenaciously to his patriarchal sense of himself as a black Baptist preacher superior to his critics, as shown by the clandestine sexual liaisons that were, as his friend Abernathy showed him,[132] one of the patriarchal privileges of such preachers—sexual proof, as it were, of a manhood otherwise in doubt.

But King's prophetic ethical voice was thus radically disengaged from his sensual, fun-loving sexual voice, a not surprising result when the ethical voice arises from relationships with maternal caretakers that are idealized and when the idealization later carries over to one's conception of marriage to a good woman. King thus bore in his psyche the burden of living a public life that must have seemed to him increasingly false, even desolating, as he was cut off from any kind of intimate sexual voice in which he could find himself in the love of another free voice. In this connection, it is revealing that King not only sharply separates agape from philia and eros but also eros from philia. Eros is a kind of highly idealized, absorbing sensuality, but friendship "is an intimate affection between personal friends, it is reciprocal love. On this level you love because you are loved."[133] It is as if eros requires no sexual voice, let alone friendship, in either of the partners, which is to do something with sexuality that King condemned in all other relationships of dehumanized objectification that failed, as Buber put it, to take seriously one another's individuality.

I earlier observed that James Baldwin said of King that he was not like any black preacher Baldwin had ever met. The writer was struck by King's remarkable wedding of religious voice with loving ethical voice, whereas he had known in his stepfather a religion distorted by anger and hatred. But he also noticed a surprising conventionality in King's public sexual voice, which failed to see the connections between racism and the abridgment of basic human rights to sexual freedom (for example, antimiscegenation laws).[134] No one wrote more eloquently than Baldwin of the way racism locked black men into a sexual cage in which relationships based on free and equal sexual voice and emotional presence were impossible. An artist and a gay man, Baldwin was sufficiently outside the patriarchal arrangements that King uncritically assumed that he could see the roots of the psychic conflicts King experienced but could not understand or resolve. King had, in fact, deeply challenged conventional patriarchal manhood, but like other men we have studied in his position (Tolstoy and Gandhi), his psyche was plunged into conflict when the ethical voice that motivated him could challenge most forms of structural injustice but not the unjust impact of that injustice on free sexual voice. This is, as it were, the last redoubt of patriarchal manhood, and no one pays a higher price for leaving it in place than the men who otherwise have challenged the violence of manhood. King, who had found in nonviolence the key to unlocking so many of the cages of racism, could not find the key to unlocking the sexual cage that imprisoned him.

5:18.80

//CHAPTER FIVE

Churchill's Resisting Voice

Winston Churchill towers above other leaders of twentieth-century democracies in the power and truth of his voice calling for and mobilizing resistance to the forms of political totalitarianism that he identified in both the communism of the Soviet Union and the fascism of Hitler's Germany.[1] My interest here is in understanding the thought and psychology of this resisting voice, in particular the form it took in his understanding of and resistance to the aggressively militaristic politics of Hitler based on an injustice—anti-Semitism—enforced by violence. Churchill's voice in politics certainly did not take the form of nonviolence we have studied in Garrison, Tolstoy, Gandhi, and King. Like Garrison and King, he was not a pacifist, but he cogently indicted the dominant pacifism of interwar Britain precisely because it failed to understand and resist the aggressively unjust violence that was mobilizing against its peace and political liberalism. But like all the men studied here, Churchill strikingly found a voice that resisted forms of structural injustice based on violence, a violence directed at and provoked by a sense of male honor insulted by such voice. What is of enormous interest to this study is that his resistance rested on a thought and psychology strikingly similar, albeit with important variations, to that we have so far studied.

Putting Churchill in this perspective clarifies what is remarkable in all the men studied in this volume, namely, that they found a voice that resisted the role of a violent conception of manhood in enforcing structural injustice. A man who is capable of this kind of voice questions, explicitly or implicitly, the traditional conceptions of manhood that repress such voice and questioning. Churchill, like Abraham Lincoln, will forever live in the history of liberal democracy because he found a voice that enabled democracies to understand and resist the most fundamental challenges to their best values. I have chosen to closely study Churchill

p. 182

rather than Lincoln because while Lincoln's close relationships with his mother and stepmother was very much in line with the psychology we have been studying, we know much less about these relationships than we do about Churchill's.[2] There is, however, an even more compelling reason for the study of Churchill: his relationship with his mother was probably closer yet less idealized than any such relationship among the group of men I treat here. We can thus explore in Churchill the consequences for a son of an ongoing relationship with a mother that is based not only on unusual common interests, ambitions, and tastes but also on an uncommon honesty about the mother's robust sexual interests and life with men outside marriage.

Churchill's Background and Early Life

Two striking similarities between Leo Tolstoy and Winston Churchill are relevant to our study: first, both were born into aristocratic families with distinguished histories of service to their imperial governments, Russian and British, respectively; second, as young men, both found their first vocations in courageous military service in imperial wars. These aristocrats also found a vocation in writing while in military service, Tolstoy as a novelist (initially writing about military service), Churchill as a historian (also writing about his military service). Tolstoy's development as a novelist chronicled a growing skepticism about the military life and sexual life he had once glorified. Churchill, who was born to much less wealth than Tolstoy, earned his income from his journalism and histories, depicting his military service in Britain's imperial wars, then the traditions of his family and nation, and finally his political life both in Parliament and in government. His career as a parliamentary politician and leader was highlighted by his speeches, many of them now famous for their voice calling for resistance, whether against the rise of communism and German fascism before World War II, against Hitler's aggressive onslaught on Britain during World War II, or against the resurgent power of the Soviet Union after World War II.[3]

Churchill's father was Randolph Churchill, the second son of the Duke of Marlborough, whose ancestry included the eighteenth-century British military commander John Duke of Marlborough. One of Churchill's best histories is a four-volume study of this ancestor, and much of his childhood was spent at Blenheim, the palace that a grateful nation had built for his ancestor and his spirited wife, Sarah.[4] The sense of his aristocratic family's service to the nation was very much alive in Winston, heightened by his father's short-lived but brilliantly erratic career in Parliament and, briefly, in other branches of government (including the important cabinet position of chancellor of the exchequer). Much of the family's wealth had been dissipated over the years, and Churchill's father thus turned, as did other impecunious British aristocrats, to a suitable marriage to a young woman of wealth. After a very short courtship, Randolph impetuously proposed marriage to Jennie Jerome, the daughter of a wealthy American businessman, Leonard Jerome of New York City.[5] Despite resistance by his family (the Jeromes were not as wealthy as his parents would have expected), Randolph married Jennie, a beautiful woman ambitious for her husband's political success. His choice undoubtedly rested on Jennie's personal appeal to him as a spirited American woman, including her strong sexual interests. She was certainly not a patriarchally good woman in comparison to the many other women he could have married, women who also would have provided much greater enhancement of both his aristocratic status and his finances. Like many otherwise patriarchal men, Randolph was excited by a woman who was not conventionally good. What was unusual about him was that, unlike Tolstoy, he himself resisted patriarchy by marrying such a woman. Jennie had lived much of her life as a young woman in Europe, moving in aristocratic circles in Paris and London in which she grew to admire the freedom, including the sexual freedom, of the men and women she met, married and unmarried. Leonard Jerome, himself quite a philanderer (Jennie was named after one of his lovers, the soprano Jenny Lind), complained at one point to his wife about his wild daughters, to which his wife responded, "Well, dear, they are *your* daughters."[6]

Randolph Churchill, absorbed by his growing success in parliamentary politics, took even less interest in his two sons, Winston and John, than most aristocratic fathers did. His distance from Winston in particular was chilling, sometimes brutally hostile.[7] Jennie was very much absorbed in her husband's political career and social life during this period, but she took much more of an interest in her sons than her husband did; among other things, she removed Winston from a school where he had been cruelly treated. Jennie closely followed the advice of Mrs. Everest, the nanny who lavished intimate affection on the young Winston and whom he adored. (In his autobiography, he wrote: "My mother made the same brilliant impression upon my childhood's eye. She shone for me like the Evening Star. I loved her dearly, but at a distance. My nurse was my confidante.")[8] Winston drew a sharp contrast between his parents in a conversation with author and editor Frank Harris (a close friend of his father's) years later: "[My father] wouldn't listen to me or consider anything I said. There was no companionship with him possible to me and I tried so hard and so often. He was so self-centered no one else existed for him. . . . My mother was everything to me."[9] The Churchills' marriage had actually deteriorated rapidly, a fact not unrelated to Randolph's contraction of syphilis, from which he would die in 1895; there is also some suggestion that he had homosexual connections.[10] Jennie continued to support her husband's political career actively (even giving speeches for him and forming the Primrose Society, which supported his politics of Tory democracy), but she turned her sexual attentions to a number of other men in her aristocratic social circle, a circle that included the Prince of Wales, later King Edward VII. Roy Jenkins observes: "George Moore, the Anglo-Irish novelist, said she had 200 lovers, but apart from anything else the number is suspiciously round."[11] Despite their marital estrangement and increasingly separate lives, Jennie devoted herself to the care of her husband during the frightful last three years of his life (taking a world tour with him near the end, during which he deteriorated into insanity and finally succumbed to death).

After the death of her husband, Jennie shifted her thwarted ambitions for Randolph to her elder son (she had refused to surrender her husband's chancellor of exchequer robes, saving them for Winston, who would, in fact, serve in that position from 1924 to 1929).[12] She drew on her wealth of associations with some of the most influential political figures of the age (some of them current or former lovers) to afford him the opportunities and political education in leadership that he needed. She also hosted dinner parties with prominent politicians who were often publicly supposed to be deadly enemies; Jennie would coax these individuals into a sense of camaraderie and fellowship, enabling her son to receive the kind of political education, including ongoing relationships with diverse politicians and even the Prince of Wales himself, he had never received from his father.[13] She attempted to fill the emotional vacuum his father's distance and hostility had inflicted on Winston, in effect giving him experiences of relationship with caring men very like the good fathering that he craved but never received from Randolph Churchill. Concerned that her son was "a mama's boy," Jennie cultivated his close friendship with one of her most serious lovers, Count Charles Kinsky.[14]

By the time of his father's death, Churchill, now a young man of twenty-one, had completed his formal education at Harrow and the Royal Military Academy of Sandhurst, and he departed for India for his first commission as a second lieutenant in the Fourth Hussars in 1896. It was Jennie who sent Winston the various books he requested, including the complete volumes of Edward Gibbon and Thomas Macaulay, which he read and studied closely with a "permanent impact of both of them, different although he may have found their styles, upon his writing and oratory."[15] Winston also called on her "to use all possible influence to get him to every scene of military action in the world," not only because of his extragant adventurism but also so he could begin writing journalistic pieces about his adventures, which would enable him to earn needed money.[16]

In fact, his mother played important roles as adviser and stage manager in all his early military adventures, adventures intentionally designed to bring Winston public fame in Britain that would yield dividends in terms of his carefully planned entrance into parliamentary politics. It was Jennie who secured Churchill's first adventure observing the Spanish war against rebels in Cuba; she also had him meet, in New York, one of her lovers, the U.S. politician Bourke Cockran, who, as another of Jennie's lover-fathers to her son, made "a profound impact on Churchill."[17] Winston's second martial adventure was with the Malakand Field Force against rebellious Pathan tribesman in the Swat Valley close up against the Afghanistan frontier with India, during which he both served in the military and wrote about his service as a journalist. These experiences led to Churchill's first book, *The Story of the Malakand Field Force,* for which his mother had secured rapid publication.[18] Urged on by her son, Jennie then used all her connections (including with Lord Horatio Herbert Kitchener and Prime Minister Robert Salisbury) in a concerted campaign that finally succeeded in enabling him to serve in his third military adventure, in the Sudan;[19] that tour of duty resulted in the publication of his *River War.*[20] Churchill's military campaigns, journalism, and books were evidently not yet sufficient to secure his aim of being elected to Parliament, for his first try in 1899 failed.[21] A fourth military campaign,

p. 186

this time in the Boer War, would finally bring Churchill his first great international fame for pluck and bravado (a daring escape from a Boer prison that thrilled Britain), a fame that finally led to his election to Parliament in 1900.[22] (In the three years between 1898 and 1900, Churchill published no less than five books—*The Story of the Malakand Field Force, The River War,* a romantic novel entitled *Savrola,* and two books of South African war reportage.)[23]

Jennie played a more public role than usual in the fourth of her son's adventures. She was a central participant in the planning, support, and actual execution of a proposal for an American-British hospital ship that ministered to the wounded in the Boer War.[24] She had already sought some independent stature as the editor of a literary journal and would later write a highly expurgated memoir of her life, *Reminiscences,* and two plays that were produced (plays about the situation of creative, powerful women in marriages); she was also an accomplished pianist, sometimes giving public concerts.[25] But her work in politics, including that in the Primrose Society, had always been in the campaigns of her husband (and she would continue to work energetically in these roles for her son once he entered politics). Her work on the hospital ship project marked a new kind of independent political agency, one that undoubtedly appealed to her personally because it was connected with a war in which not only both her sons but also her new lover and future husband, George Cornwallis-West, served. But the project also appealed to Jennie because it had been suggested to her that she would thus make a new kind of history for women, one that Florence Nightingale had begun in organizing a unit of nurses for the Crimean War in 1854, as well as defending such work by women in emancipatory terms:"Why have women passion, intellect, moral activity—these three—and a place in society where no one of these can be exercised?" (Martin, *Jennie,* 2:190). Jennie herself spoke of the role of women in nursing men injured in war in strikingly maternal terms:

> We may differ as to the policy which necessitates the sending of
> so many gallant soldiers to the front. It is always easy to criticize,
> but as a gifted compatriot wrote to me, "The wounded are the
> wounded, irrespective of creed and nationality." And, indeed, we
> can have but one mind in this matter: If we can alleviate suf-
> ferings and at the same comfort the many aching and anxious

hearts at home, shall we not be fulfilling our greatest mission in life? These are "Women's Rights" in the best sense of the word. We have heard of the friendship between England and America. These are better than words, and we greatly hope that the hospital-ship *Maine* may do more to cement that friendship than years of flag-waving and pleasant amenities. (2:193)

Jennie spoke of the typical soldier she worked with on the ship as a mother would of a son: "Out of his uniform he is a big child, and wants to be kept in order, and not too much spoilt. I am afraid we were inclined to do this! . . . I had long and frequent talks with many of them" (2:209). Winston strikingly gave his mother a resonance for her motives in undertaking this new kind of agency: "Your name will be long remembered with affection by many poor broken creatures. Besides, it is the right thing to do, which is the great point"(2:209). We get a sense of a remarkable level of understanding and support between son and mother and a common sense of humane values about relationship and the need to bring men traumatized by violence back into relationship. Later, during World War I, Jennie took her grandson to a hospital "where she was spending most of her time. Jennie wanted her young grandson to balance his heroic view of war by seeing some of the casualties" (2:337).

This close working relationship continued in Churchill's early political career. Jennie actively campaigned for her son as she had for her husband and gave public speeches in support of his candidacy (2:171–74, 237, 278). She also drew on her social contacts to open doors for him (the Prince of Wales, later King Edward VII, would take an interest in his career), and she was a sounding board for his speeches and an adviser on his political career, in particular his move from the Tory Party of his father to the Liberal Party in which he spent his early years in politics, including his first service in government.[26] In writing of his early life, Churchill observed that he initially found his political voice in organizing students at Sandhurst to resist "the Purity Campaign of Mrs. Ormiston Chant" against young men and women meeting in a public theater, insisting that right to be free from prudish moralism was one of the central rights guaranteed to English citizens.[27] It was certainly very much Jennie's son who would think of legitimate politics in terms of protecting a right of that type as well as the right of free speech, in which

Churchill, as a writer and parliamentarian, would brilliantly find his distinctive public voice. No British politician of his age would, as we shall see, more courageously demand and exercise that right against the complacent majoritarian politics of his age (when he returned to the Tory Party, he often spoke, as in the 1930s, in opposition to its policies).[28] But when Churchill was appointed president of the Board of Trade, his political liberalism was also expressed in seeking social reform legislation, including unemployment insurance.[29] His *People's Rights,* published in 1909, defended many of the policies of the liberal political and constitutional reform he then advocated.[30] Churchill voted for women's suffrage but did not support it unequivocally (he was put off by the violence of British suffragettes such as the Pankhursts); by contrast, the value he placed on his mother's free sexual voice would have put him well ahead of his time, including well ahead of many less equivocal advocates of women's suffrage.[31] A notable lapse, however, in Churchill's liberalism was his attitude to trade unions.[32]

Jennie's close working relationship with her son drew to a close with his 1908 marriage to Clementine Hozier. Clementine took on the role of confidante and close political adviser, and her perspective, like that of Eleanor Roosevelt, was often more liberal than that of her husband. Clementine and Winston had mothers who were similar in one striking respect. Clementine's mother, Blanche Hozier, had had "at least nine lovers," one of whom almost certainly fathered Clementine.[33] Roy Jenkins observes, "It is remarkable that the offspring of two such libertines should have made one of the most famously long-lasting and faithful marriages in history."[34] Churchill had certainly been interested in other women before Clementine (and possibly in men as well), and Clementine had certainly been interested in other men.[35] What Jenkins may not take sufficiently seriously is the effect on attitudes to women of a son like Churchill or attitudes to men of a daughter like Clementine, both of whom understood and appreciated sexual women like their mothers. Mothers of this type, whose voices and lives resist patriarchal conceptions of women's sexuality, may impart to their children a comparable sense of resistance, leading them to seek partners who respond to deep personal need.

Certainly, in Churchill's case, he and Jennie shared not only political ambition but also a common love of pleasure and a willingness to spend money in pursuit of it (Churchill wrote to his mother along such lines:

"I sympathise with all your extravagances—even more than you do with mine").[36] It was Jennie who introduced Winston to painting, an artistic activity that was to absorb and compose him as a creative alternative to the compulsive verbal fireworks characteristic of the rest of his frenetic life.[37] When Jennie was considering marriage to a much younger man, George Cornwallis-West, against the strong objections of the Prince of Wales and many others, Churchill was remarkably supportive, urging his mother "to consult your own happiness," supporting in her "the longing of a romanticist to return to one of the most unequivocal feelings she had known" (she would marry in 1900).[38] After Jennie's divorce from Cornwallis-West in 1914, Churchill would also support his mother's next marriage, three years later, again to a much younger man, Montague Porch (Jennie died in 1921 at age sixty-seven). Such respect for the role romantic sexual feeling had played in his mother's life imparted to Churchill an unusual feeling and respect for free voice and intelligence in women generally.

In his romantic novel, *Savrola,* written in 1897, he offers a thinly disguised portrait of his mother as Lucile. Lucile is locked in a loveless marriage to a tyrant, President Antonio Molara (a portrait, surely, of his father), but is awakened to a new sense of life by her adulterous love for the novel's republican rebel, Savrola. (Her husband conveniently is killed in the rebellion.) Their love is portrayed as a breaking of disassociation— she from the sense of being a goddess on a pedestal, he from an abstracted philosophy—as they move into loving relationship.[39] Churchill's sense of the possibility and importance of this type of relationship may have guided his choice of a partner. Jennie had confided to a close friend her view of Clementine as her son's mate: "You see my Winston is not *easy;* he is very difficult indeed and she is just right."[40]

Churchill's Voice of Resistance

Churchill's entrance into politics arose, as we have seen, from a shrewd public campaign drawing on his military adventures and the journalism and books he penned that reflected on those adventures. He was a remarkably courageous soldier, but in reflecting on courage, his account is deflationary: "The courage of the soldier is not really contempt for physical evils and indifference to danger. It is a more or less successful attempt to simulate these habits of mind. Most men aspire to be good actors in the play. There are a few who are so perfect that they do not seem to be actors at all. This is the ideal after which the rest are striving. It is one very rarely attained."[41] Yet few soldiers, however courageous, could write as well as Churchill does about the values that inspirit taking such a military role in Britain's imperial wars:

> What enterprise that an enlightened community may attempt is more noble and more profitable than the reclamation from barbarism of fertile regions and large populations? To give peace to warring tribes, to administer justice where all was violence, to strike the chains off the slave, to draw the richness from the soil, to plant the earliest seeds of commerce and learning, to increase in whole peoples their capacities for pleasure and diminish their chances of pain—what more beautiful ideal or more valuable reward can inspire human effort? The act is virtuous, the exercise invigorating, and the result often extremely profitable.[42]

We have seen this combination of writer and soldier before, in Leo Tolstoy. As noted, both Churchill and Tolstoy found their first vocations as soldiers, and they gloried in military service to the ambitions of their respective imperial states. But whereas Tolstoy glories in serving a theocratic absolutist state, Churchill, even in his early works, thinks of the legitimacy of war, when legitimate, in terms of the aims of liberal justice: "To administer justice where all was violence, to strike the chains off the slave." Unlike Tolstoy, Churchill is never tempted, in reflecting on his experience in war, to embrace pacifism, but his experience as a soldier was of a very different sort from Tolstoy's, motivated, under the guidance of his mother, by ultimate ambitions to advance liberal ends through political service in a democratic state.

As Churchill made the transition from soldier to parliamentarian, he had to decide what kind of democratic politician he would be, and for him, assuming that role was as much a matter of acting on a public stage as soldiering was. The sense of his own voice in politics arose, as we have seen, from liberal impulses to resist injustice, but that voice, formed in relationship with his mother, was to be publicly framed by him in terms of the aristocratic traditions of his father's family. This combination of invention and tradition is peculiarly Churchillian. Usually, his invention of

P 191

self takes the form of interpreting history in a certain way; at other times, however, his invention extends to history itself. Churchill barely knew his father and always regarded his mother as the pivotally important influence in his life, personal and political. Nonetheless, consistent with the patriarchal pieties of the age in which he lived, he was to publish, in 1906, a two-volume study of his father's political life, *Lord Randolph Churchill,* that barely mentions his mother and prominently omits any discussion of his parents' private life.[43] Yet its historical sins are not just those of omission. The work is an exercise in what R. F. Foster calls "the politics of piety."[44] As Foster makes clear, Lord Randolph Churchill was a brilliantly erratic, opportunistic politician without any guiding political principles other than his own political success.[45] Churchill's picture of his father ignores these uncomfortable facts in order to invent a person like the politician he was becoming: a rebel against the tyranny of the Tory Party, a party that had no place for men of ideas, in particular men of liberal ideas. (In fact, as Foster puts it, "what ideas were actually possessed by Lord Randolph—that most instinctive and febrile of politicians—had often been grounded in pure Toryism").[46] What Churchill took from his father was ambition, independence, and great style (for example, he imitated his father's manner in making public speeches[47]) but nothing of moral substance. His book about his father, quite well written, was warmly received, enhancing his own career in politics.[48] His later writing of history is much more genuinely interpretive but always guided by his own struggle for clarifying to others, as well as himself, the place of his public voice in long-standing traditions.

Churchill was to have a distinguished early career in government. As a Liberal, for instance, he served as president of the Board of Trade (1908–10), as home secretary (1910–11), and as first lord of the Admiralty (1911–15); as a Tory, he served as chancellor of the exchequer (1924–29). His governmental service during World War I, when he was hounded out of government after the Gallipoli debacle, was the subject of his five-volume *World Crisis and the Aftermath* (1923–31).[49] (He insisted on military service at the front after his dismissal.) But it was in the period after he left government in 1929 that he again found his resisting political voice in terms not only of family but also of national traditions (including his father's British traditions and his mother's American traditions). His four-volume *Marlborough: His Life and Times* (1933–38) interpreted his great ancestor's role in history as forging a national tradition of resistance to European tyrannies, and his four-volume *History of the English-Speaking Peoples* (largely written in the 1930s but not published until 1956–58) interpreted the British and American traditions in terms of the overall aims of a struggle for liberal democracy, at home and abroad.[50] His work on both these books, as mentioned earlier, enabled him to find his distinctive voice of resistance to Hitler's fascism in terms of long-standing family and national traditions. As he put the point in a 1936 speech (focusing only on Britain):

> For four hundred years the foreign policy of England has been to oppose the strongest, most aggressive, most dominating Power on the Continent, and particularly to prevent the Low Countries falling in the hands of such a Power. Viewed in the light of history, these four centuries of consistent purpose amid so many changes of names and facts, of circumstances and conditions, must rank as one of the most remarkable episodes which the records of any race, nation, state, or people can show. Moreover, on all occasions England took the more difficult course. Faced by Philip II of Spain, against Louis XIV under William III and Marlborough, against Napoleon, against William II of Germany, it would have been easy and must have been very tempting to join with the stronger and share the fruits of his conquest. However, we always took the harder course, joined with the less strong Powers, made a combination among them, and thus defeated and frustrated the Continental military tyrant whoever he was, whatever nation he led. Thus we preserved the liberties of Europe, protected the growth of its vivacious and varied society, and emerged after four terrible struggles with an every-growing fame and widening Empire. Here is the wonderful unconscious tradition of British foreign policy. All our thoughts rest in that tradition today. I know of nothing that has happened to human nature which in the slightest degree alters the validity of their conclusions. I know of nothing in military, political, economic, or scientific fact which makes me feel that we might not, or cannot, march along the same road. I venture to put this very general proposition before you because it seems to me that if it is accepted, everything else becomes much more simple.

Observe that the policy of England takes no account of which nation it is that seeks the overlordship of Europe. The question is not whether it is Spain, or the French Monarchy, or the French Empire, or the German Empire, or the Hitler regime. It has nothing to do with rulers or nations; it is concerned solely with whoever is the strongest or the potentially dominating tyrant.[51]

Churchill invented himself as a public voice in history by showing how that voice elaborated a long-standing family and national tradition. Nothing in the historical traditions he offered us compelled the view that Hitler would be such an aggressive tyrant. It is Churchill's remarkably original insight that he accurately gave voice to the truth that Hitler was such a tyrant, perhaps the worst the world had yet seen. The important question here is not tradition but how and why Churchill found a compelling, indeed prophetic moral voice to interpret the tradition in the way he did. Churchill had earlier had the same insight about totalitarianism in the Soviet Union, regarding fascism as "the shadow or ugly child of Communism."[52] How and why did he so powerfully give voice to the political resistance to fascism?

Churchill's most important book, his six-volume *The Second World War* (1948–54), is his own narrative of this resistance, culminating in his astonishing political leadership of Great Britain in World War II. It merits close study both in terms of Churchill's quite early insight into the appeal and power of Hitler's fascism, rooted in political anti-Semitism, and his remarkably early call for resistance against both Hitler and Mussolini, braving and indicting the majoritarian forces arrayed against him, including the dominant pacifism of interwar Britain. The theater for Churchill's resistance was the House of Commons, in which parliamentarians enjoyed traditional privileges of free speech much broader than those those accorded ordinary citizens.[53] What places Churchill's resistance so clearly in the line of Garrison, Tolstoy, Gandhi, and King is his demand for and exercise of the broadest right of free speech—free from any coercion or intimidation arising from a sense of insult at the speaker's conscientious views about public matters and issues. His original draft of the Atlantic Charter makes clear his own personal views that people must "respect the right of all peoples to choose the form of government under which they will live. They are only concerned to defend the right of freedom of speech and thought, without which such choice must be illusory."[54] This liberal conception of respect for basic rights of this type frames Churchill's interpretive history of the traditions of family and nation in which he placed himself, and this conception and his own experience framed his early sense of the aggressive threat Hitler's fascism posed to Britain's peace and values.

This is shown by the ways in which Churchill sensitively describes the roots of Hitler's fascism:

> As he lay sightless and helpless in hospital during the winter of 1918 [injured after fighting for four years on the Western Front in World War I], his own personal failure seemed merged in the disaster of the whole German people. The shock of defeat, the collapse of law and order, the triumph of the French, caused this convalescent regimental orderly an agony which consumed his being, and generated those portentous and measureless forces of the spirit which may spell the rescue or the doom of mankind. The downfall of Germany seemed to him inexplicable by ordinary processes. Somewhere there had been a gigantic and monstrous betrayal. Lonely and pent within himself, the little soldier pondered and speculated upon the possible causes of the catastrophe, guided only by his narrow personal experiences. He had mingled in Vienna with extreme German Nationalist groups, and here he had heard stories of sinister, undermining activities of another race, foes and exploiters of the Nordic world—the Jews. His patriotic anger fused with his envy of the rich and successful into one overpowering hate.[55]

Hitler's politics, as described clearly in *Mein Kampf*, is thus "simple":

> Man is a fighting animal; therefore the nation, being a community of fighters, is a fighting unit. Any living organism which ceases to fight for its existence is doomed to extinction. A country or race which ceases to fight is equally doomed. The fighting capacity of a race depends on its purity. Hence the need for ridding it of foreign defilements. The Jewish race, owing to its universality, is of necessity pacifist and internationalist. Pacifism is the deadliest sin; for it means the surrender of the race in the

fight for existence. The first duty of every country is therefore to nationalise the masses; intelligence in the case of the individual is not of first importance; will and determination are the primary qualities. . . . The aristocratic principle is fundamentally sound. Intellectualism is undesirable. The ultimate aim of education is to produce a German who can be converted with the minimum of training into a soldier.[56]

Churchill understood this psychology so well and took its demonic appeal so seriously because he had himself been a soldier. But he had also been much else, drawing on traditions and relationships Hitler never knew. What apparently appalled him about Hitler's politics was the rationalization of its violence in terms of irrationalist anti-Semitism. When one of Hitler's followers offered to introduce him to the German leader, Churchill, who then knew little about Hitler, thought of him as he did about all his enemies in war: "I admire men who stand up for their country in defeat, even though I am on the other side. He had a perfect right to be a patriotic German if he chose." But Churchill went on to say: "Why is your chief so violent about the Jews? I can quite understand being angry with Jews who have done wrong or are against the country. And I understand resisting them if they try to monopolise power in any walk of life; but what is the sense of being against a man simply because of his birth? How can any man help how he is born?"[57] Hitler apparently was told about the comment and refused to meet with him.

Churchill had been powerfully influenced, both as a soldier and as a politician, by his mother's sense of ongoing social relationship with persons of diverse backgrounds and politics, including his father's and his own political enemies. His attempt to humanize even Hitler, as a victim of war trauma and humiliation, bespeaks a general tendency both in his writing about his military service and in his political life as a war leader to be magnanimous to his enemies. With respect to Jews in particular, his father's closest and most supportive friends were Rothschilds, especially Nathan Meyer Rothschild.[58] What clearly struck Churchill about Hitler was his inability to extend to him, let alone to the Jews, the sense of a common humanity. Hitler's refusal of relationship with anyone who spoke on behalf of the humanity of Jews rested on a denial of any ethical principles superior to ethnic conscience.[59] Hitler's war on the Jews was a war on the values of universal human rights (represented, for Hitler,

P.196

by the Jews), including the right of free speech, and for Churchill, respect for those rights was a necessary condition for the legitimacy of any government. What made Hitler so dangerous, as Churchill saw it, was that the psychology of his personal turn to fascism resonated with a larger political psychology of national humiliation among the German people. What Churchill saw with such clarity was that the heart of Hitler's appeal for German men in particular was a psychopathic therapy of aggressive militarism that, in service of an ethnic conscience drained of any larger sense of ethics, rested on the use of violence in a ruthlessly opportunistic way.[60] The only test for such opportunism would be its success or failure. Churchill saw clearly that this type of militarism would be emboldened by any failure to resist it.

In his public call for resistance, Churchill made this point as early as 1932, and he repeated it with an increasing sense of imminent calamity at every stage of Germany's rearmament and expansionism until World War II.[61] His calls for coercive resistance were never bellicose in the aggressive style of Hitler but were always made in terms of the necessity and proportionality of the resistance, earlier rather than later, in order to forestall what he prophetically saw as an escalation of violence in the absence of resistance. As he starkly put the point, "If you will not fight for the right when you can easily without bloodshed; if you will not fight when your victory will be sure and not too costly; you may come to the moment when you will have to fight with all the odds against you and only a precarious chance of survival. There may even be a worse case. You may have to fight when there is no hope of victory, because it is better to perish than live as slaves."[62] Even as a leader during World War II, "although exhilarated by military problems, [Churchill] was . . . never a warmonger. He disliked the loss of life in a way that Haig would have found soft-hearted, Stalin incomprehensible, and even Roosevelt a little over-cautious."[63] When he visited the carnage caused by the Germans' bombing of the East End of London, his eyes filled with tears; "a bomb blasted local woman called out, 'Look, he really cares,' and the assembled crowd burst into spontaneous cheers."[64]

The analytic power of Churchill's call for resistance during this period was tied to his understanding of the political psychology of fascism, namely, that the success of Hitler's opportunistic militarism increased his support in Germany and elsewhere (Italy and Japan) as he achieved his ends, at least until World War II, without military resistance by the liberal democracies; Hitler was then popularly known as "General Blood-less" in Germany.[65] In this period, both Hitler and Mussolini were em-boldened by what they saw as the dominance of pacifism in Britain, reflected in the 1933 passage by the students of the Oxford Union of what Churchill called "their ever-shameful resolution, 'That this House refuses to fight for King and country.'"[66] Churchill's indictment of this pacifism was that it failed to take political reality seriously, in particular to face the facts about the character of fascism, as a form of radical po-litical evil.[67] Pacifism was read by fascists in a way that confirmed and emboldened their contempt for liberal democracy: "Mussolini, like Hitler, regarded Britannia as a frightened, flabby old woman, who at the worst would only bluster and was, anyhow, incapable of making war."[68]

Churchill certainly saw the idealistic ethical appeal of pacifism: "The Sermon on the Mount is the last word in Christian ethics. Everyone re-spects the Quakers."[69] But, he argued, in the face of an enemy such as political fascism, pacifism was an irresponsible position for political lead-ers in liberal democracies: "Their duty is first so to deal with other na-tions as to avoid strife and war and to eschew aggression in all its forms, whether for nationalistic or ideological objects."[70] It does not fol-low that nonviolent resistance would not be an ethically appealing and even effective position for reformers to take in certain contexts, as it was for Garrison and King. But Churchill did object to the form it took in Gandhi.[71] Indeed, one of the reasons for his political isolation in the 1930s (in addition to his calls for resistance to fascism) was his opposi-tion to the dominant position in Britain that the proper response to Gandhi's movement was to free India from colonial rule; he argued pre-sciently that freedom would lead to sectarian violence, for which Britain would be responsible.[72]

Churchill's skepticism about Gandhi's pacifism was, like his comparable objection to British pacifism as a response to political fascism, that it failed to take seriously the irrationalist forces of religious intolerance in India in the same way that British pacifism failed to take seriously the irrationalist force of political anti-Semitism in Hitler's politics. (Churchill tartly dismissed Gandhi as "a seditious Middle Temple lawyer, now pos-ing as a fakir of a type well known in the East.")[73] Gandhi's pacifism was, as we earlier saw, much more successful when its audience was composed of Britons (to Churchill's chagrin) rather than Indians. Gandhi, who had preposterously urged civil disobedience by the Jews against Hitler, may no more have understood the dimensions of irrationalist religious hatred in Germany than he did that in India. One of the sharpest wartime exchanges between Franklin Delano Roosevelt and Churchill was over the question of India; Roosevelt had written Churchill that he should take as a model the U.S. experience under the Articles of Confederation, to be followed by something like the U.S. Constitution.[74] Churchill thought such a position would be politically irresponsible for Britain in light of the circumstances in India for the same reason that he thought Gandhi's pacifism in India was irresponsible: it failed to take seriously the irrationalism of religious hatred as a force in politics. He reflected: "The human race cannot make progress without idealism, but idealism at other people's expense and without regard to the consequences of ruin and slaughter which fall upon millions of humble homes cannot be considered as its highest or noblest form."[75] In light of the tragic dimensions of the ethnic violence in India at the time of partition, Churchill's skepticism about Gandhi's role in Indian independence was, at the end, shared by Gandhi himself, who, as a broken, remorseful man, longed for death.

Churchill's Resisting Voice, Jennie's Free Sexual Voice

Churchill is united with the other remarkable men studied here through his thought and his psychology, shown in both the demand for and the exercise of a voice that powerfully called for resistance to forms of injustice based on violence. The importance of Churchill to my study is that he shows how this thought and psychology clarify not only the voice of men who call for nonviolent resistance but also the distinctive voice of a man calling, when necessary and proportional, for violent resistance. What is common to these men is, first, a voice that resists forms of structural injustice based on violence and, second, an insistence on a courageously independent moral voice as the way to reveal how such injustice has been and continues to be maintained by violence directed against any voice that contests it.

Churchill's voice is as much directed at understanding, analyzing, and resisting the unjust force of such violence as is the voice of Garrison, Tolstoy, Gandhi, or King. Unlike these other men, he does not self-consciously appeal to the authority of the Sermon on the Mount as support for his voice. To the contrary, as we have seen, he acknowledges its

p. 199

ethical appeal but denies that it can be a basis for politically responsible action by a leader in a liberal democratic state opposing an evil such as political fascism. However, after stating and elaborating this position, he goes on to discuss the ethical obligation of a nation to keep its word in accordance with its treaty obligation, and he calls this ethical guide "honour." But honor, Churchill sees, can be given a range of interpretations—some ethical, some clearly not: "It is baffling to reflect that what men call honour does not correspond always to Christian ethics. Honour is often influenced by that element of pride which plays so large a part in its inspiration. An exaggerated code of honour leading to the performance of utter vain and unreasonable deeds could not be defended, however fine it might look."[76] We may reasonably connect these remarks with Churchill's analysis of the force and appeal of Hitler's fascism, an interpretation of a humiliated injury to a sense of male honor that expresses itself in violent moral atrocity. Churchill, like the other men we have studied, rejects this sense of honor and connects this rejection, as they do, with "Christian ethics." His alternative conception of honor, to which he appeals throughout his life as the ground for resistance to injustice, is based on the place of human rights in democratic manhood, often expressly criticizing the role honor plays in patriarchal manhood (as the rationale for the violence of a humiliated manhood). Churchill does not directly appeal, as the other men do, to the Sermon on the Mount, but the same point is implicit in what he says. Like them he insists on a free moral voice directed against codes of male honor rationalized by violence directed against any such voice. If I am right about this, Churchill, like Garrison, Tolstoy, Gandhi, and King, finds his distinctive public voice by rejecting an interpretation of male honor under which insult must lead to violence. 21:43.92

What makes Churchill distinctive is not that we can reasonably connect his voice to his mother's care; rather, it is that, in his case, the mother's care was strikingly different from any we have so far seen. It is as though with Jennie life finally imitates art, as Hester Prynne enters life only now as the mother of a son and a woman sexually freer than any Hawthorne could have imagined. It was a prominent feature of the impact of maternal care and voice on Tolstoy, Gandhi, and King that such care and voice were highly idealized and arose (as also in the case of Garrison) in the form of a mother's highly personal religion, a form of hidden transcript in which these women, like other subordinated groups, find their own ethical voice in resistance to the patriarchal voice of established churches. Tolstoy and Gandhi, for example, notably find their ethical voice in a maternal caring voice but a voice not imagined as sexual, and the interpretation ultimately accorded such voice is, for them, one that calls for the repudiation of sexuality. Churchill certainly finds his voice in relationship to his mother, but their relationship was not based on her highly personal religion; nor was it based on a mother's voice idealized as lacking free sexual voice. Thus, his voice does not call for any repudiation of sexuality. What makes Churchill's relationship to Jennie remarkable is that he related to a mother whose robust sexual voice and life were her hidden transcript. Her power as a woman was hidden in the sense that it was carefully kept by mother and son from public knowledge during the period in which they lived. (An example of the punishment visited on a woman who publicly acknowledged such values is the American punitive response to the free love arguments of Victoria Woodhull; strikingly, Woodhull escaped these horrors by emigrating to Britain and marrying there a man who knew nothing of her background.)[77] Jennie certainly both believed in and practiced what Woodhull defended in public, but this family secret between Churchill and his mother was not only carefully guarded, it was affirmatively buried under his public invention of a father in his biography of Randolph Churchill, which distorted not only his father's life but also his relationship with his son. Jennie thus kept hidden the transcript of her sexual voice and life in the same way other mothers in our study held on to a highly personal sense of religion, the transcripts of which were the relational basis on which their sons found their creative ethical voices as public men.

As mentioned earlier, Churchill always had a closer relationship with his mother than with his father.[78] He wrote of her as he saw her during this period, as "a radiant being possessed of limitless riches and power. . . . More of the panther than of the woman in her look, but with a cultivated intelligence unknown to the jungle."[79] "More of the panther than of the woman" captures exactly how unlike conventional Victorian womanhood his mother seemed to the young Churchill; for him, she was certainly not on an idealized asexual pedestal but centered in a magnetic psychic vitality that was at once dangerously alive and yet highly cultivated and intelligent. During this period, Jennie was, to be sure, preoccupied with advancing her husband's political career, but given the deterioration of the marriage, she was also focused on an intense social and sexual life with other men, including several she apparently loved deeply (notably, Count Charles Kinsky).[80] Like other children of aristocrats, Churchill was sent away to school, and his letters show "a constant hoping for visits which did not take place, of wishing for more attention in the future, and of being shunted around rather than of being automatically welcomed at home for short or long holidays."[81] Unlike her husband, however, Jennie paid closer attention to her children, changing Winston's school when he complained about brutality and insisting to her husband that they take their son with them on their European vacation.[82] After the death of her husband, Jennie's interests and ambitions shifted to her son, and he characterizes their relationship during this stage as one of remarkable equality: "I was now in the main the master of my fortunes. My mother was always at hand to help and advise; but I was now in my 21st year and she never sought to exercise parental control. Indeed she soon became an ardent ally, furthering my plans and guarding my interests with all her influence and boundless energy. She was still at forty, beautiful and fascinating. We worked together on even terms, more like brother and sister than mother and son. At least so it seemed to me. And so it continued to the end."[83]

To advance her husband's career, Jennie had innovated the "dinner of deadly enemies" alluded to earlier:

> It was thought a hazardous experiment. It proved a complete success. They were all well-bred people. They all recognized their obligations to their hostess as paramount for the time being. They were Lady Randolph's guests; that was enough. There were no hostilities. The talk flowed on smoothly. When a man found himself sent into dinner with a woman he did not speak to, his tongue was somehow unloosed; it was a truce. In some cases, ancient animosities were softened. In all, they were suspended. The guests all knew each other; and as they looked about the table, they all saw that Lady Randolph had attempted the impossible, and had conquered. A social miracle had been performed.[84]

Now, she undertook the same sort of dinners for her son: "My mother gathered constantly around her table politicians of both parties, and leading figures in literature and art, together with the most lovely beings on whom the eye could beam."[85]

Churchill certainly gives us some sense here and elsewhere of his mother's remarkable gifts at relationship, what her biographer calls "an adhesive web of love. . . . It was instinctive in everything she did, and it drew women as well as men to her."[86] What Churchill does not tell us is that her adhesive powers were an expression of her free sexual voice and that some of the men drawn into her web were current or former lovers. What we do know is that this web of love afforded her son a brilliant political education as well as connections that he was to use to advance his ambitions. At least some of these men (lovers of Jennie such as Kinsky and Cockran) offered Winston more paternal care than he had ever received from his natural father.

There is very little reliable empirical research about married women who have adulterous affairs and even less about the effects of such affairs on their relationships with their children. Dalma Heyn's *The Erotic Silence of the American Wife* (New York, 1997), for example, is based on interviews of such married women and largely focuses on the consequences, good and bad, for them and for their marriages. Heyn finds adultery is often a positive experience for women. As one woman put it, "I felt like I had been born. Like I was alive for the first time" (257). Another said, "I got my brain back" (264). Heyn observes, "If my findings of the women are surprising, perhaps subsequent findings about children will be surprising too" (178). Heyn worries that our assumptions that the effects must be negative reflects unjust gender stereotypes "because the Perfect Mother is as tenacious an icon as the Perfect Wife" (178). To do reliable research on this question, "we must examine our assumptions about a mother who rejects the role, and whether so hurts her child. The power of goodness to silence pleasure in relationships may be as detrimental to children as it is to their mothers. Children may pick up their mother's anxiety about the consequences of losing this goodness, including her fear that she may lose the capacity to be a good mother—or they may pick up their mother's excitement about finding pleasure" (178). In researching these questions empirically, Heyn herself interviews one woman about the effects of her adultery on her children. That woman, Eleanor, observes that she is less interested in a teacher's assessment of her children's work or behavior and more interested in the children themselves, listening to them and their feelings more, and she ascribes this change to her affair. Before the affair, she would "detach from my children because of my own insecurity and depression, buying the teacher's verdict about

people I knew better than she." After the affair, she sees her former attitude to her children as "a gross injustice, such a betrayal of the people I
care about, such a betrayal of my own feelings." Her previous attitude
rested on "manufactured feelings . . .—This is what a mother feels; this
is what a wife feels. The affair has made me feel the feelings of the outsider, while still giving me the authority and concern of the insider" (278).

There is every reason to think that Jennie's affairs had for her many
of the positive features Heyn's women describe, freeing her sexual voice
to find and give pleasure and thus sustaining an emotional and intellectual robustness in circumstances of a marriage turned nightmare that
would otherwise have been intolerable. Jennie's affairs may also have had
positive effects on her sons, of the type Heyn suggests. A son such as
Winston may have been excited by his mother's sense of pleasure and its
brilliant consequences for her person and way of life and indeed for his
way of life as her son. His thinly disguised portrait of his mother as Lucile in his romantic novel, *Savrola,* written in 1897, supports this view;
Churchill writes of Lucile's adulterous love for Savrola as an awakening
from disassociation (as a goddess on a pedestal) into loving relationship.[87]
Though the marriage had deteriorated, Jennie powerfully continued to
support her husband's political ambitions. She was also a much better
parent to her children than her husband was. Winston did not have the
emotional intimacy with her, as a child, that he had with Mrs. Everest,
his nanny, and his letters from school bespeak a deep longing for such
intimacy that was not fulfilled. But he knew his mother cared for and
listened to him, and early on, he may have developed a realistic sense of
her as a person whose love for her son was one among other needs and
attachments (certainly, not mythologically self-sacrificing) and that he
would have to listen and attend to her as an expression of his love and
to win her love. His ambitions for a political life like his father's were
undoubtedly formed by the political ambitions of Jennie, just as Randolph's had been.[88]

In his first vocation, military service, Churchill showed himself to be a
young man who was very conscious of himself as an actor inventing a
heroic persona on the public stage of Britain, an identity that he would
use to serve his political ambitions. There is every reason to think that the
formative audience for this performance then, as it had been in the past,
was his mother. But for this reason, Churchill was a soldier with a great
psychological difference from other soldiers who had a more familiar

patriarchal background. His ambition for a heroic manhood did not arise from a traumatic break with his mother, resolved by identification with his father; rather, his ambition arose in loving relationship to his mother's voice, including her sexual voice, which he both acknowledged and accepted. There was no psychological place here for the mythological fantasies of gender that idealize one's mother as an asexual being who is infinitely self-sacrificing—fantasies that arise from the traumatic break of any real relationship to one's mother's voice, with identification with gender stereotypes covering over the loss of such a relationship (indeed, requiring such a loss of voice and relationship). For Churchill, the psychology of manhood developed in relationship to a mother's sexual voice, a voice that made possible an adhesive web of love in terms of which the ambitions of manhood were formed and understood. We have already seen how extensive his mother's involvement was with shaping and supporting his military and political career, including her role on the nursing ship during the Boer War in which her care and concern for the wounded men bespoke the kind of maternal care she had taken with her sons (she certainly spoke of the soldiers as she would of her sons). Jennie's eye for the vulnerabilities of men as soldiers (the boy in the man) clarifies the sources of Winston's psychological gifts, including his truthful reading of the glorification of aggressive violence in Hitler's fascism.

This psychology showed itself in Churchill's sense, as an adult, of egalitarian friendship with his mother, based on an acknowledgment that, as a man and a woman, they shared so much—for example, their love of pleasure (including sexual voice and pleasure) and their political ambition. The sense of the importance of a sexual loving voice and relationship to a human life explains Churchill's remarkable voice first spoken in defense of men and women meeting in public (in opposition to the purity leagues) and later raised in parliamentary debates in defense of the right of Edward VIII to marry the woman he loved (the hostility of these debates was so intense that Churchill reported, "[It was] almost physically impossible to make myself heard").[89] This psychology explains as well why Churchill was the most relational of soldiers and of politicians, always seeking to see his enemy as human and, if feasible, resolving differences through dialogue and relationship. How far Churchill carried this relationality is shown by his observation: "I hate nobody except Hitler—and that is professional."[90] In fact, Churchill, as we have seen, had achieved remarkable insight into Hitler's demonic psychology and its appeal to Germans. Indeed, the same relationality explains his voice of resistance, in particular resistance to injustice enforced by a violently aggressive code of patriarchal manhood.

This psychology is illuminated by connecting our discussion of it in Churchill to perhaps the most psychologically profound exploration by an artist of the difficulties men have with such resistance—Joseph Conrad's *Heart of Darkness*.[91] Conrad's voice in this novel is Marlowe. Marlowe's journey into the Congo to find Kurtz is his own journey into his psychological difficulties, as a man, in coming to terms with how Kurtz, an idealist, could have been so corrupted by his experience as a colonialist to have become a genocidal murderer, writing, as an expression of his corruption, "Exterminate all the Brutes."[92] Conrad shows us that the psychology of Kurtz depends, crucially, on a mythological division between an idealized conception of women, the Intended in Belgium, and a denigrated conception, the black woman with whom Kurtz has had an affair, "savage and superb, wild-eyed and magnificent."[93] Such mythology is sustained by lies whose power derives from a code of manhood resting on a rigid gender binary that upholds the unjust demands of the code by violence against any voice that might reasonably contest its demands. The force of this mythology in Marlowe is revealed by the way in which he cannot speak the truth to the Intended about what has happened to Kurtz but instead supports her in her own mythology about Kurtz the idealist. Conrad shows us how much violent patriarchal manhood depends on the repression of such voice in men, a repression keyed to the role gender plays in patriarchal manhood (in particular the pedestal, dividing women in terms of sexual voice). Such repression of intimate voice leads to men prone to a psychology of illusion about themselves and others, including their relationships not only with women but also with men (the illusion among men, for example, of the intimacy of one's secret sharer, with whom, in fact, one has no real relationship).[94]

It is an interesting question why Conrad was even able to describe such difficulties of resistance, certainly a competence well beyond most men of his period or of any historical period. What we do know is that the striking truth of his artistic voice cost him dearly in terms of breakdowns after writing such books, which relived traumatic experiences of his childhood (the death of his own mother and later his father from imprisonment occasioned by their resistance to Russian tyranny in Poland).[95] Churchill was, like Conrad, an aristocrat and had served in the military in his first vocation (Conrad served in the British merchant marine for some twenty years); both came to regard British institutions as justified because of their liberalism, though Churchill was an insider and Conrad very much an outsider; both made sense of their military experience as men of letters; and both regarded Germany and Russia as political cultures aggressively hostile to liberal values.[96] Their greatest difference involves Churchill's relationship with his remarkable mother, which led to a psychology that did not divide women in terms of sexual voice. What may have incurred such strain for Conrad in reviving traumatic memories arose in Churchill as the more natural expression of his relationship to his mother's sexual voice. Stripped of this psychology of gender idealization and denigration, Churchill did not, like Kurtz or Marlowe, sharply divide women into idealized and denigrated, asexual and sexual. His mother, whom he loved and admired, was not therefore an asexual being but was instead admired and sexual, brilliantly humane. Churchill's way of describing his mother ("more of the panther than of the woman in her look") thus echoes Conrad's description of Kurtz's black mistress ("savage and superb, wild-eyed and magnificent"). The Intended and the mistress have, as it were, become one, known and admired through sexual voice. The psychological consequence for Churchill was that, freed of the distorting prism the honor code imposes on the human psyche, he could, like his mother, truthfully read relationship and see, as a man, how the unjust force and appeal of the patriarchal honor code rests on breaking relationship.

Churchill recognized the unjust force of such a code in Hitler's refusal to even discuss with him the question of his political anti-Semitism. The refusal showed that this personal and political psychology rested on the repression of what were, for Churchill, the most fundamental of human rights, the rights of free thought and voice; indeed, it rested on the violent attack on these human rights. Churchill's voice of resistance arose on the moral basis of such rights but also on the basis of an astonishing psychological insight into how this personal and political psychology of wounded patriarchal manhood had to aggressively war on human rights of this type both in Germany and abroad.

We can see this insight in the way Churchill described Hitler's fascism as rooted in his psychology of traumatic injury and humiliating defeat in World War I, a trauma that, building on the earlier trauma of patriarchal separation of son from mother, resolved itself in a psychologically even more extreme identification with patriarchal manhood. Claudia Koonz has recently shown, to great effect, how much the moral atrocities of Hitler's fascism were made possible by a racist conception of ethnic conscience that psychologically depended on a self-conscious program of hardening the armor of patriarchal manhood. Such hardening supported the demands of ethnic conscience by deflecting and repressing the voice of ethical conscience.[97] Hitler's fascism depended on this ideology and a supporting sociology of all-male, sometimes highly educated packs that would harness collective intelligence to the aims of moral atrocity.[98] This atrocity, Churchill saw, was made possible psychologically by an extreme conception of patriarchal manhood that rationalized aggressive violence against any voice that might reasonably protest its injustice, including the unjust ethnic and religious stereotypes that rationalized the violence (turning innocent victims into aggressors).[99] Such irrationalism was made possible by the unjust enforcement of patriarchal gender stereotypes, rationalizing aggressive violence as a response to any insult to such stereotypes, including any challenge to them.

Churchill formed his ambitions for heroic manhood, both as a soldier and as a politician, in a way quite different from the usual psychology of patriarchal manhood. The usual psychology involves the son's renouncing his relationship and identification with his mother, a traumatic break that is resolved through identification with patriarchal manhood and acceptance of gender stereotypes. These stereotypes take the form of the idealization of women in terms of those who are asexual and self-sacrificing and the denigration of those who are sexual and self-interested. Churchill came to a sense of heroic manhood in loving relationship to his mother's sexual voice, and thus he was not psychically encumbered by the mythology of gender that rationalizes patriarchal manhood. For this reason, I believe, he so clearly saw both the normative and psychological dangers posed by the extreme form of patriarchal manhood that motivated the personal and political psychology of Hitler's fascism. A psychology based on the irrationalism of remaking the world in the image of its gender mythology must war on the human relationships and voices inconsistent with its image, which is to say that it must war on liberal democracy itself. It was because Churchill was so psychologically unencumbered by patriarchal gender stereotypes, as a soldier and a politician himself, that he saw Hitler's fascism so realistically and, as it turned out, so prophetically. The same thought and psychology in Churchill explains as well why he was so brilliantly critical of the dominant British pacifism of the interwar years. He put his criticism not only in terms of a "refusal to face facts" and an "obvious lack of intellectual vigour" but also in terms of an underlying political irresponsibility, living in "illusions about an ideal world" and in "dreams."[100] Churchill indicted a political leadership incapable of the leadership required by the looming challenge of fascist aggression, a leadership delighting "in smooth-sounding platitudes, . . . desire for popularity and electoral success irrespective of the vital interest of the State, genuine love of peace and pathetic belief that love can be its sole foundation."[101] He saw in this pacifism in general what he criticized in Gandhi's pacifism in particular: the failure to take seriously the political irrationalism of extreme religious or ethnic intolerance. It was precisely because Churchill's sense of manhood arose, unlike Gandhi's and that of others, from relationship to his mother's sexual voice that he was less burdened by a gender mythology that, in repressing sexual voice, failed to take seriously the nature and appeal of structural injustices such as religious and ethnic intolerance that rested on the repression of such voice.

Churchill's voice lives on in history because, when more politically motivated leaders pandered to majoritarian opinion, his voice courageously called for resistance, by force if necessary, to the threat Germany's fascism posed to Britain's peace and liberal democracy. Churchill was, of course, a great war leader of Britain. But unlike the more politically astute Roosevelt, who was four times elected as president, Churchill was, unelected, summoned by King George VI to lead a coalition government after Prime Minister Neville Chamberlain fell in the crisis of 1940. When an election did occur in 1945, the British people, after the solidarity born of their war experience, wanted a program of social redistribution akin to what Americans had had in the New Deal, and thus they voted for the Labour candidate, rejecting Churchill. (He won the election of 1951, however, and served as prime minister from 1951 to 1955.)[102] A voice like Churchill's is not always combined with the appeal of a democratic politician precisely because such a voice often finds and speaks its truth against the opinion of democratic majorities. That makes such a voice more, not less, important to the integrity of democratic liberalism.

I have argued that what made Churchill's resisting voice possible was a relationship to his mother's sexual voice that empowered his own voice, including its critical insights into the challenge to Britain of Hitler's fascism (as well as his insights into the challenge of totalitarian communism, in notable speeches in 1919 and 1946 ["an Iron Curtain has descended"]).[103] Churchill's voice, unlike that of the other men studied in this work, called for resistance to fascism by force (and later to communism by armed deterrence). But his appeal was only for the amount of force that was necessary to stop an enemy—an enemy that, had he been listened to, could have been stopped early and without anything like the catastrophic loss of life that World War II was to involve. As a war leader, Churchill was much more concerned with human life than other leaders were, insisting that Anglo-American carnage be reduced by postponing the Second Front until 1944; later on, he was shocked by Gen. Dwight D. Eisenhower's evident willingness to use atomic weapons (his most controversial wartime decision, founded on the belief that it would decisively shorten the war, was unleashing the bombing on German cities in 1944, including the obliteration of Dresden).[104] Churchill's interest was not the force he thought necessary but the voice he, as a man, found in himself to appeal to the most basic values of human rights in speaking so brilliantly against the aggressive violence threatened, as he saw it, by the wounded patriarchal manhood of Hitler's fascism. We can see as well the force of this resisting voice when Churchill responded in the same way to Stalin's suggestion that the German problem after the war would be resolved by shooting the fifty thousand leading German officers and technicians. Churchill recorded: "On this I thought it right to say, 'The British Parliament and public will never tolerate mass executions. . . . I would rather . . . be taken out into the garden here and now and be shot myself than sully my own and my country's honour by such infamy.'"[105] As early as 1919, he had spoken about the need to resist "Bolshevist atrocities,"[106] and after World War II's opportunistic alliance between Britain, the United States, and the Soviet Union had achieved its ends, he once again powerfully called for resistance to totalitarian communism, through forms of deterrence and new forms of international (the United Nations) and European unity (including the North Atlantic Treaty Organization and a proposed United States of Europe).[107] Resisting Hitler as well as Stalin, Churchill spoke from a new conception and psychology of democratic manhood, one that found its eloquent ethical voice in relationship to the voices, including the sexual voices, of free and equal women. It is for this reason that he diagnosed with such astonishing lucidity the patriarchal heart of darkness out of which arose the monstrous political violence of both the political totalitarianisms of the twentieth century, Hitler's and Stalin's.

It is surely of interest that a man with such a relationship with his mother should have found, in his marriage to a woman with a mother quite similar to his own, one of the happiest of companionate lifetime partnerships. While Churchill's life had its periods of depression (his "black dog"), these episodes were keyed to frustrations in his political ambitions, a vulnerability not unrelated, surely, to the early conditions of his mother's love.[108] But the depressions were balanced by a remarkably happy marriage, to a woman to whom he could always turn for understanding, consolation, and often excellent political advice and support.[109] He also found much satisfaction in painting, an art his mother had taught him. It was only Churchill's relationship with his son, Randolph, that was difficult, a not unsurprising consequence, perhaps, of his own relationship (or lack thereof) with his own father.[110] On balance, Churchill found a way, as a man and a politician, to live as his mother had lived, truthful to his voice in a life both of personal happiness and astonishing political service.

//p. 211

//CHAPTER SIX

Disarming Manhood

The men studied in this volume—Garrison, Tolstoy, Gandhi, King, and Churchill—found their ethical voices through disarming manhood, in particular through stripping themselves as men of the traditional conception of manhood that regards any insult to that manhood as sufficient cause for violence. These men spoke in a new ethical voice made possible by a thought and psychology disarmed of the role violence plays in patriarchal manhood. The consequences of such voice have now been studied in some depth, empowering new types of resistance to forms of structural injustice sustained by the violence of patriarchal manhood. My argument has suggested a certain developmental psychology, shared by all these men, that illuminates how and why they came to speak in this new voice.

Opening oneself to women's antipatriarchal voices, on the view I have explored in the argument of this book, has remarkable consequences for the ethical voice of men who are thus brought to question conventional manhood and the role violence plays in manhood. But it also has potentially tragic dimensions, as we can see in the marital misery of Tolstoy, Gandhi, and King and in the growing loneliness, depression, and crippling sense of failure these men experienced. Of the five modern men studied here, only Garrison and Churchill found their voice in relationships not only with maternal caretakers but also with real women; both were in quite happy marriages, and Garrison enjoyed collaborative work with women as a radical abolitionist and abolitionist feminist. How are we to understand why disarming manhood has such benefits and costs?

The key, I believe, is that unjust gender stereotypes about men bear heavily on the voice of men in order to hold them in their patriarchal roles and on women only to the extent required to enable men to maintain

those roles. But there are many women who, though living under patriarchy, are not subject to close patriarchal regulation and thus enjoy some
freedom of voice, especially within the domain marked off as that of
women. These women give expression to an ethical voice, based on their
experience, in the form of a personal religion or a way of life exemplifying the hidden transcripts through which subordinated groups nourish
a voice of ethical resistance to their subordination. When men like those
studied here, as boys and sometimes later, give ethical significance and
weight to the voices of such women, not suppressing them as patriarchy
requires, they develop in themselves an ethical voice (giving a public expression to perceptions rooted in maternal hidden transcripts); this voice
raises questions of justice about gender itself because the voices of the
women with whom the men identify express an ethical voice independent and often critical of patriarchy (which accords authority only to the
voice of hierarchical fathers). To be in this position is so psychologically
and ethically liberating because the ethical voice of such men challenges
the role of manhood in rationalizing forms of political violence and thus
raises questions about the many forms of structural injustice that depend
on that violence.

The claim is not, then, that women enjoy a moral superiority over
men but that, standing in a different relationship to patriarchy, their
voices in their own domain are ethically freer and thus can be the basis
for a comparable freedom in the men who stay in closer relationship to
those voices despite the strictures of patriarchy to the contrary. The injustice of conventional gender stereotypes is that they divide men and
women unfairly from a sense of their common humanity. To the extent
women's voices are held less rigidly in thrall to this injustice, they give
men in relationship to them a sense of the ethical values of a common
humanity not divided by the terms of structural injustice. It is not, then,
surprising that opening one's psyche to women's voices has been necessary for the forms of ethical voice we have studied in depth in this book.
It is a feature of our developmental psychology under patriarchy that relationships with women play this role. And there is every reason to believe that the point is as urgent and important today as it has ever been,
as we are poised between patriarchal and democratic manhood both at
home and abroad.

The great historical lesson of the totalitarianisms of the twentieth
century, which almost brought civilization as we know it to cataclysmic

destruction on several occasions, is the terrifying price we pay when our technology is so much more advanced than our ethics and politics. But we know that the political violence of fascism, for example, with its genocidal murder of 6 million innocent Jews, was motored fundamentally by an aggressively political anti-Semitism and that it fed on and cultivated a sense of manhood based on codes of honor at least as old as *The Iliad*. As we saw earlier, unjust gender stereotypes were quite central to a Nazi manhood hardened even to the genocidal murder of millions.[1] And the bloody totalitarianism of Stalin's communism (including the starvation of at least 5 million peasants) was crucially fueled by an indoctrination into an ideal of the soldier constantly on duty that, as with Hitler's fascism, bizarrely justified state-imposed mass killing as self-defense.[2] It is no accident that there were close links in totalitarian political method between fascism and Soviet communism,[3] based as they were on conceptions of a hardened manhood rooted in violence against any dissent to or doubt about the terms of state-enforced structural injustice.[4]

There is every reason to believe that this political psychology remains very much in place after the end of the Cold War, for similar patterns of violence still exist, rooted in a sense of a manhood whose honor rests on violence in support of forms of structural injustice; consider the extreme religious intolerance, racism, and ethnic hatred in Bosnia, Yugoslavia, and Rwanda, as well as various forms of secular and religious terrorism and other types of state-sponsored violence.[5] Mark Juergensmeyer has persuasively analyzed the rise of fundamentalist violence, at home and abroad, in terms of a highly gendered armoring of humiliated men in a cosmic war. What triggers the violence are perceived threats to manhood: "Nothing is more intimate than sexuality, and no greater humiliation can be experienced than failure over what one perceives to be one's sexual role. Such failures are often the basis of domestic violence; and when these failures are linked with the social roles of masculinity and feminity, they can lead to public violence. Terrorist acts, then, can be forms of symbolic empowerment for men whose traditional sexual roles—their very manhood—is perceived to be at stake."[6]

The terrorism of Islamic fundamentalism is a good example of the toxic combination of technological know-how with deplorable ethical and political values, rooted, inter alia, in extreme religious intolerance (most obviously anti-Semitism). Most believers in Islam condemn such terrorism, but there is a larger problem of political culture here—a problem that makes such fundamentalism possible and that must be responsibly addressed. The political culture of most Islamic nations is problematic on two scores: its lack of separation of church and state and its sexism.[7] These are certainly interdependent problems, as it is the elaboration of the argument for toleration (underlying the separation of church and state) that makes possible the protest of forms of structural injustice, including sexism. Any religion can, I believe, be corrupted to unjust ends when political leaders corruptly use religion to entrench and legitimate their own power. Islam is only the most notable contemporary example of a phenomenon that has, at earlier historical points, afflicted other religions, notably, the various forms of Christianity before constitutional developments within dominantly Christian nations called for a separation of church and state as much in the interest of a just politics as of an authentic Christianity based on the historical Jesus of Nazareth. It would, of course, be a great mistake to suppose that these nations are still not afflicted by sectarian religious, ethnic, and gender intolerance and that such intolerance sometimes fosters ethnocentric forms of unjust imperialism. And there is no reason to think that believers in Islam cannot reasonably free themselves of the corrupt politicians who afflict them. There is also reason to think that one place to start would be in taking seriously the antipatriarchal voices of Islamic women usually not attended to.[8]

The argument of this book is that we are now in a position to make reasonable choices about manhood and thus womanhood. A conventional patriarchal manhood was once hegemonic; its codes of honor mythologically divided women into good and bad, traumatically separated men from real relationships with women, and invested the energy of manhood in violence as a response to any threat to that manhood. Such threats included any challenge to the terms of structural injustice, and they triggered a violence that repressed ethical voice. There is, however, another kind of manhood available—the democratic manhood that is illustrated in the psychology and ethics of the men under study in this book. This new genre of manhood is much less easily co-opted into forms of violence that, in fact, rest on and enforce structural injustice. Indeed, the distinctive feature of this kind of manhood is its moral competence in resisting forms of structural injustice.

We have now studied in some depth five individuals who exemplify this new conception of manhood. All of them struggled with the tradi-

p. 215

tional conception of manhood in which one's virtues as a man, including courage, were defined in terms of a sense of honor that responded to any insult by violence. What they came to see is that this conventional conception of courage crucially required the suppression of ethical voice and conscience, effectively conscripting men into the service of group aims that were never deliberatively accepted as just. If courage is the virtue that overcomes fear, these men demonstrated the courage of democratic manhood: they overcame their fear of being humiliated as men and discovered in that freedom a new and creative ethical voice, rooted in their relationships with women.

Tolstoy and Churchill, who had comparable aristocratic backgrounds and a history of military service in their nations' imperial wars, exemplify forms of such resistance—but of rather different kinds. Tolstoy came to a sense of remorse over his military career, as he increasingly saw the wars he participated in as fundamentally unjust types of theocratic imperialism, rooted in forms of structural injustice, religious intolerance, and ethnic hatred; after his ethical crisis, he turned to pacifism and celibacy. Churchill thought of Britain's imperial wars in a quite different way, believing they were justified, when they were justified, "to administer justice where all was violence, to strike the chains off the slave."[9] He criticized Gandhi for failing to take seriously the evil of the religious and ethnic intolerance that his pacifism never responsibly addressed. Churchill found his voice of resistance not in pacifism (which he powerfully criticized) and certainly not in celibacy but in resisting an extreme form of aggressive patriarchal manhood that, insulted in its humiliated sense of male honor, rationalized violence to ends of moral atrocity. Both these aristocrats and former soldiers, having disarmed manhood of violence as a response to insult, found a new ethical voice in themselves that protested the structural injustices rationalized by patriarchal manhood. This made possible a new psychology and a new conception of the virtues of manhood (including courage), one that showed itself in resistance to injustice rather than in complicity with or acquiescence in forms of unjust violence, whether as a soldier (Tolstoy) or as a political leader (Churchill).

One of the most interesting consequences of the approach I have taken to studying these men is that the virtue of courage they remarkably exemplify drew its strength from relationships with women, both maternal caretakers and the women who figured prominently in the movements

several of them energized and led. The psychology I describe thus clarifies not only the personal psychology of these men but also the larger
political psychology of the mass movements they led, including the pathbreaking role of women in those movements. The nonviolent voice of
Garrison, Gandhi, and King so empowered women to become moral
and political agents because it arose from women's experience and gave
a new ethical scope, significance, and resonance to their experience and
voices.

Finding one's ethical voice, in the way we have seen throughout this
book, does not occur in a solipsistic vacuum—for example, in the close
study of religious texts, independent of other experiences in one's life.
Four of the men I have analyzed (Garrison, Tolstoy, Gandhi, and King)
did find authority for their voices through studying the Sermon on the
Mount, but what they interpretively found in this text was a voice that
arose in relationship to maternal voices of attentive, caring love. Finding,
as a man, a voice that resists structural injustice never follows simply from
a reading of religious texts. For example, Dietrich Bonhoeffer initially
thought that Christian texts required pacifism.[10] His change in view,
which led him actively to support the abortive plot to kill Hitler, arose
from the call of his lived moral experience in confronting Hitler's mur-
derous regime, an experience that required him "to see the great events
of world history from below, from the perspective of the outcast, the sus-
pects, the maltreated, the powerless, the oppressed, the reviled—in short,
from the perspective of those who suffer."[11] Among those experiences
were his relationships within his family, in particular with his mother and
grandmother, who experienced Hitler's anti-Semitic policies as an outrageous breaking of long-standing, humane ethical relationships with
Jews (his brother-in-law was, in fact, a leader of the plot to kill Hitler
and certainly confronted Bonhoeffer with the genocidal reality of Hitler's
programs).[12] Conversely, nothing in the Huguenot theology of the
French minister Andre Pascal Trocme called for pacifism in general or
active resistance to the enforcement of Hitler's anti-Semitic programs in
Vichy France. But both his relationship with his mother and his relationship with his rather nonreligious Italian wife (who insisted that Jewish
children be given refuge and help in escaping from the police who were
rounding them up for transport to camps in Germany) fundamentally
clarify how Trocme took the important role he did in resisting Hitler's
anti-Semitic programs.[13]

Our study shows us that resistance becomes psychologically and ethically possible when the human psyche finds its voice in experiences of ethical presence in relationship to other loving, attentive persons and their voices. It is when men hold on to the truth of that ethical voice in relationship that they come to question and reject conceptions and practices, such as conventional manhood and womanhood, that not only are false by that test but that *require* the suppression of truthful voice. What underlies the psychology and ethics of resistance is the voice of the psyche revolting at conceptions and practices that rest on lies and must, to survive, kill the psyche's sense of relational truth and presence. When I speak of the armor of manhood that can be disarmed, I mean a kind of disassociation in men's experience that is so common that we have ceased to notice it, thinking that it is part of man's nature. But our study of men resisting patriarchal manhood shows us that this disassociation confuses unjust cultural arrangements with nature, in effect naturalizing injustice. Such disassociation can creatively be broken by voices arising from new forms of association and relationship, including relationships with women.

It is the psychic imperative of truth in relationship that explains why such resistance, with all its costs, is undertaken. Resistance, as we have seen throughout this study, maintains this truthful relational voice, often demanding, as King certainly did, that relations (for example, to our intimate companions and families) be accorded respect as the ties that make us human. Resistance to the terms of structural injustice protests the dehumanizing terms of irrational stereotypes that strip such relations of their human dignity. Living in the truth of such relationships requires resistance to the lies on which structural injustice thrives. It is in that sense that Gandhi was quite right to locate the resisting energy behind his protests in a sense of truthful voice.

Some of the men we studied pioneered this kind of resistance, and the truth of their voice called for voice against many forms of structural injustice—but not against one of its most pivotally important forms, sexism. Such a voice is divided against itself; it is a truthful voice tainted by elements of falsity, with the consequences we have seen (an advocacy of nonviolence that, in Tolstoy and Gandhi, myopically treated women close at hand violently). It seems a charitable but true reading of the psychology of Tolstoy and Gandhi that, even in their sexism, they held to ethical voice, despite the disastrous personal consequences they inflicted on themselves and others, because they believed, however wrongly, that the same voice that required their criticism of various forms of structural injustice required this as well. They at least had the integrity to see that the ethical voice in them, based on relational truth and presence, was fundamentally in conflict with the terms of patriarchal marriage as they knew it. Rather than compromise their ethical voice, they killed their sexuality, opting for celibacy. Martin Luther King Jr. faced a similar sense of conflict, but he opted not for celibacy but for a life of patriarchal marriage and clandestine sexuality that betrayed his sense of ethical values (and brought shame on his wife). The extremity of the choices, so destructive of their personal happiness, to which these men felt driven must show the destructive and indeed tragic power of patriarchy in intimate life against even the most profound critics of forms of structural injustice. Any injustice can be questioned except, apparently, an injustice resting on the suppression of sexual voice. The failure to question this injustice rendered Tolstoy, Gandhi, and King, who otherwise brilliantly challenged the terms of patriarchal manhood, psychologically vulnerable to the return of the repressed. Their residual assumptions of patriarchal manhood shamed and terrorized them into an isolating psychological solipsism, an emotionally ascetic discipline of celibacy or promiscuity that cut them off from intimate relationships. For this reason, each of them came to a psychological place as suicidally alone as Anna Karenina's. Friedrich Nietzsche thought the motivation to such asceticism was the revenge of the psyche against the inhuman demands of an ethics of equal respect.[14] The truth is more honorable and more pitiable: a moral contradiction in humane values of equal respect, crippling the psyche's need for voice and relationship. If even the most well-intentioned nonviolent men have difficulty coming to terms with this problem, one sees the good sense in Hester Prynne's view that, if the relations between men and women are to be put on a sound basis, men must work, as Garrison did, at hearing and listening to real women speaking in their own ethical voices, including their free sexual voices.

Our study of Winston Churchill shows us a path to democratic manhood free of these psychic contradictions, one importantly made possible by his relationship to his mother's free sexual voice lived on a scale of free love that Hawthorne could not have imagined. Her voice and life were the bases of formative relationships that enabled her son to find his own remarkable voice as a soldier and later as a statesman. Put another way, Churchill found his voice in loving relationship to his mother's sexual voice and the web of love she wove. His voice arose from a sense of real relationship to his mother's voice, the sense of excitement and pleasure he took in her brilliance and courage: "More of the panther than of the woman in her look, but with a cultivated intelligence unknown to the jungle. Her courage not less great than that of her husband."[15] For this reason, Churchill's voice was less distorted by the mythological idealization of a mother's voice that led to such contradictions in the life and psychology of Tolstoy, Gandhi, and King. Because he related to his mother on terms of respect and love for her complex individuality, he came to be, as a soldier and statesman, better able to read real relationships and individuals such as Hitler who demonically warred on all such humane relationships. Churchill was also, of course, better able as a man to stay in a loving relationship with a woman as complex as he—companion, indispensable adviser, and lover until his end. The contrast between Tolstoy and Churchill, despite the similarities in their backgrounds, could not be more stark or more instructive: one ended in a life that was ascetic and tragic, the other in a life of pleasure and relationship.[16]

My argument suggests that relationships between sons and mothers have been and may be among the most important sources of resistance to injustice, a resistance based on an ethically freer voice in both men and women. The thesis of the book is how manhood becomes armed (the violence of patriarchal manhood) and how it can be disarmed when violence is countered as the honorable response to an insulted or shamed manhood, making possible ethical voice and resistance to injustices supported by patriarchal violence. Such disarmament has been recognized and explored in each of the men studied in this work. It was made possible by a resistance learned from their mothers, but for this reason, it was also complicated when the sons' sense of their mothers' resistance was patriarchally compromised. The difficulties of such resistance arise, as we see in the problems in Tolstoy and Gandhi and even King, when relationships with women and their own sexuality reflect an idealization of motherhood that in turn reflects the patriarchal split between good and bad women. Sigmund Freud's essay *On the Universal Tendency to Debasement in the Sphere of Love* ties men's splitting of women into madonnas and whores to the so-called resolution of the Oedipus complex.[17] Freud's argument is universal only in its reflection of the near universality of patriarchal cultures. But my argument suggests that it is not universal among men and that in Churchill, for example, we may consider how the absence of this splitting of women into the idealized and de-graded enhanced the ability to read the human world (Churchill's read-ing of Hitler) and reflected the ability to stay in relationship (manifested both in Churchill's understanding of Hitler and also in his personal life—notably, his marriage). What was key here was a real relationship of a son to his mother's sexual voice and life, a sexuality that freed her to enter into a different kind of relationship to her son—neither abusive nor idealized. A mother capable of such sexual resistance to patriarchal idealization and denigration imparts the same powers of resistance to her son. It is when mothers and sons break through idealization into real, lov-ing relationship that ethical voice and emotional intelligence are brought into mutually supportive harmony rather than conflict.

There is an inherent contradiction between idealization and relation-ship. What we see in Tolstoy, Gandhi, and King is how their resistance, though rooted in relationships with women, was compromised by the idealization implicit in aspects of those relationships. Idealization covers loss, as we see so starkly in Tolstoy's loss-filled developmental psychology. If idealization is thus read as the hallmark of loss, then it becomes easier to understand why, in Tolstoy and Gandhi as well as King, relationships with women and with sexuality became so fraught with suppressed anger and anger displaced on women.

What is most original in my story about these men and their political impact is its method: the primacy I accord gender and voice in an inter-disciplinary theory that combines developmental psychology with femi-nist liberal political theory. My argument is that this political theory, usually limited to the interpretation of constitutional democracies, in fact explains important political leaders and their impact—a voice that calls on and expands the values of political liberalism, as King certainly did in the United States and Churchill did for Britain and the civilized world.[18]

Feminism, as a serious development within political liberalism, has been of growing importance since the liberal political revolutions of the late eighteenth century, a development reflected in the American struggles stretching from the work of the antebellum abolitionist feminists to the recognition of many of the central claims of justice of such feminism under current judicial interpretations of U.S. constitutional law.[19] I have analyzed the ethical voice of Garrison, Tolstoy, Gandhi, King, and Churchill as arising importantly in relationship to such developments. Only Gar-rison really saw or understood the relationship as a matter of democratic political theory. Churchill may have grasped some of the connections, but, consistent with the patriarchal pieties of the age, he wrote and published a highly distorted history of the father he barely knew, not of the mother he knew and loved so well. Churchill's actions, however, bespeak some sense of the values of liberal feminism; he voted for women's suffrage but did not support it wholeheartedly (he was alienated by the violence of British suffragettes such as the Pankhursts);[20] by contrast, the value he placed on his mother's free sexual voice would have placed him well ahead of his time and well ahead of many less ambivalent advocates of women's suffrage. We should recall that Churchill first found his political voice in arguing for a fuller freedom of men and women to associate in opposition to "the Purity Campaign of Mrs. Ormiston Chant," and that his mother had lived a life he respected that was at least as scandalous as her friend Oscar Wilde's, though she maintained a discretion about her sex life that Wilde did not.[21] (In one of his letters to her, Wilde said men were dull in comparison to a woman like her, "beautiful and brilliant" and thus "verbally inspired").[22] Churchill, consistent with his liberalism, also objected to the moralism underlying American Prohibition.[23] Some of the men here studied, notably Tolstoy, were quite antagonistic to the feminism they saw about them. But even so reactionary a figure as Tolstoy thought himself to be was, on my view of him, motivated by a search for ethical voice that questioned traditional gender stereotypes of manhood, and he should be understood as struggling with issues of voice as a man that many women were, as feminists, struggling with as women. It is Tolstoy's tragedy that he did not see the connection, but his struggle clarifies the deep relationships of often conflicted ethical men to a feminism that has a much greater impact on them than they can, as men, acknowledge.

We are now in a position to understand these connections. Garrison, Tolstoy, Gandhi, King, and Churchill discovered their ethical voices on the basis of an implicit political theory of the argument for toleration and the protest of structural injustice. This theory of political liberalism is the normative theory that justifies democratic constitutionalism, and thus these men (Tolstoy excepted) directed their arguments against citizens of the democratic constitutionalism of the United States or Britain, seeking ethically to persuade them to acknowledge and remedy policies, in particular support of forms of structural injustice, that were inconsistent with these deeper ethical values; Tolstoy shared their political liberalism but brought it to bear to criticize all forms of politics that violated his understanding of pacifism. Feminism is itself, however, an elaboration of the principles of political liberalism, as the abolitionist feminists clearly saw. All these men drew implicitly on these principles when, as men, they criticized a conception of patriarchal manhood that legitimated violence as a response to insults, upholding a code of honor that rationalized forms of structural injustice. Each of them struggled to a sense of ethical voice, developed on the basis of the authority of women's voices, that put them in critical opposition to dominant stereotypes of manhood and thus womanhood. What is so striking is the power this ethical voice had for all these men, the courage (inspired by the moral experience of women) they showed in drawing out its implications, and the prices they were willing to pay to follow its demands. A contemporary feminism will be richer and more profound when it is able to understand the place of these remarkable men in its project and when it sees the ethical power of its project in terms of the price such men have borne to do justice, as they understood justice, to its liberating insights.

Such a feminism focuses on the impact of unjust gender stereotypes not only on the voices of women and the men traditionally regarded as feminine (gay men) but also on the ferocious, even catastrophic impact of such unjust gender stereotypes on the voices of straight men, rigidly holding them into conformity with the requirements of patriarchal authority (authority deriving from the hierarchical relationships between sons and fathers). What this book has now studied in some depth is a set of men who did something very difficult for men to do, namely, resist the role accorded patriarchal authority in order to follow an ethical voice that arose from the authority they accorded the usually marginalized voices of women. It is revealing that women's voices were often accorded such authority by their sons through the hidden transcripts of a personal religion centering on an antipatriarchal interpretation of the life and teaching of Jesus of Nazareth.

It seems likely that men more fully capable of democratic manhood, as Garrison certainly was, will also be better fathers because their relationships with their wives or partners and with women generally express a freer voice that resists patriarchal demands; thus, they may themselves bring to child rearing a loving care that fosters and respects free and equal voice, including sexual voice. A mother supported by such a man need not conceal her resistance in a personal religion or way of life under the radar of patriarchy but can live such resistance more publicly in loving union with her spouse and children on terms of justice. The contemporary challenge of manhood is not the same as that faced by Garrison, Tolstoy, Gandhi, King, and Churchill because our circumstances are different today. However, what is central to their achievement (the liberating ethical powers of a free voice in men inspired by their relationships to the antipatriarchal voices of women) is very much our continuing challenge and opportunity. We face, much more self-consciously than they, the one issue that so threatened their manhood, namely, relating to women on just terms. If the issue so threatened such men, we can perhaps see why it still so threatens us, in particular as we face forms of reactionary fundamentalist political violence, at home and abroad, motored by a sense of patriarchal honor in part outraged by our values, including our liberalism and its corollary, feminism.

Such violence, when successful, challenges our manhood, a manhood now self-consciously in transition between patriarchal and democratic forms. The worry is that our response will be inconsistent with our considered values, values that include traditions of nonviolent dissent that we rightly honor. Arundhati Roy recently put the worry in the following terms: "Any government's condemnation of terrorism is only credible if it shows itself to be responsive to persistent, reasonable, closely argued, nonviolent dissent. And yet, what's happening is just the opposite. The world over, nonviolent resistance movements are being crushed and broken. If we do not respect and honor them, by default we privilege those who turn to violent means."[24] We need now, more than ever, to refresh our memories of the traditions that Roy worries we may otherwise irresponsibly forget. Americans in particular must remember our nonviolent traditions that, as in the American civil rights movement of the 1960s, were brilliantly successful at a cost in human life that, though unjustified, was small compared with "a single day of battle in the Civil War or World War II."[25] Nonviolence, in comparison to violence, may better and more humanely advance and secure justice. We need now, more than ever, to keep such nonviolent alternatives clearly, lucidly in mind. In contrast, Roy points acidly to the rise of religious fascism in Gandhi's democratic India, as politicans manipulatively encourage and fail to punish pogroms that use political violence to sustain religious and ethnic intolerance.[26] What Roy sees in her native India (the resort to violence rather than nonviolent protest) she claims to see in democratic America's comparable betrayal of the politics of Martin Luther King in its response to terrorism, both the war in Afghanistan and the war in Iraq: wounded manhood turning without compelling reason to violence.[27] Roy, a feminist, is asking the right questions, as she does, for example, when she insists we face Churchill's contradictions and our own.[28] In particular, she sees in the American wars in Afghanistan and Iraq a patriarchally grounded corruption of judgment about the aims and means of the just use of force, a corruption made possible by overwhelming feelings of shame and humiliation at the unjust use of violence against ourselves. A nation that is so patriarchally corrupted in its judgments confuses its justice and power with legitimacy in the use of force, resorting to violence unnecessarily and in ways that fuel further violence, not voice and dialogue.

Our traditions, I have argued, include both nonviolent and violent forms of ethical resistance, based on speaking in a voice, empowered by relationships to the voices of antipatriarchal women, that resists the injustices supported by the violence of patriarchal manhood. These traditions certainly include the resistance to fascism that Churchill led, which was surely a reasoned, last resort and one that should, as he urged, have been undertaken earlier when aggression was clearly threatened. But they include as well the remarkably effective forms of nonviolent resistance that we have investigated in Garrison, Tolstoy, Gandhi, and King (all inspired by Jesus of Nazareth).

What marks the psychology of these nonviolent forms of ethical resistance is a disarming of manhood that frees ethical voice not only in speakers but also in audiences. This psychology is distinguished by the justice of the claims made in their own incomparable voices, their willingness to speak truthfully in resistance to injustice, and their willingness to endure unjust treatment for thus speaking, exposing themselves to bullying condemnation, violence, and even death (Gandhi and King were murdered), thus making clear the roots of such injustice in violence against ethical voice. The values of such men are shown by the primacy they accord voice in ethical resistance, exposing their voice to free testing before impartial arbiters; they always seek reasonable consensus through dialogue in preference to the violence of wounded manhood that humiliates, provoking a cycle of violence that feeds on itself. When such voices ethically persuade in a way patriarchal violence does not, it is because their very willingness to speak in these ways enables them to address a voice in their audiences that is still alive and responsive under the armor of patriarchal manhood. Roy asks us, Are we keeping faith with such traditions, or are we allowing an enemy through insult to remake ourselves in his violently repressive patriarchal image (undertaking preemptive wars, unsupported by imminent and proportional threat, and conducting such wars in ways that contradict the values of democratic equal dignity we claim to uphold)? We need to understand ourselves and our traditions and to ask, as Roy does, the right questions, which interrogate our own psyches, including our vulnerabilities to shame and violence. If our foreign policies are based in fear and not on reasonable judgment, such corrupting fear must have, Roy suggests, a wider pernicious impact on our public life—a corruption of judgment strikingly exemplified recently, for instance, by populist support in Utah for legislation forbidding universities to ban students from carrying guns to classes.[29] Does not such a domestic public judgment, corrupted by patriarchally induced fear, thus also foster a violence it claims to combat when it demands that universities (the forums for voice and dialogue under constitutional democracy) should become yet another war zone of American contradictions? Does this situation not exemplify a larger problem in domestic policy, shown by America's highly retributive conception of criminal justice (including inhumanely excessive prison terms and conditions and the retention of the death penalty), institutions that may worsen the problem of violence they claim to combat?[30] We will not be able to ask and answer such questions, addressed to our domestic as well as foreign policies, in a responsible manner until we speak in a voice as free as those of a Garrison or King or Churchill, finding in ourselves a courage that understands and is not bullied into silence by our fears as men in transition as we are between patriarchal and democratic manhood. We need to find a courage that allows us to speak from an ethical voice rooted firmly in our democratic values. To do so, we must deliberatively map for ourselves the complex normative and psychological terrain we are negotiating.[31] I have used the close study of these five men to suggest that there is in our experience, as there was in theirs, an alternative developmental psychology, perhaps always implicit in human psychology, that can be called on and developed in ways consistent with our considered ethical values. It is not at all foreign to us but very present in their lives and movements and, to the extent these men and movements affect us, very much present in our own psychology.

00:09:46.46

When some American men protested the injustice of the Vietnam War (as King himself did[32]), we can reasonably understand the ethically creative tension in their psyches as something caused by the presence in themselves of two roads in their developmental psychology, roads that divided over patriarchal support of the war and an inner voice that called for resistance. Some of them were, notably, Catholic priests, one of whom, James Carroll, identified the priesthood with his father's patriarchal authority, experienced a growing sense of a voice rooted in his mother's religious piety that repudiated the war, and eventually left the priesthood and married.[33] Others, among them Thomas Merton, found their voice in opposition to the war very much in terms of the role Jesus played in their sense of vocation. In Merton's case, this was a sense psychologically connected to his feeling for his caring father and his sense of loss at his death.[34] Merton's life and teachings were in turn a source of the resistance to the war of other Catholic priests, notably, Daniel and Philip Berrigan (the latter eventually left the priesthood to marry).[35] Daniel Berrigan himself understood his journey into an ethical voice of resistance as breaking "bars to manhood."[36] I see in the ethics and psychology of all these men both the ethics and the psychology we have now traced in the lives of the men and movements studied in this book. It is a pattern increasingly in our midst, one that ever greater numbers of men feel moved to develop and take seriously as an alternative to a conventional manhood that they find more and more questionable, both ethically and personally.

I am one of those men, a gay man in an almost thirty year loving relationship with a partner. It is not my view that gay men are, by virtue of their sexual orientation, less drawn to patriarchy than are straight men. But one of the range of ethical and personal choices faced by gay men is the extent to which they will insist on their identity as gay men against the terms of the homophobia that afflicts them. If they make the choice to protest such homophobic disadvantage, as I have,[37] they may make the choice as a way of pursuing what I have here called democratic manhood, something they have come to value in their personal relationships; their choice reflects, in my view, the ethics and psychology we have now studied at length in this book. There is nothing inevitable or necessary in this choice. As it did in the case of all the men studied in this book, the choice may involve costs, both external and internal, that a more silent, assimilationist identity would not impose. But choices of this sort are never made in terms of such costs, which, from the perspective of a psyche rooted in what I have called free ethical voice, are not worthy considerations. There is, no doubt, a kind of courage here, but it is not the courage of conventional patriarchal manhood. In my case, though I think of both my mother and my father as maternal caretakers whose loving voices gave resonance to my sense of antipatriarchal voice, I know that whatever courage was involved in my choice was a courage I had learned not from my father but from the free ethical voice of my Italian American mother, who had an informed and intelligent view on everything and let you know it. Her religion was a very personal form of Roman Catholicism in which the sacred heart of Jesus was the voice of ethics, a voice I, otherwise quite unreligious, carry in my psyche. Her ultimate criticism of an evil such as anti-Semitism or, closer to hand, homophobia, was directed at its heartlessness. When I was considering how public a role I should take in protesting homophobia, a conversation with my mother proved decisive. It was not that she supported my choice. She was much too protective of me to sacrifice her son so easily for what seemed to her like crackpot liberal ideology. But when I confronted her with the question of whether she wanted me to lead a life that seemed to me a cowardly failure to stand by my convictions, she responded forcefully that she did not want *that*. She knew by then that my life with my companion was very like the life of loving care, passion, and egalitarian voice she had had with my father (he was deceased by then). And because she had lived with us for long periods during her desolating loneliness after my father's death, she could see how much our love meant to each of us and how much it showed itself in our love and care of her, when she most needed this kind of support. My mind was made up, then, not by what she wanted me to do but by my sense of what the ethical voice she had imparted to me required. My mother is now gone, but her voice is always with me, testing relationships in the way she did for their truth. It is the voice of this book. Isn't my story in microcosm the same one I have been telling all along?

I certainly do not think of myself as having either the voice or the courage of the men studied in this book, but they move me deeply, touching something alive in my psyche, as I trust in yours. My argument is that their psychology is much more common than we may like to think—all too ordinary, as ordinary as I am or any man is when he comes into ethical conflict with the sense of conventional manhood he has inherited, as all men today do at some point or other. It is with the commonplace, ordinary character of this conflict that I want to end this book. Democratic manhood will have a larger appeal to the extent its demands are more in line with what men reasonably want in a good life rather than the alternative. To the extent one can show that its demands are so bearable by the most ordinary of men and so rewarding, one will have made a better case for its ethical and personal appeal.

When men come to question a manhood that endorses violence against any threat to manhood (as I did when I questioned the violence of homophobia both in others and in myself), they come to experience the authority of a voice from within that is a psychology as much part of the human psyche as that of the patriarchal Oedipal psychology that represses that voice. In light of reflective ethical and personal values, the psychological route one takes is a matter of choice. What I have tried to show is that such values include the sense of oneself as a man of emotional presence in caring, loving relationship and that the psychology and ethics of resistance rest on the protection in oneself and in one's relationships of the integrity of such loving care. It is no part of my argument that, after feminist transformation on terms of justice, gender differences between men and women will not exist, but neither will the absurd and inhuman supposition that men's psyches do not as much live, breathe, and grow in loving relationship to other persons at all points in their lives as do the psyches of women. A manhood that could live in the truth—a truth women have always known—that all human psyches thrive only in such conditions is surely a manhood worth having. And if we do not have it yet in hand, it is well worth struggling for through a love, political and personal, that will bring it to birth in our psyches.

//p 229

NOTES

INTRODUCTION

1. See, for example, Leo Braude, *From Chivalry to Terrorism: War and the Changing Nature of Masculinity* (New York: Alfred A. Knopf, 2003).

2. Arundhati Roy, *War Talk* (Cambridge, MA: South End Press, 2003), 4.

3. David L. Chappell, *A Stone of Hope: Prophetic Religion and the Death of Jim Crow* (Chapel Hill: University of North Carolina Press, 2004), 153.

4. See David Lodge, *Consciousness and the Novel: Connected Essays* (Cambridge, MA: Harvard University Press, 2002), 42, 45, 51–52, 56, 58–61.

5. See, for my own works along these lines, David A. J. Richards, *Toleration and the Constitution* (New York: Oxford University Press, 1986); *Foundations of American Constitutionalism* (New York: Oxford University Press, 1989); *Conscience and the Constitution: History, Theory, and Law of the Reconstruction Amendments* (Princeton: Princeton University Press, 1993); *Women, Gays, and the Constitution: The Grounds for Feminism and Gay Rights in Culture and Law* (Chicago: University of Chicago Press, 1998); and *Free Speech and the Politics of Identity* (Oxford: Clarendon Press, 1999).

6. See, on this development, Richards, *Women, Gays, and the Constitution.*

7. For feminist works that anticipate the analysis I offer, see Dorothy Dinnerstein, *The Mermaid and the Minotaur: Sexual Arrangements and Human Malaise* (New York: Harper & Row, 1976); Nancy J. Chodorow, *The Reproduction of Mothering: Psychoanalysis and the Sociology of Gender* (Berkeley: University of California Press, 1978).

8. See Carol Gilligan, *In a Different Voice: Psychological Theory and Women's Development* (Cambridge, MA: Harvard University Press, 1982).

9. See Carol Gilligan, *The Birth of Pleasure: A New Map of Love* (New York: Vintage Books, 2003).

10. Richards, *Women, Gays, and the Constitution.*

11. For an excellent recent study on which I draw throughout my argument, see Henry Mayer, *All on Fire: William Lloyd Garrison and the Abolition of Slavery* (New York: St. Martin's Griffin, 1998).

CHAPTER ONE

1. For a fuller discussion of the abolitionists in general and the radical abolitionists in particular, see Richards, *Conscience and the Constitution.*

2. For a fuller discussion of this development, see Richards, *Women, Gays, and the Constitution.*

3. Mayer, *All on Fire,* 222–28.

4. Ibid., 577–80.

5. For a fuller examination of the argument in Locke and Bayle and its American elaboration, notably by Jefferson and Madison, see Richards, *Toleration and the Constitution,* 89–128.

6. See Gavin I. Langmuir, *Toward a Definition of Anti-Semitism* (Berkeley: University of California Press, 1990), and *History, Religion, and Anti-Semitism* (Berkeley: University of California Press, 1990).

7. See Richards, *Women, Gays, and the Constitution.*

8. William H. Chafe, *Women and Equality: Changing Patterns in American Culture* (New York: Oxford University Press, 1977), 77; on the similar methods of repression, see ibid., 58–59, 75–76.

9. Cited in Langmuir, *History, Religion, and Anti-Semitism,* 294.

10. On segregated education, see *Brown v. Board of Education,* 347 U.S. 483 (1954); on miscegenation laws, see *Loving v. Virginia,* 388 U.S. 1 (1967); cf. *McLaughlin v. Florida,* 379 U.S. 184 (1964).

11. For citations and commentary, see Richards, *Conscience and the Constitution,* 80–89, and *Women, Gays, and the Constitution,* 182–90.

12. For citations and commentary, see Richards, *Women, Gays, and the Constitution,* 182–90.

13. See Harriet A. Jacobs, *Incidents in the Life of a Slave Girl,* ed. Jean Fagan Yellin (1861; reprint, Cambridge, MA: Harvard University Press, 1987). For important commentaries, see Deborah M. Garfield and Rafia Zafar, eds., *Harriet Jacobs and "Incidents in the Life of a Slave Girl"* (Cambridge: Cambridge University Press, 1996).

14. See C. Vann Woodward and Elisabeth Muhlenfeld, *The Private Mary Chesnut: The Unpublished Civil War Diaries* (New York: Oxford University Press, 1984), 42.

15. *Thoughts on African Colonization* (1832; reprint, New York: Arno Press and the New York Times, 1968).

16. Mayer, *All on Fire,* 69.

17. Ibid., 134.

18. For Garrison's identification with Jesus, see ibid., 125, 204–5, 210, 224, 449.

19. Mayer, *All on Fire,* 203–5.

20. Ibid., 207.

21. Ibid., 202.

22. See Richards, *Women, Gays, and the Constitution,* 102–14; Mayer, *All on Fire,* 285–99.

23. See, for example, Kenneth S. Greenberg, *Honor and Slavery* (Princeton: Princeton University Press, 1996); Joanne B. Freeman, *Affairs of Honor: National Politics in the New Republic* (New Haven: Yale University Press, 2001); and Bertram Wyatt-Brown, *Southern Honor: Ethics and Behavior in the Old South* (New York: Oxford University Press, 1982).

24. Mayer, *All on Fire,* 264–69.

25. See Adin Ballou, *Christian Non-resistance, in All Its Important Bearings, Illustrated and Defended* (1848; reprint, Philadelphia: Jerome S. Ozer, 1972).

26. Mayer, *All on Fire,* 266, 557–58.

27. Ibid., 356.

28. Ibid., 465.

29. See William Lloyd Garrison, "Declaration of Sentiments of the American Anti-Slavery Convention," reprinted in Garrison, *Selections from the Writings and Speeches of William Lloyd Garrison* (Boston: R. F. Wallcut, 1852), 68–69.

30. Ibid.

31. Richards, *Conscience and the Constitution,* 50–51.

32. Garrison, "Declaration of Sentiments," 67, and Garrison, *Thoughts on African Colonization,* 94 (emphasis in original).

33. See, for full discussion of this development and its legitimacy, Richards, *Free Speech.*

34. Mayer, *All on Fire,* 498, 503, 520.

35. See, on the shifts in Garrison's position over time, ibid., 222–28, 249–51, 264, 448–50, 479–80, 520–21.

36. Ibid., 249–51, 264.

37. Ibid., 249–51.

38. Ibid., 250.

39. See, in general, David Potter, *The Impending Crisis, 1848–1861,* ed. Don E. Fehrenbacher (New York: Harper & Row, 1976).

40. Mayer, *All on Fire,* 306–7, 413.

41. Elizabeth Hall Witherell, ed., *Henry David Thoreau: Collected Essays and Poems* (New York: Library of America, 2001), "Civil Disobedience," 203–24, quote at p. 211.

42. For Thoreau's speeches in praise of Brown, see "A Plea for Captain John Brown," in Henry D. Thoreau, *Reform Papers,* ed. Wendell Glick, 111–38 (Princeton: Princeton University Press, 1973); "Martyrdom of John Brown," ibid., 139–43; "The Last Days of John Brown," ibid., 145–53. For commentary on Thoreau's support of Brown and his abolitionist stance in general, see Daniel Walker Howe, "Henry David Thoreau on the Duty of Civil Disobedience," an inaugural lecture delivered before the University of Oxford on May 21, 1990 (Oxford: Clarendon Press, 1990).

43. Thoreau, *Walden,* in *Henry David Thoreau,* ed. Robert F. Sayre, 321–588 (New York: Library of America, 1985), 490–500. For illuminating commentary, see Stanley Cavell, *The Senses of Walden* (Chicago: University of Chicago Press, 1992), 83–87.

44. See Nathaniel Hawthorne, *The Scarlet Letter* (1850; reprint, New York: Penguin, 1983).

45. For a discussion that has inspired mine, see Carol Gilligan, *The Birth of Pleasure,* 131–35.

46. Ibid., 154.

47. See Nina Baym's introduction to Hawthorne, *The Scarlet Letter,* vii–xxix.

48. Leila Ahmed, *A Border Passage: From Cairo to America—A Woman's Journey* (New York: Farrar, Straus and Giroux, 1999), 120–27.

49. See James G. Scott, *Domination and the Arts of Resistance: Hidden Transcripts* (New Haven: Yale University Press, 1990).

50. Gilligan, *The Birth of Pleasure* (2002 ed.), 4–5.

51. J. G. Peristiany, ed., *Honour and Shame: The Values of Mediterranean Society* (Chicago: University of Chicago Press), 66–67.

52. Ibid., 253–54, 256–57.

53. Ibid., 42–53.

54. See David I. Kertzer, *Sacrifices for Honor: Italian Infant Abandonment and the Politics of Reproductive Control* (Boston: Beacon Press, 1993).

55. See David D. Gilmore, ed., *Honour and Shame and the Unity of the Mediterranean* (Washington, DC: American Anthropological Association, 1987), 110.

56. See David A. J. Richards, *Tragic Manhood and Democracy: Verdi's Voice and the Powers of Musical Art* (Brighton, UK: Sussex Academic Press, 2004).

57. Gilligan, *The Birth of Pleasure* (2002 ed.), 14–17, 89–91, 161–63, 178–79, 204.

58. I explore both this ethics and its associated moral psychology in David A. J. Richards, *A Theory of Reasons for Action* (Oxford: Clarendon Press, 1971).

59. Virginia Woolf, *Three Guineas* (San Diego: Harcourt Brace, 1938), 102.

60. Sara Ruddick, *Maternal Thinking: Toward a Politics of Peace* (Boston: Beacon Press, 1989), 38.

61. Ibid., 41.

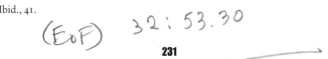

(EoF)   32: 53.30

62. Ibid., 119–23.

63. See, on this phenomenon in infancy, Daniel N. Stern, *The Interpersonal World of the Infant: A View from Psychoanalysis and Developmental Psychology* (New York: Basic Books, 1985).

64. See Sara Ruddick, *Maternal Thinking,* 148–51, 166, 182–83, 169–70.

65. Ibid., 176.

66. This might show itself in reading this alternative developmental story as a narrative of the etiology of homosexuality. In my view, it would be a developmental strength in gay men if their development included a maternal care like that described by Ruddick, but it is clear that not all gay men come from such a background; further, it is certainly quite clear that many straight men also profit from such backgrounds (as we see in the men studied in this book). For one plausible view of the character of close relations with their mothers of gay men, see Richard Green, *The "Sissy Boy Syndrome" and the Development of Homosexuality* (New Haven: Yale University Press, 1987).

67. See William Ian Miller, *Bloodtaking and Peacemaking: Feud, Law, and Society in Saga Iceland* (Chicago: University of Chicago Press, 1990), 305.

68. See William Ian Miller, *Humiliation and Other Essays on Honor, Social Discomfort, and Violence* (Ithaca, NY: Cornell University Press, 1993), 196.

69. See, in general, Kenneth S. Greenberg, *Honor and Slavery* (Princeton: Princeton University Press, 1996); Pieter Spierenburg, *Men and Violence: Gender, Honor, and Rituals in Modern Europe and America* (Columbus: Ohio State University Press, 1998); Richard E. Nisbett and Dov Cohen, *Culture of Honor: The Psychology of Violence in the South* (Boulder, CO: Westview Press, 1996).

70. See Joanne B. Freeman, *Affairs of Honor: National Politics in the New Republic* (New Haven: Yale University Press, 2001); Bertram Wyatt-Brown, *Southern Honor: Ethics and Behavior in the Old South* (New York: Oxford University Press, 1982).

71. See James Gilligan, *Violence: Reflections on a National Epidemic* (New York: Vintage Books, 1997); Chris Hedges, *War Is a Force That Gives Us Meaning* (New York: Public Affairs, 2002); Mark Juergensmeyer, *Terror in the Mind of God: The Global Rise of Religious Violence* (Berkeley: University of California Press, 2000); Amin Maalouf, *In the Name of Identity: Violence and the Need to Belong,* trans. Barbara Bray (New York: Arcade Publishing, 2000); and Michael Ignatieff, *The Warrior's Honor: Ethnic War and the Modern Conscience* (New York: Henry Holt, 1997).

72. See Scott, *Domination and the Arts of Resistance.*

73. Cited in Mayer, *All on Fire,* 224.

74. See Leo Tolstoy, *The Kingdom of God Is within You: Christianity Not as a Mystic Religion but as a New Theory of Life,* trans. Constance Garnett (1894; reprint, Lincoln: University of Nebraska Press, 1984), 101; Robert Ellsberg, ed., *Gandhi on Christianity,* (Maryknoll, NY: Orbis Books, 1991), 19; and Martin Luther King Jr., "Loving Your Enemies," in *A Knock at Midnight: Inspiration from the Great Sermons of Reverend Martin Luther King, Jr.,* ed. Clayborne Carson and Peter Holloran, 41–60 (New York: Warner Books, 2000), quote at p. 41.

75. Thomas à Kempis, *The Imitation of Christ,* ed. Paul M. Bechtel (Chicago: Moody Press, 1984), 168–73.

76. For a good historical study, see Roland H. Bainton, *Christian Attitudes toward War and Peace: A Historical Survey and Critical Re-evaluation* (Nashville, TN: Abingdon Press, 1960). Also see, for example, John Howard Yoder, *The Original Revolution: Essays on Christian Pacifism* (Scottdale, PA: Herald Press, 1998); Stanley Hauerwas, *The Peaceable Kingdom: A Primer in Christian Ethics* (Notre Dame, IN: University of Notre Dame Press, 1983); Stanley Hauerwas, *With*

the Grain of the Universe: The Church's Witness and Natural Theology (Grand Rapids, MI: Brazos Press, 2001).

77. On Garrison in this regard, see Mayer, *All on Fire,* 448–50, 479–80, 520–21; on King and his consistent defense of this position throughout his life, see Martin Luther King Jr., *A Testament of Hope: The Essential Writings of Martin Luther King, Jr.,* ed. James M. Washington (San Francisco: Harper & Row, 1986), 56, 389, 390–91, 571, 589–90.

78. For Tolstoy's most sustained discussions of his conception of religion and ethics, see *My Religion,* in Tolstoy, *My Religion; On Life; Thoughts on God; On the Meaning of Life,* trans. Leo Wiener (Boston: Dana Estes, 1904), 3–224, and *On Life,* ibid., 225–408; for an illuminating commentary, see Richard F. Gustafson, *Leo Tolstoy: Resident and Stranger* (Princeton: Princeton University Press, 1986), especially 403–55. On Gandhi, see Mohandas K. Gandhi, *An Autobiography: The Story of My Experiments with Truth,* trans. Mahadev Desai (Boston: Beacon Press, 1993), 136–37.

79. See Paula Fredriksen, *From Jesus to Christ,* 2nd ed. (New Haven: Yale University Press, 2000), 177–204. Other important studies along these lines are: Geza Vermes, *Jesus the Jew: A Historian's Reading of the Gospels* (1973; reprint, Philadelphia: Fortress Press, 1981); Vermes, *Jesus and the World of Judaism* (London: SCM Press, 1983); Vermes, *The Religion of Jesus the Jew* (Minneapolis: Fortress Press, 1993); Vermes, *The Changing Faces of Jesus* (New York: Viking Compass, 2001); David Flusser, *Jesus* (Jerusalem: Hebrew University Magnes Press, 2001); Flusser, *Judaism and the Origins of Christianity* (Jerusalem: Hebrew University Magnes Press, 1988); Paula Fredriksen, *Jesus of Nazareth, King of the Jews: A Jewish Life and the Emergence of Christianity* (New York: Alfred A. Knopf, 2000); E. P. Sanders, *Jesus and Judaism* (Philadelphia: Fortress Press, 1985); Sanders, *The Historical Figure of Jesus* (London: Allen Lane, 1993); John P. Meier, *A Marginal Jew: Rethinking the Historical Jesus,* 3 vols. (New York: Doubleday, 1991–2001); David Daube, *The New Testament and Rabbinic Judaism* (Peabody, MA: Hendrickson, 1998); and A. N. Wilson, *Jesus: A Life* (New York: Fawcett Columbine, 1992).

80. See Flusser, *Judaism,* 509–14, and Vermes, *Religion of Jesus,* 40–41.

81. See, for a good examination of this contrast, Walter Kaufmann, *Critique of Religion and Philosophy* (Princeton: Princeton University Press, 1958), 278–85.

82. Vermes, *Religion of Jesus,* 152.

83. Vermes, *The Changing Faces of Jesus,* 174.

84. Ibid., 220.

85. Martin Buber, *I and Thou,* trans. Walter Kaufmann (New York: Scribner's, 1970), 66–67.

86. Ibid., 117.

87. For a good discussion, see Meier, *A Marginal Jew,* 1:332–42 (for comment on Matt. 19–12, see 342–43).

88. Ibid., 3:73–80.

89. Ibid., 3:75.

90. For a good discussion, see Ben Witherington III, *Women and the Genesis of Christianity* (Cambridge: Cambridge University Press, 1990), 52–64.

91. For good discussion of both these events, see ibid., 65–74.

92. A. N. Wilson, *Jesus: A Life* (New York: Fawcett Columbine, 1992), 5; see also 67–68.

93. Ibid., 151.

94. See Witherington, *Women,* xiv; see also 153.

95. For plausible arguments along these lines, see Rosemary Radford Ruether, *Sexism and God-Talk: Toward a Feminist Theology* (Boston: Beacon Press, 1993); Elisabeth Schussler Fiorenza, *Jesus: Miriam's Child, Sophia's Prophet* (New York: Continuum, 1994); Fiorenza, *In Memory of*

p234 Notes to pages 32–36

Her: A Feminist Theological Reconstruction of Christian Origins (New York: Crossroad, 2002); Fiorenza, ed., *Searching Scriptures,* vol. 1, *A Feminist Introduction* (New York: Crossroad, 1993); Fiorenza, ed., *Searching the Scriptures,* vol. 2, *A Feminist Commentary* (New York: Crossroad Publishing, 1994); and Karen L. King, *The Gospel of Mary of Magdala: Jesus and the First Woman Apostle* (Santa Rosa, CA: Polebridge Press, 2003).

96. Moses thus speaks to God of his loving demands as maternal: "Did I conceive all these people? Did I give birth to them, that you should say to me, 'Carry them in your bosom, as a nurse carries a sucking child,' to the land that you promised on oath to their ancestors?" (Num. 10:11). *The New Oxford Annotated Bible* (New York: Oxford University Press, 1991), 181. For relevant commentary, see Aaron Wildavsky, *The Nursing Father: Moses as a Political Leader* (Tuscaloosa: University of Alabama Press, 1984). Isaiah not only describes the human response to God in terms of a woman in labor (Isa. 12:8, 21:3, 26:17) but also describes God's prophetic love in such terms: "I will cry out like a woman in labor, / I will gasp and pant" (Isa. 42:14). *The New Oxford Annotated Bible,* 923. See also Isaiah 40:11: "He will feed his flock like a shepherd; / he will gather the lambs in his arms, / and carry them in his bosom, and gently lead the mother sheep." Ibid., 918. A Qumran hymn speaks of God's love as maternal: "And as a woman who tenderly loves her babe, so does Thou rejoice in them." Cited in Vermes, *Religion of Jesus,* 177.

97. Erik H. Erikson, "The Galilean Sayings and the Sense of 'I,'" *Yale Review* 70, no. 3 (1981): 321–62, quote at p. 349.

98. W. E. Albright and C. S. Mann, *The Anchor Bible: Matthew* (New York: Doubleday, 1971), 68.

99. Ibid., 69, n. 39. Perhaps, as Joachim Jeremias argues, Jesus is speaking not of a general insult but "of a quite specific insulting blow: the blow given to the disciples of Jesus as heretics." Joachim Jeremias, *The Sermon on the Mount* (London: Athlone Press, 1961), 27.

100. David Daube, *The New Testament and Rabbinic Judaism* (Peabody, MA: Hendrickson, 1998), 258–59.

101. See W. D. Davies, *The Setting of the Sermon on the Mount* (Cambridge: Cambridge University Press, 1964), 427.

102. See Flusser, *Judaism,* 193–201.

103. See Vermes, *The Changing Faces of Jesus,* 275.

104. Meier, *A Marginal Jew,* 2:149.

105. Cited in ibid., 2:148–49.

106. See Raymond E. Brown, *The Anchor Bible: The Gospel According to John I–XII* (New York: Doubleday, 1966), 332.

107. Ibid., 335.

108. On this tradition, see Abraham Heschel, *The Prophets* (New York: Perennial Classics, 2001).

109. *The Bible: Authorized King James Version,* edited with an introduction and notes by Robert Carroll and Stephen Prickett (Oxford: Oxford University Press, 1998), 45.

110. Meier, *A Marginal Jew,* 3:495, 623.

111. *The Bible: Authorized King James Version,* 40.

112. Cited in Flusser, *Jesus,* 166.

113. See Richard Alston, "Arms and the Man: Soldiers, Masculinity, and Power in Republican and Imperial Rome," in *When Men Were Men: Masculinity, Power and Identity in Classical Antiquity,* ed. Lin Foxhall and John Salmon, 205–23 (London: Routledge, 1998), and Aldo Schiavone, *The End of the Past: Ancient Rome and the Modern West,* trans. Margery J. Schneider (Cambridge, MA: Harvard University Press, 2000).

114. For an illuminating discussion, see Flusser, *Jesus,* 155–73.

115. On the Zealots and Jesus's relation to them, see Meier, *A Marginal Jew,* 3:205–8, 565–69.

116. See Donald S. Lopez Jr., *The Story of Buddhism: A Concise Guide to Its History and Teachings* (San Francisco: Harper, 2001), 73–74. See also Walpola Rahula, *What the Buddha Taught* (New York: Grove Press, 1974), 97, on universal love: "Just as a mother would protect her own child even at the risk of her own life, even so let one cultivate a boundless heart towards all beings."

117. Iris Murdoch, *Metaphysics as a Guide to Morals* (New York: Allen Lane, 1992), 484 (emphasis in original).

118. Iris Murdoch, *The Sovereignty of Good* (London: Routledge, 1971), 29.

119. Ibid., 51–52, 93, 100.

120. On the capacity for love, see ibid., 65; on attachments, see ibid., 69, 89, 100.

121. Gandhi, *Autobiography,* 68.

122. See Caroline Walker Bynum, *Jesus as Mother: Studies in the Spirituality of the High Middle Ages* (Berkeley: University of California Press, 1982).

123. The New Oxford Annotated Bible (New York: Oxford University Press, 1991), 15.

124. See Sigmund Freud, "On the Universal Tendency to Debasement in the Sphere of Love," in *The Standard Edition of the Complete Psychological Works of Sigmund Freud,* ed. James Strachey, vol. 11, 177–90 (London: Hogarth Press, 1975).

125. See, on the first point here, Judith Herman, *Trauma and Recovery* (New York: Basic Books, 1997), for example, 105–6.

CHAPTER TWO

1. His support included assistance to the persecuted Dukhobors religious sect, to whom he donated the proceeds of his late novel *Resurrection,* making possible their emigration to Canada. See A. N. Wilson, *Tolstoy: A Biography* (New York: W. W. Norton, 1988), 433–34, 437, 445.

2. See Martin Green, *Tolstoy and Gandhi, Men of Peace: A Biography* (New York: Basic Books, 1983); Green, *The Origins of Nonviolence: Tolstoy and Gandhi in Their Historical Settings* (University Park: Pennsylvania State University Press, 1986).

3. See Henri Troyat, *Tolstoy,* trans. Nancy Amphoux (New York: Grove Press, 1967) (first published in French in 1965), and Wilson, *Tolstoy.* The shorter studies include Romain Rolland, *Tolstoy,* trans. Bernard Miall (Port Washington, NY: Kennikat Press, 1911), and John Bayley, *Leo Tolstoy* (Plymouth, UK: Northcote House, 1997).

4. Wilson, *Tolstoy,* 11.

5. Ibid.

6. Troyat, *Tolstoy,* 4.

7. Wilson, *Tolstoy,* 12.

8. Ibid., 24.

9. Ibid., 27.

10. Quoted in ibid., 88.

11. Troyat, *Tolstoy,* 62, 66, 86, 99.

12. Ibid., 34.

13. Ibid., 88, 336.

14. Ibid., 136, 209–12.

15. Wilson, *Tolstoy,* 130. The event involved pushing one of the Islavin children, Lyubov Islavin, off the balcony where they were playing, allegedly to spare her the attentions of other little boys. Wilson asks of this memory: "At the age of ten (and she eleven) is this probable?" (130). The incident shows, Wilson suggests, Tolstoy's tendency to make girls into symbols of purity and innocence, who must, by violence, be protected from corruption by other boys.

16. Troyat, *Tolstoy,* 261.

17. Quoted in ibid., 396.

18. Quoted in Wilson, *Tolstoy,* 83.

19. See Leo Tolstoy, *Childhood, Boyhood, Youth,* trans. Rosemary Edmonds (London: Penguin, 1964), and *The Sebastopol Sketches,* trans. David McDuff (London: Penguin, 1986).

20. See Leo Tolstoy, *The Cossacks,* in Leo Tolstoy, *Great Short Works,* trans. Louise and Aylmer Maude, with an introduction by John Bayley (New York: Perennial Library, 1967), 83–243.

21. His work dealing with domestic life before his marriage, *Family Happiness,* while written from the point of view of a woman, lacks the kind of penetrating insight into women and sense of their complexity and contradictions that we find in these later great novels; see John Bayley, *Tolstoy and the Novel* (Chicago: University of Chicago Press, 1988), 288–93. See Leo Tolstoy, *Family Happiness,* in *Great Short Works,* 3–81.

22. Wilson, *Tolstoy,* 123–41; 145–74.

23. Ibid., 132–33.

24. Quoted in ibid., 126.

25. Troyat, *Tolstoy,* 88.

26. Leo Tolstoy, *War and Peace,* trans. George Gibian, Norton Critical Edition, 2nd ed. (New York: W. W. Norton, 1996), 175–86, 834–48, 1006–19.

27. S. A. Tolstaia, *The Diary of Tolstoy's Wife, 1860–1891,* trans. Alexander Werth (New York: Payson and Clarke, 1928), 42.

28. Ibid., 48–49.

29. Ibid., 229–30.

30. Wilson, *Tolstoy,* 206.

31. Troyat, *Tolstoy,* 257.

32. Ibid., 274, 469.

33. Tolstaia, *Diary,* 262.

34. Leo Tolstoy, *What Then Must We Do?* trans. Aylmer Maude (Devon, UK: Green Books, 1991), 230.

35. Cited in Wilson, *Tolstoy,* 466–67.

36. Ibid., 213–28.

37. Bayley, *Tolstoy and the Novel,* 104.

38. Ibid., 105.

39. Wilson, *Tolstoy,* 217.

40. Tolstoy, *War and Peace,* 419–23, 498–534.

41. See Alexander Pushkin, *Eugene Onegin,* trans. Charles Johnson with an introduction by John Bayley (London: Penguin, 1979). On Pushkin's influence and achievement, see John Bayley's introduction to *Eugene Onegin,* 9–28. See also Bayley, *Pushkin: A Comparative Commentary* (Cambridge: Cambridge University Press, 1971).

42. Bayley, *Tolstoy and the Novel,* 181.

43. Tolstoy, *War and Peace,* 1020, 1022.

44. Ibid., 989.

45. Quoted in Wilson, *Tolstoy,* 249–50.

46. Leo Tolstoy, *Anna Karenina: A Novel in Eight Parts,* trans. Richard Pevear and Larissa Volokhonsky (New York: Viking, 2000), 1.

47. Ibid., 41, 162, 488–90; cf. Levin's meeting his dying brother's mistress, a former prostitute, ibid., 88–92.

48. Ibid., 637–39, 747–48.

49. Tolstoy, *What Then Must We Do?* 230.

50. Tolstoy, *Anna Karenina,* xxii.

51. Wilson, *Tolstoy,* 216–17.

52. Tolstaia, *Diary,* 231.

53. Tolstoy, *Anna Karenina,* 327, 387–89, 391.

54. See Amy Mandelker, *Framing Anna Karenina: Tolstoy, the Woman Question, and the Victorian Novel* (Columbus: Ohio State University Press, 1993).

55. Wilson, *Tolstoy,* 287–88.

56. Hawthorne, *The Scarlet Letter,* 141.

57. Tolstoy, *Anna Karenina,* 694, 700, 695, 695–96, 700, 701.

58. Sigmund Freud, "'Civilized' Sexual Morality and Modern Nervous Illness," in *The Standard Edition of the Complete Psychological Works of Sigmund Freud,* vol. 9 (1906–1908), ed. James Strachey (London: Hogarth Press, 1959), 181–204, quote at p. 199.

59. For a similar view of Tolstoy's identification with Anna, see Bayley, *Tolstoy and the Novel,* 201.

60. Leo Tolstoy, *Confession,* trans. David Patterson (New York: W. W. Norton, 1983).

61. Wilson, *Tolstoy,* 299.

62. Ibid., 312.

63. Ibid.

64. Tolstoy, *Confession,* 25.

65. Wilson, *Tolstoy,* 313.

66. Tolstoy, *Confession,* 27.

67. Wilson, *Tolstoy,* 313.

68. Tolstoy, *Confession,* 32.

69. Ibid., 30–31.

70. Ibid., 33.

71. Ibid., 73.

72. Tolstoy, *Anna Karenina,* 238, 678, 681.

73. Bayley, *Tolstoy and the Novel,* 201–3.

74. Troyat, *Tolstoy,* 257.

75. See, for relevant psychoanalytic exploration of this *kind* of identification, Juliet Mitchell, *Mad Men and Medusas: Reclaiming Hysteria* (New York: Basic Books, 2000).

76. Tatyana Tolstaya, *Pushkin's Children: Writings on Russia and Russians,* trans. Jamey Gambrell (Boston: Houghton Mifflin, 2003), 82, 83.

77. In Leo Tolstoy, *Great Short Works,* see *The Death of Ivan Ilych,* 245–302, *The Kreutzer Sonata,* 353–449, *Father Sergius,* 501–46, and *Hadji Murad,* 547–668.

78. Troyat, *Tolstoy,* 547–48.

79. Ibid., 415.

80. Tolstoy, *Confession,* 32.

81. Ibid., 73.

82. See Richard F. Gustafson, *Leo Tolstoy: Resident and Stranger—A Study in Fiction and Theology* (Princeton: Princeton University Press, 1986), 14, 30, 66–67, 202, 210, 455.

83. See Wilson, *Tolstoy,* 314–16.

84. For an illuminating treatment of Tolstoy's theological views in relation to his fiction, see Gustafson, *Leo Tolstoy.*

85. See Leo Tolstoy, *The Four Gospels Harmonized and Translated,* vol. 1, trans. Leo Wiener (Boston: Dana Estes, 1904); Tolstoy, *The Four Gospels Harmonized and Translated,* vol. 2, trans. Leo Wiener (New York: Colonial Press, 1904); Tolstoy, *My Religion,* 3–221; and Tolstoy, *On Life,* 225–405.

86. Leo Tolstoy, *The Gospel in Brief,* trans. Isabel Hapgood (Lincoln: University of Nebraska Press, 1997), 80.

87. Ibid., 75.

88. *The Bible: Authorized King James Version, The New Testament,* 8.

89. Meier, *A Marginal Jew,* 2:149.

90. Cited in ibid., 2:148–49.

91. Joachim Jeremias, *The Sermon on the Mount,* trans. Norman Perrin (Philadelphia: Fortress Press, 1963), 33.

92. Ray Monk, *Ludwig Wittgenstein: The Duty of Genius* (New York: Free Press, 1990), 115–16, 117, 132, 136, 213.

93. Tolstoy, *My Religion,* 17.

94. Ibid., 11–12.

95. Ibid., 269.

96. Ibid., 210.

97. Tolstoy, *On Life,* 334.

98. See Wilson, *Tolstoy,* 347–48, 373–74, 375–76, 391.

99. Ibid., 270, 339.

100. See Gustafson, *Leo Tolstoy,* 14, 30, 66–67, 202, 210, 455.

101. Wilson, *Tolstoy,* 348–49.

102. See Tolstoy, *Kingdom of God.*

103. On this influence, see Wilson, *Tolstoy,* 411, 490–91.

104. See Tolstoy, *Kingdom of God,* 3; for another tribute by Tolstoy to Garrison, see Fanny Garrison Villard, *William Lloyd Garrison on Non-resistance* (New York: Nation Press Printing, 1924), 46–55.

105. See, for example, ibid., 105, 115–16, 190, 244.

106. Wilson, *Tolstoy,* 358–60, 420–21, 437–39.

107. Ibid., 420–21. The Russian government forcibly separated members of the Molokan religious sect from their children to ensure the young were brought up in the Orthodox faith; see ibid., 437–39.

108. Tolstoy, *My Religion,* 143.

109. On the right to conscience, see Tolstoy, *Kingdom of God,* 353, 368.

110. Leo Tolstoy, "A Letter to a Hindu," in *I Cannot Be Silent: Writings on Politics, Art, and Religion by Leo Tolstoy,* ed. and trans. W. Gareth Jones (Bristol, UK: Bristol Press, 1989), 213–24.

111. Tolstoy, *On Life,* 244, 248–49, 321–22.

112. Tolstoy, "A Letter to a Hindu," 222.

113. For these prefaces, see *The Collected Works of Mahatma Gandhi,* vol. 10, November 1909–March 1911 (Delhi, India: The Publications Division, 1963), 1–5.

114. See B. Srinivasa Murthy, *Mahatma Gandhi and Leo Tolstoy Letters* (Long Beach, CA: Long Beach Publications, 1987).

115. Wilson, *Tolstoy,* 347.

116. Ibid., 344–45, 350–51, 353–54, 492.

117. Ibid., 494.

118. See, for example, Tolstoy, *War and Peace,* 222, 250, 263, 361, 391, 432, 565, 600; Tolstoy, *Anna Karenina,* 308, 309, 311, 346, 435, 516, 520, 693.

119. Wilson, *Tolstoy,* 505–17.

CHAPTER THREE

1. See Erik H. Erikson, *Gandhi's Truth: On the Origins of Militant Nonviolence* (New York: W. W. Norton, 1993).

2. See, for biographies of Gandhi, Stanley Wolpert, *Gandhi's Passion: The Life and Legacy of Mahatma Gandhi* (Oxford: Oxford University Press, 2001); Judith M. Brown, *Gandhi: Prisoner of Hope* (New Haven: Yale University Press, 1989); Rajmohan Gandhi, *The Good Boatman: A Portrait of Gandhi* (New Delhi: Penguin, 1995); Bhikhu Parekh, *Gandhi: A Very Short Introduction* (Oxford: Oxford University Press, 1997); Romain Rolland, *Mahatma Gandhi,* trans. Catherine D. Groth (New Delhi: The Publications Division, 1990); William L. Shirer, *Gandhi: A Memoir* (New York: Washington Square Press, 1979); Louis Fischer, *Gandhi: His Life and Message for the World* (New York: Penguin, 1982). Gandhi's autobiography is *An Autobiography: The Story of My Experiments with Truth.*

3. Gandhi, *Autobiography,* 4.

4. Wolpert, *Gandhi's Passion,* 13.

5. Parekh, *Gandhi,* 1.

6. Brown, *Gandhi,* 27, 86, 194, 393; R. Gandhi, *The Good Boatman,* 39, 66, 196–97, 199, 454, 457; Erikson, *Gandhi's Truth,* 63, 90.

7. Erikson, *Gandhi's Truth,* 111.

8. Ibid., 111–12.

9. Wolpert, *Gandhi's Passion,* 13–14.

10. Ibid., 5.

11. Gandhi, *Autobiography,* 204–11.

12. R. Gandhi, *The Good Boatman,* 179–87; Brown, *Gandhi,* 201.

13. Brown, *Gandhi,* 23.

14. See, for a general perspective, Lawrence James, *The Rise and Fall of the British Empire* (New York: St. Martin's Griffin, 1994).

15. On the role of Lockean liberal political theory in constitutionalism, see Richards, *Toleration and the Constitution* and *Conscience and the Constitution.*

16. Ellsberg, *Gandhi on Christianity,* 19, 28, 29–30.

17. Brown, *Gandhi,* 25–26.

18. Gandhi cites Carpenter's book in *Hind Swaraj;* see Gandhi, *Hind Swaraj and Other Writings,* ed. Anthony J. Parel, xliii, n. 34. See also Gandhi's letter to H. S. L. Polak, dated September 8, 1909, in *The Collected Works of Mahatma Gandhi,* vol. 9, September 1908–November 1909, 394–96; Edward Carpenter, *Civilisation: Its Cause and Cure and Other Essays* (New York: Scribner's, 1921).

19. Carpenter, *Civilisation,* 1, 219, 221–22, 229, 270–71.

20. Carpenter's importance to the historical emergence of arguments for feminism and the rights of gay/lesbian persons is discussed in Richards, *Women, Gays, and the Constitution,* 310–27. For the impact on Carpenter of a trip to India, see Edward Carpenter, *From Adam's Peak to*

Elephanta: Sketches in Ceylon and India (London: George Allen & Unwin, 1892); for his feminism focusing on sexual voice, see Carpenter, *Love's Coming of Age: A Series of Papers on the Relations of the Sexes* (Chicago: Charles H. Kerr, 1912); for a helpful biography, see Chushichi Tsuzuki, *Edward Carpenter, 1844–1929: Prophet of Human Fellowship* (Cambridge: Cambridge University Press, 1980). On E. M. Forster, see P. N. Furbank, *E. M. Forster: A Life* (San Diego: A Harvest Book, 1978).

21. Brown, *Gandhi,* 55.

22. Parekh, *Gandhi,* 3.

23. Brown, *Gandhi,* 26–27.

24. Ibid., 27, 25, 28.

25. Ibid., 30–31.

26. Ibid., 31.

27. See M. K. Gandhi, *Satyagraha in South Africa,* translated from the Gujarati by Valji Govindji Desai (Ahmadabad, India: Navajivan Publishing House, 1928).

28. Parekh, *Gandhi,* 6.

29. Gandhi, *Autobiography,* 137, 160.

30. Parekh, *Gandhi,* 8.

31. Gandhi, *Satyagraha in South Africa,* 20–21, 30–32, 66.

32. Cited in Parekh, *Gandhi,* 8; see ibid., 85–86.

33. Gandhi, *Autobiography,* 4.

34. Ibid., 78.

35. Parekh, *Gandhi,* 7.

36. See William Mackintire Salter, *Ethical Religion* (Boston: Roberts Brothers, 1891).

37. See John Ruskin, *Unto This Last,* Clive Wilmer ed. (London: Penguin, 1997).

38. George Orwell, "Reflections on Gandhi," in George Orwell, *A Collection of Essays* (San Diego: A Harvest Book, 1981), 171–80, at p. 173.

39. Parekh, *Gandhi,* 6.

40. Brown, *Gandhi,* 55.

41. Gandhi, *Satyagraha in South Africa,* 103.

42. Brown, *Gandhi,* 55.

43. Ibid., 56.

44. Gandhi, *Satyagraha in South Africa,* 100.

45. Quoted in Brown, *Gandhi,* 56.

46. Ibid.

47. Gandhi, *Satyagraha in South Africa,* 187.

48. Brown, *Gandhi,* 59.

49. Gandhi, *Satyagraha in South Africa,* 251–60.

50. Ibid., 260–85.

51. Ibid., 173.

52. Brown, *Gandhi,* 56.

53. Gandhi, *Satyagraha in South Africa,* 258.

54. Ibid., 253.

55. Brown, *Gandhi,* 32, 63–64.

56. Gandhi, *Satyagraha in South Africa,* 154–55, 187.

57. Ibid., 130.

58. Brown, *Gandhi,* 45–46.

59. See M. K. Gandhi, *Hind Swaraj,* in M. K. Gandhi, *Hind Swaraj and Other Writings,* ed. Anthony J. Parel (Cambridge: Cambridge University Press, 2000), 5–125.

60. Brown, *Gandhi,* 57.

61. See, for full discussion, Brown, *Gandhi.*

62. Ibid., 132.

63. Brown, *Gandhi,* 59.

64. Ibid.

65. Ibid., 242, 263.

66. See, for Gandhi on these points, Pushpa Joshi, *Gandhi on Women* (Ahmadabad, India: Navajivan Publishing House, 1988), 87, 93–95, 95–97, 144–45, 215, 217–18, 220, 222, 241–42, 257–58, 259, 288, 312–13, 316.

67. See, for Gandhi on child marriage, ibid., 135–36, 137–39, 140–41.

68. See, for Gandhi on these points, ibid., 149–50, 244–45, 258. See also Brown, *Gandhi,* 209–13.

69. Brown, *Gandhi,* 360.

70. See Mukulika Banerjee, *The Pathan Unarmed* (Karachi, Pakistan: Oxford University Press, 2000).

71. V. S. Naipaul, *India: A Wounded Civilization* (Vintage: New York, 1978), 169.

72. Brown, *Gandhi,* 347–48.

73. Ibid., 350.

74. Ibid., 350–51.

75. Ibid., 351.

76. Parekh, *Gandhi,* 26–27.

77. Brown, *Gandhi,* 356.

78. Ibid., 375.

79. George Orwell, "Reflections on Gandhi," 172.

80. Quoted in Joshi, *Gandhi on Women,* 142.

81. See Bhikhu Parekh, *Colonialism, Tradition, and Reform: An Analysis of Gandhi's Political Discourse,* rev. ed. (New Delhi: Sage Publications, 1999), 200.

82. See Manubehn Gandhi, *Bapu—My Mother* (Ahmadabad, India: Navajivan Publishing House, 1949), 3.

83. Ibid.

84. Quoted in Joshi, *Gandhi on Women,* 185.

85. Quoted in Erikson, *Gandhi's Truth,* 110.

86. Ibid. (emphasis in original).

87. Gandhi, *Autobiography,* 4.

88. Erikson, *Gandhi's Truth,* 111.

89. Quoted in ibid., 111.

90. Ibid.

91. Gandhi, *Satyagraha in South Africa,* 100.

92. Gilligan, *The Birth of Pleasure,* 14–17, 89–91, 161–63, 178–79, 204.

93. M. K. Gandhi, *Non-violent Resistance (Satyagraha)* (Mineola, NY: Dover Publications, 2001), 72.

94. M. K. Gandhi, *Satyagraha in South Africa,* 72, 210.

95. Ibid., 157.

96. Quoted in Parekh, *Colonialism, Tradition and Reform,* 221.

97. For a skeptical treatment of these grounds, see Joshua A. Goldstein, *War and Gender: How Gender Shapes the War System and Vice Versa* (Cambridge: Cambridge University Press, 2001).

98. Orwell, "Reflections on Gandhi," 176.

99. See Erikson, *Gandhi's Truth,* 229–54, 231–37, 237–42, 243.

100. Ibid., 132.

101. Carpenter, *Civilisation,* 222.

102. Erikson, *Gandhi's Truth,* 111.

103. *The Bhagavad-Gita,* trans. Barbara Stoler Miller (New York: Bantam Books, 1986), 24–25, 27, 29. Quote is on p. 29.

104. See Mohandas K. Gandhi, *The Bhagavad Gita According to Gandhi,* trans. John Strohmeier (Berkeley, CA: Berkeley Hills Books, 2000).

105. See Gandhi's discussion of this point, ibid., 83–84.

106. Parekh, *Colonialism, Tradition and Reform,* 181.

107. For a defense of this point, see Ashutosh Varshney, *Ethnic Conflict and Civic Life: Hindus and Muslims in India* (New Haven: Yale University Press, 2002). For other studies of Gandhi's impact on a free India, see Ved Mehta, *Mahatma Gandhi and His Apostles* (New Haven: Yale University Press, 1976), and Ramachandra Guha, *An Anthropologist among the Marxists and Other Essays* (Delhi, India: Permanent Black, 2001).

108. See, on this point in the case of Tolstoy, Wilson, *Tolstoy,* 478.

109. Gandhi, *Non-violent Resistance,* 348–50.

110. Brown, *Gandhi,* 350–51.

111. Parekh, *Colonialism, Tradition and Reform,* 220.

112. Brown, *Gandhi,* 377–78.

113. Gandhi, *Autobiography,* 4–5.

CHAPTER FOUR

1. See Taylor Branch, *Parting the Waters: Martin Luther King and the Civil Rights Movement, 1954–63* (London: Papermac, 1988); see also Branch, *Pillar of Fire: America in the King Years, 1963–65* (New York: Simon & Schuster, 1998).

2. See Richards, *Conscience and the Constitution.*

3. See *Plessy v. Ferguson,* 163 U.S. 537 (1896).

4. See *Brown v. Board of Education,* 347 U.S. 483 (1954).

5. See James M. McPherson, *The Abolitionist Legacy: From Reconstruction to the NAACP* (Princeton: Princeton University Press, 1975), 368–93; Richard Kluger, *Simple Justice: The History of "Brown v. Board of Education" and Black America's Struggle for Equality* (New York: Vintage, 1977); Genna Rae McNeil, *Groundwork: Charles Hamilton Houston and the Struggle for Civil Rights* (Philadelphia: University of Pennsylvania Press, 1983).

6. See *Gitlow v. New York,* 268 U.S. 652 (1925) (First Amendment held applicable to states under Fourteenth Amendment). For an illuminating discussion of this judicial development, see Harry Kalven Jr., *The Negro and the First Amendment* (Chicago: University of Chicago Press, 1965).

7. Even under the harsh terms of American slavery, black Americans—though brutally cut off from their native cultures as well as from the rights of American public culture—demonstrated remarkable creativity in giving ethical meaning to their plight, including grounds for resistance to it. See, on the black interpretation of Christian freedom under slavery, Eugene D. Genovese, *Roll, Jordan, Roll: The World the Slaves Made* (New York: Vintage Books, 1974), 159–284; on religious and political freedom under emancipation, see Leon F. Litwack, *Been in the Storm So Long: The Aftermath of Slavery* (New York: Vintage Books, 1979), 450–556; on the

ideals of religious and constitutional freedom of Martin Luther King, see, in general, Branch, *Parting the Waters.*

8. See, for example, Eric J. Sundquist, *To Wake the Nations: Race in the Making of American Literature* (Cambridge, MA: Harvard University Press, 1993).

9. See Anthony G. Amsterdam, "Thurgood Marshall's Image of the Blue-Eyed Child in Brown," 68 *New York University Law Review* 70 (1993): 226–36.

10. See *Loving v. Virginia,* 388 U.S. 1 (1967).

11. *Pace v. Alabama,* 106 U.S. 583 (1883) (stronger penalties for interracial, as opposed to intraracial, sexual relations not racially discriminatory, since both whites and blacks were subject to the same penalty); *McLaughlin v. Florida,* 379 U.S. 184 (1964).

12. See, for these developments, Richards, *Women, Gays, and the Constitution.*

13. Quoted in Michael Eric Dyson, *I May Not Get There with You: The True Martin Luther King, Jr.* (New York: Touchstone, 2001), 195.

14. Quoted in Glip Schulke and Penelope Ortner McPhee, *King Remembered* (New York: W. W. Norton, 1986), 9.

15. Quoted in Evelyn Brooks Higginbotham, *Righteous Discontent: The Women's Movement in the Black Baptist Church, 1880–1920* (Cambridge, MA: Harvard University Press, 1993), 173.

16. Ibid., 1.

17. See, on the black interpretation of Christian freedom under slavery, Genovese, *Roll, Jordan, Roll,* 159–284; on religious and political freedom under emancipation, see Litwack, *Been in the Storm So Long,* 450–556.

18. See, in general on this point, Higginbotham, *Righteous Discontent.*

19. Ibid., 139, 140.

20. Jacquelyn Grant, *White Women's Christ and Black Women's Jesus: Feminist Christology and Womanist Response* (Atlanta, GA: Scholars Press, 1989), 212.

21. Quoted in ibid., 213.

22. Quoted in ibid., 214 (emphasis in original).

23. Branch, *Parting the Waters,* 33.

24. On King's antipathy to violence as a young boy, see L. D. Reddick, *Crusader without Violence: A Biography of Martin Luther King, Jr.* (New York: Harper & Brothers, 1959), 59–60.

25. Branch, *Parting the Waters,* 166–67.

26. Quoted in ibid., 730.

27. See James Baldwin, *Go Tell It on the Mountain,* in Baldwin, *Early Novels and Stories,* ed. Toni Morrison (New York: Library of America, 1998), 1–215.

28. David Leeming, *James Baldwin: A Biography* (New York: Alfred A. Knopf, 1994), 9.

29. Ibid.

30. James Baldwin, *The Fire Next Time,* in James *Collected Essays,* ed. Toni Morrison (New York: Library of America, 1998), 291–347, at p. 304.

31. Ibid., 304.

32. Ibid., 311–12 (emphasis in original).

33. James Baldwin, "The Dangerous Road before Martin Luther King," in Baldwin, *Collected Essays,* ed. Toni Morrison (New York: Library of America, 1998), 638–58, at p. 638.

34. Ibid., 639.

35. Ibid., 655.

36. Ibid., 656. The purging of Rustin from the Southern Christian Leadership Conference, where King had wanted him appointed as coordinator and publicist, was King's response to a

grotesque threat by Adam Clayton Powell that, otherwise, he would publicly state that King and Rustin had had a homosexual affair; see Branch, *Parting the Waters,* 328–29.

37. Baldwin, "The Dangerous Road before Martin Luther King," 638–58, at p. 653.

38. Ibid., 653–54.

39. See Marisa Chappell, Jenny Hutchinson, and Brian Ward, "'Dress modestly, neatly . . . as if you were going to church': Respectability, Class and Gender in the Montgomery Bus Boycott and the Early Civil Rights Movement," in *Gender in the Civil Rights Movement,* ed. Peter J. Ling and Sharon Monteith, 69–100 (New York: Garland Publishing, 1999).

40. See Orlando Patterson, *The Rituals of Blood: Consequences of Slavery in Two American Centuries* (Washington, DC: Civitas, 1998).

41. See, for her brilliant analysis, Richards, *Women, Gays, and the Constitution,* 182–90.

42. See Walter Rauschenbusch, *Christianity and the Social Crisis* (1907; reprint, Louisville, KY: Westminster John Knox Press, 1991).

43. Branch, *Parting the Waters,* 73.

44. Rauschenbusch, *Christianity and the Social Crisis,* 53.

45. Branch, *Parting the Waters,* 74.

46. Ibid., 75, 76.

47. Ibid., 75–78.

48. Ibid., 77.

49. See Reinhold Niebuhr, *Moral Man and Immoral Society: A Study in Ethics and Politics* (1932; reprint, Louisville, KY: Westminster John Knox Press, 2001).

50. See David A. J. Richards, *Foundations of American Constitutionalism* (New York: Oxford University Press, 1989), 32–39.

51. On Niebuhr's impact on King, see Branch, *Parting the Waters,* 87.

52. Ibid., 90.

53. Ibid., 91.

54. For King on Buber, see King, *Testament of Hope,* 119, 147, 284, 293, 478, 625, 629–30.

55. See King, *Testament of Hope,* 86, 96, 135–36, 146, 161–62, 183, 318, 364, 468–69.

56. Ibid., 56, 389, 390–91, 571, 589–90.

57. See, in general, Jervis Anderson, *Bayard Rustin: Troubles I've Seen: A Biography* (New York: HarperCollins, 1997). See also Bayard Rustin, *Down the Line: The Collected Writings of Bayard Rustin* (Chicago: Quadrangle Books, 1971); Rustin, *Strategies for Freedom: The Changing Patterns of Black Protest* (New York: Columbia University Press, 1976); James Haskins, *Bayard Rustin: Behind the Scenes of the Civil Rights Movement* (New York: Hyperion Books, 1997).

58. See Frederick Douglass, "The Meaning of July Fourth for the Negro," speech delivered July 5, 1852, and reprinted in *The Life and Writings of Frederick Douglass,* vol. 2, ed. Philip S. Foner (New York: International Publishers, 1950), 200.

59. Branch, *Parting the Waters,* 128–34, 139, 655.

60. See Mary Fair Burks, "Trailblazers: Women in the Montgomery Bus Boycott," in *Women in the Civil Rights Movement,* ed. Vicki L. Crawford, Jacqueline Anne Rouse, and Barbara Woods, 71–84 (Bloomington: Indiana University Press, 1993); Belinda Robnett, *How Long? How Long?: African-American Women in the Struggle for Civil Rights* (New York: Oxford University Press, 1997), 53–70; Lynne Olson, *Freedom's Daughters: The Unsung Heroines of the Civil Rights Movement from 1830 to 1970* (New York: Scribner's, 2001), 87–131; Branch, *Parting the Waters,* 149.

61. Branch, *Parting the Waters,* 136.

62. Constance Baker Motley, *Equal Justice under Law* (New York: Farrar, Straus and Giroux, 1998), 157.

63. See Andrew Young, *An Easy Burden: The Civil Rights Movement and the Transformation of America* (New York: HarperCollins, 1996), 295.

64. On this important constitutional development, see Kalven, *The Negro and the First Amendment.*

65. See King, *Testament of Hope,* 50, 71, 88, 265, 266, 290, 294, 300, 328, 347, 349.

66. Branch, *Parting the Waters,* 188, 193.

67. See, for fuller discussion of these events, ibid., 143–205.

68. See Krishnalal Shridharani, *War without Violence: A Study of Gandhi's Method and Its Accomplishments* (New York: Harcourt Brace, 1939); Branch, *Parting the Waters,* 171.

69. On studies of the movements, see, for example, Richard B. Gregg, *The Power of Nonviolence* (1935; reprint, New York: Schocken Books, 1971); Joan B. Bondurant, *Conquest of Violence: The Gandhian Philosophy of Conflict* (1958; reprint, Princeton: Princeton University Press, 1988). Also see, in general, Sudarshan Kapur, *Raising Up a Prophet: The African-American Encounter with Gandhi* (Boston: Beacon Press, 1992).

70. Branch, *Parting the Waters,* 179.

71. Ibid., 179–80.

72. Ibid., 250, 250–55, 259, 260, 261–64, 274.

73. See David J. Garrow, *Bearing the Cross: Martin Luther King, Jr. and the Southern Christian Leadership Conference* (New York: Quill/William Morrow, 1986), 227.

74. Ibid., 226–28.

75. Quoted in ibid., 229.

76. Quoted in ibid., 229.

77. Ibid., 236.

78. Ibid.

79. Ibid., 240.

80. Quoted in Branch, *Parting the Waters,* 729.

81. Quoted in Garrow, *Bearing the Cross,* 242.

82. Quoted in ibid., 242.

83. Quoted in ibid., 242.

84. Quoted in ibid., 243.

85. Ibid., 243–44.

86. Ibid., 738–45. See Martin Luther King Jr., "The Letter from Birmingham City Jail," in *Testament of Hope,* 289–302.

87. See Richard Wright, *Black Boy,* reprinted in Arnold Rampersad, ed., *Richard Wright: Later Works* (New York: Library of America, 1991), 5–365. For illuminating commentary, from which I have profited, see William H. Chafe, *Women and Equality: Changing Patterns in American Culture* (Oxford: Oxford University Press, 1977), 59–65, 73–74.

88. For commentary, see Chafe, *Women and Equality,* 62–65.

89. See, for useful commentary on this and related points, Leeming, *James Baldwin.*

90. King, *Testament of Hope,* 211, 358–59, 471, 478, 489.

91. See Martin Luther King Jr., "Loving Your Enemies," in *A Knock at Midnight,* ed. Carson and Holloran, 41–64.

92. See, on this point in King's thinking, *Testament of Hope,* 140, 144, 336, 358, 484, 514, 593.

93. See Branch, *Parting the Waters,* 756–802.

94. Ibid., 752.

95. Ibid., 750–51.

96. Ibid., 755.

97. For the settlement, see Garrow, *Bearing the Cross,* 259.

98. Ibid., 269.

99. Branch, *Parting the Waters,* 892–93.

100. Young, *An Easy Burden,* 369–74.

101. See, for example, Garrow, *Bearing the Cross,* 173–230, 287–355, 431–624.

102. For a discussion of these free speech principles, see Richards, *Free Speech,* and Kalven, *The Negro and the First Amendment.*

103. On the role of this text in King's statements, see *Testament of Hope,* 38, 47, 90, 140, 216, 256, 297, 436, 447.

104. King, "Loving Your Enemies," 59.

105. Motley, *Equal Justice under Law,* 157.

106. See, for example, Joseph R. Washington Jr., *Black Religion: The Negro and Christianity in the United States* (Boston: Beacon Press, 1964).

107. See, for an autobiography of one such woman who participated, as a student, in the civil rights movement, Charlayne Hunter-Gault, *In My Place* (New York: Vintage Books, 1993). For a rather different perspective by an activist woman who was not part of the nonviolent civil rights movement, see Angela Davis, *An Autobiography* (1974; reprint, New York: International Publishers, 1988).

108. Reddick, *Crusader without Violence,* 131.

109. See, for important studies, Ling and Monteith, *Gender in the Civil Rights Movement;* Olson, *Freedom's Daughters;* Robnett, *How Long? How Long?;* Crawford, Rouse, and Woods, *Women in the Civil Rights Movement;* Bettye Collier-Thomas and V. P. Franklin, eds., *Sisters in the Struggle: African American Women in the Civil Rights–Black Power Movement* (New York: New York University Press, 2001); Paula Giddings, *When and Where I Enter: The Impact of Black Women on Race and Sex in America* (New York: William Morrow, 1984).

110. On Baker, see Branch, *Parting the Waters,* 231–33, 258, 264, 273–76, 292–93, 317, 392, 466–67, 487, 518; Branch, *Pillar of Fire,* 192–93, 439, 457. On Clark, see Branch, *Parting the Waters,* 263–64, 290, 381–82, 573, 576–77, 899; Branch, *Pillar of Fire,* 124, 191. On Nash, see Branch, *Parting the Waters,* 279–80, 295, 392, 424, 428–29, 437, 439, 449, 455, 466–67, 487, 559, 588, 712, 754, 892–93; Branch, *Pillar of Fire,* 54–55, 68, 139–41, 165, 285, 524, 553, 559, 579, 587, 599. On Hamer, see Branch, *Parting the Waters,* 636, 819; Branch, *Pillar of Fire,* 57, 71, 74, 109, 179, 219, 240, 329, 458–59, 461, 465, 474, 481, 547–48.

111. See, on this development, Sara Evans, *Personal Politics: The Roots of Women's Liberation in the Civil Rights Movement and the New Left* (New York: Vintage Books, 1980).

112. See, on this point in King's statements, *Testament of Hope,* 210, 254, 269, 290, 474, 588, 594, 626.

113. For a work along these lines influential on King, see Abraham J. Heschel, *The Prophets* (1962; reprint, New York: Perennial Classics, 2001). For King's friendship with Heschel and Heschel's participation in the Selma march, see Branch, *Pillar of Fire,* 30–32, 611.

114. Branch, *Parting the Waters,* 197n.

115. See King, *A Testament of Hope,* 88, 141, 207, 252, 277, 480, 523.

116. Ibid., 102; see also 109, 125, 164, 281, 282, 334, 335, 484, 592–93.

117. Ibid., 140, 144, 336, 358, 484, 514, 593.

118. King, "Loving Your Enemies," 59.

119. See Dyson, *I May Not Get There with You.*

120. See Branch, *Parting the Waters,* 239.

121. See Dyson, *I May Not Get There with You,* 189, 222.

122. See Ralph David Abernathy, *And the Walls Came Tumbling Down* (New York: Harper-Perennial, 1989), 474–75.

123. Ibid., 467.

124. Ibid., 468.

125. For an early statement, see King, "Loving Your Enemies."

126. Ibid., 48.

127. Branch, *Parting the Waters,* 773.

128. King, *A Testament of Hope,* 62.

129. Branch, *Pillar of Fire,* 13, 80, 86, 255, 257, 547–48, 574.

130. King, *A Testament of Hope,* 579, 580, 582.

131. For a powerful description of this violence, both public and private, see Elaine Brown, *A Taste of Power: A Black Woman's Story* (New York: Anchor Books, 1992).

132. Branch, *Parting the Waters,* 239.

133. King, *A Testament of Hope,* 46.

134. For an example of King's downplaying of this issue, see ibid., 478.

CHAPTER FIVE

1. See Roy Jenkins, *Churchill: A Biography* (New York: Farrar, Straus and Giroux, 2001).

2. Lincoln's mother died before he was ten years old. She was known as brilliant and intellectual, and Lincoln referred to her as his "angel mother" and said of her, "God bless my mother; all that I am or ever hope to be I owe to her." See David Herbert Donald, *Lincoln* (New York: Simon & Schuster, 1995), 23. The love of his stepmother was also significant in his life. See ibid., 27–28. For an illuminating study of Lincoln's psychology, including his struggles with honor, see Douglas L. Wilson, *Honor's Voice: The Transformation of Abraham Lincoln* (New York: Alfred A. Knopf, 1998).

3. For a good collection of these speeches, see Winston S. Churchill, *Never Give In! The Best of Winston Churchill's Speeches* (New York: Hyperion, 2003).

4. Winston S. Churchill, *Marlborough: His Life and Times,* 4 vols. (1933; reprint, New York: Scribner's, 1968).

5. See Ralph G. Martin, *Jennie: The Life of Lady Randolph Churchill,* vol. 1, *The Romantic Years, 1854–1895* (New York: New American Library, 1970) and vol. 2, *The Dramatic Years, 1895–1921* (New York: New American Library, 1972).

6. Quoted in Martin, *Jennie,* 1:32.

7. Ibid., 1:133.

8. Winston Churchill, *My Early Life: 1874–1904* (1930; reprint, New York: Touchstone, 1996), 5.

9. Quoted in Martin, *Jennie,* 1:247.

10. Ibid., 1:174–75, 237.

11. Jenkins, *Churchill,* 8.

12. Martin, *Jennie,* 1:221.

13. Ibid., 1:172–73, 295–96.

14. Ibid., 1:273.

15. Jenkins, *Churchill,* 25.

16. Ibid., 28.

17. Ibid., 29.

18. Winston Churchill, *The Story of the Malakand Field Force* (1898; reprint, New York: Barnes and Noble, 1993).

19. Martin, *Jennie,* 2:99–101, 133–35; Jenkins, *Churchill,* 38.

20. See Winston S. Churchill, *The River War: The Reconquest of the Sudan* (1899; reprint, London: Four Square Books, 1960).

21. Jenkins, *Churchill,* 47–50.

22. Ibid., 51–64, 65.

23. Winston S. Churchill, *Savrola* (1900; reprint, London: Beacon Books, 1957). See Jenkins, *Churchill,* 98.

24. Martin, *Jennie,* 2:189–216.

25. See ibid., 2:147–54, 155–70, 178–80, 259–62, 285–86, 298, 300–308, 324–25, 1:278–82.

26. Jenkins, *Churchill,* 65–125.

27. Churchill, *My Early Life,* 50–59.

28. See, on the importance for Churchill of this right of moral independence in thought and action, Winston S. Churchill, *The Second World War,* vol. 1, *The Gathering Storm* (Boston: Houghton Mifflin, 1948), 112, 180, 218–19. For the range of his speeches in opposition to governmental policies, see Churchill, *Never Give In!*

29. Jenkins, *Churchill,* 142–66. See also Lord Roy Jenkins, *The British Liberal Tradition: From Gladstone to Young Churchill, Asquith, and Lloyd George—Is Blair Their Heir?* (Toronto: University of Toronto Press, 2001).

30. See Winston S. Churchill, *The People's Rights* (1909; reprint, New York: Taplinger Publishing, 1971).

31. Jenkins, *Churchill,* 109, 185.

32. For example, during the General Strike of the mid-1920s, Churchill not only preached fiscal discipline—as you would expect any Conservative chancellor of the exchequer to do—but actually went out and organized strike-breaking gangs. This was at a time of mass unemployment, hunger marches, and the like. See, on this period in Churchill's public service, Jenkins, *Churchill,* 393–417.

33. Ibid., 133.

34. Ibid., 134.

35. See, on charges brought against Churchill for homosexuality while in the army (which Jennie had suppressed), Martin, *Jennie,* 2:58–59, 176.

36. Cited in Jenkins, *Churchill,* 37.

37. Martin, *Jennie,* 1:175 and 2:341.

38. Cited in Martin, *Jennie,* 2:184, 181.

39. Churchill, *Savrola,* 215–17.

40. Cited in Martin, *Jennie,* 2:293.

41. Churchill, *The Malakand Field Force,* 207.

42. Churchill, *The River War,* 13.

43. Winston Spencer Churchill, *Lord Randolph Churchill,* 2 vols. (London: Macmillan, 1906).

44. See R. F. Foster, *Lord Randolph Churchill: A Political Life* (Oxford: Clarendon Press, 1981), 382–403.

45. See, in general, ibid.

46. Ibid., 402.

47. Martin, *Jennie,* 2:251.

48. Jenkins, *Churchill,* 102–3.

49. See Winston S. Churchill, *The World Crisis, 1911–1918,* 2 vols. (London: Odhams Press, 1938).

50. See Winston S. Churchill, *A History of the English-Speaking Peoples,* vol. 1, *The Birth of Britain* (New York: Bantam Book, 1963), vol. 2, *The New World* (New York: Bantam Books, 1974), vol. 3, *The Age of Revolution* (London: Cassell, 1957), vol. 4, *The Great Democracies* (New York: Bantam Books, 1974).

51. See Winston Churchill, *The Second World War,* 6 vols. (Boston: Houghton Mifflin, 1948–53), 1:207–8.

52. See his 1919 speech against "Bolshevist atrocities," in *Never Give In!* 77; quote is from Churchill, *Second World War,* 1:15.

53. See, on parliamentary privilege, A. W. Bradley and K. D. Ewing, *Constitutional and Administrative Law,* 13th ed. (Edinburgh: Pearson Education, 2003), 214–32, and Dawn Oliver and Gavin Drewry, *The Law and Parliament* (London: Butterworths, 1998). On the rather narrow understanding of the free speech rights of ordinary citizens during this period, see K. D. Ewing and C. A. Gearty, *The Struggle for Civil Liberties: Political Freedom and the Rule of Law in Britain, 1914–1945* (Oxford: Oxford University Press, 2001).

54. Quoted in Churchill, *Second World War,* 3:434.

55. Churchill, *Second World War,* 1:52–53.

56. Ibid., 1:55–56.

57. Ibid., 1:83–84.

58. See Foster, *Lord Randolph Churchill,* 30, 159, 194–95, 203, 211, 286, 331; on Nathan Rothschild in particular, see, for example, ibid., 194, 241, 246, 248, 270, 277, 284, 288–89, 291, 375, 394–95.

59. See Claudia Koonz, *The Nazi Conscience* (Cambridge, MA: Belknap Press, 2003).

60. For Churchill's remarkable 1932 parliamentary speech to this effect, see Churchill, *Never Give In!* 100–102.

61. See Churchill, *Second World War,* 1:72–73, 76, 112–13, 204–5, 265–67, 272–74, 327–28.

62. Ibid., 1:348.

63. Jenkins, *Churchill,* 505.

64. Ibid., 635.

65. Koonz, *Nazi Conscience,* 256–57.

66. Churchill, *Second World War,* 1:85.

67. Ibid., 1:89, 254.

68. Ibid., 1:168.

69. Ibid., 1:320.

70. Ibid.

71. Jenkins, *Churchill,* 436, 439, 456.

72. For Churchill's speeches to this effect, see Churchill, *Never Give In!* 97–99, 115–17.

73. Ibid., 97.

74. Churchill, *Second World War,* 4:212–14.

75. Ibid., 4:219.

76. Ibid., 1:321.

77. See Richards, *Women, Gays, and the Constitution,* 157–64.

78. Jenkins contrasts, during Churchill's boyhood, his "non-relationship with his father" with his "semi-relationship with his mother," Jenkins, *Churchill,* 10.

79. Churchill, *My Early Life,* 4.

80. Martin, *Jennie,* 1:166–67.

81. Jenkins, *Churchill*, 9.

82. Martin, *Jennie*, 1:167.

83. Churchill, *My Early Life*, 62.

84. Quoted in Martin, *Jennie*, 1:172–73.

85. Churchill, *My Early Life*, 99.

86. Martin, *Jennie*, 1:18.

87. Churchill, *Savrola*, 215–17.

88. Martin, *Jennie*, 1:148.

89. Churchill, *Second World War*, 1:218–19.

90. Quoted in Dominique Enright, comp., *The Wicked Wit of Winston Churchill* (London: Michael O'Mara Books, 2001), 53.

91. See Joseph Conrad, *Heart of Darkness* (1902; reprint, London: Penguin, 1995).

92. Ibid., 84.

93. Ibid., 99.

94. See, for Conrad's exploration of this psychology, Joseph Conrad, "The Secret Sharer," in Joseph Conrad, *The Secret Sharer and Other Stories* (New York: Dover, 1993), 83–113.

95. See Frederick R. Karl, *Joseph Conrad: The Three Lives* (New York: Farrar, Straus and Giroux, 1979). For Conrad's own sense of his artistic voice as a voice of resistance to injustice, see ibid., 572, 646–47.

96. See, for Conrad's remarkable treatment of this issue, "Autocracy and War—1905," in Joseph Conrad, *Notes on Life and Letters* (1920; reprint, McLean, VA: IndyPublish.com, n.d.), 61–80.

97. See Koonz, *Nazi Conscience*, 147, 154, 166, 191, 210, 223, 240, 250–54.

98. Ibid., 222–23, 250–54.

99. Ibid., 145, 147.

100. See Churchill, *Second World War*, 1:89, 209, 667.

101. Ibid., 1:89.

102. See Jenkins, *Winston Churchill*, 843–97.

103. See Churchill, *Never Give In!* 77–78, 413–24.

104. See Jenkins, *Churchill*, 505, 846, 873, 777–78.

105. Quoted in ibid., 723.

106. Churchill, *Never Give In!* 77–78.

107. Ibid., 413–25, 427–30, 433–34, 436–44, 449–50.

108. Jenkins, *Churchill*, 427, 466, 819, 868.

109. Ibid., 293–94, 362, 308.

110. Ibid., 10, 209, 658, 804.

//CHAPTER SIX

1. For a general study of this gender issue in German fascism, see Koonz, *Nazi Conscience;* see also Claudia Koonz, *Mothers in the Fatherland: Women, the Family, and Nazi Politics* (New York: St. Martin's Press, 1987).

2. See Robert Conquest, *Stalin: Breaker of Nations* (New York: Penguin, 1991), 163–65; Walter Laqueur, *The Dream That Failed: Reflections on the Soviet Union* (New York: Oxford University Press, 1994), 13; and, on all these points, Francois Furet, *The Passing of an Illusion: The Idea of Communism in the Twentieth Century,* trans. Deborah Furet (Chicago: University of Chicago Press, 1999).

3. See Furet, *The Passing of an Illusion,* 174–75, 178, 189–90.

4. See Arthur Koestler, *Darkness at Noon,* trans. Daphne Hardy (1941; reprint, New York: Bantam Books, 1968), 124–29, 134–37, 153, 182–85, 189–90, 205.

5. See Chris Hedges, *War Is a Force;* Michael Ignatieff, *The Warrior's Honor;* Amin Maalouf, *In the Name of Identity;* Daniel Pipes, *Militant Islam Reaches America* (New York: W. W. Norton, 2002); Kanan Makiya, *Cruelty and Silence: War, Tyranny, Uprising, and the Arab World* (New York: W. W. Norton, 1993); Avishai Margalit, "The Suicide Bombers," *New York Review of Books* 50, no. 1 (January 16, 2003): 36–39; and Bernard Lewis, *What Went Wrong? Western Impact and Middle Eastern Response* (Oxford: Oxford University Press, 2002).

6. Mark Juergensmeyer, *Terror in the Mind of God: The Global Rise of Religious Violence* (Berkeley: University of California Press, 2000), 195.

7. See Lewis, *What Went Wrong?*

8. See, for example, Leila Ahmed, *A Border Passage: From Cairo to America—A Woman's Journey* (New York: Farrar, Straus and Giroux, 1999); Fatema Mernissi, *Islam and Democracy: Fear of the Modern World,* trans. Mary Jo Lakeland (Cambridge, MA: Perseus, 1992); and Fatema Mernissi, *The Veil and the Male Elite: A Feminist Interpretation of Women's Rights in Islam* (Cambridge, MA: Perseus, 1991).

9. Churchill, *The River War,* 13.

10. See John W. deGruchy, ed., *The Cambridge Companion to Dietrich Bonhoeffer* (Cambridge: Cambridge University Press, 2002), 158.

11. Dietrich Bonhoeffer, *Letters and Papers from Prison,* ed. Eberhard Bethge (New York: Touchstone, 1971), 17.

12. See Renate Bethge, "Bonhoeffer's Family and Its Significance for His Theology," in *Dietrich Bonhoeffer—His Significance for North Americans,* ed. Larry Rasmussen, 1–30 (Minneapolis, MN: Fortress Press, 1990).

13. See Philip P. Hallie, *Let Innocent Blood Be Shed: The Story of the Village of Le Chambon and How Goodness Happened There* (New York: Harper & Row, 1979).

14. See Friedrich Nietzsche, *On the Genealogy of Morals,* trans. Douglas Smith (Oxford: Oxford University Press, 1996), 77–136 (endorsing a shame-based ethics of misogynist heroes against a guilt-based ethics of equal rights and obligations).

15. Churchill, *My Early Life,* 4.

16. On these psychological alternatives in the lives of women as well as men, see Gilligan, *The Birth of Pleasure.*

17. Ibid.

18. See, for my own works along these lines, Richards, *Toleration and the Constitution; Foundations of American Constitutionalism; Conscience and the Constitution; Women, Gays, and the Constitution;* and *Free Speech.*

19. See, on this development, Richards, *Women, Gays, and the Constitution.*

20. Jenkins, *Churchill,* 109, 185.

21. Churchill, *My Early Life,* 50.

22. Cited in Martin, *Jennie,* 2:51.

23. Churchill, *Never Give In!* 99.

24. Roy, *War Talk,* 13.

25. Chappell, *A Stone of Hope,* 153.

26. Roy, *War Talk,* 18–19, 34, 50, 105.

27. See, in general, ibid.

28. On Churchill's rather racist way of dismissing the claims of the Palestinians, see ibid., 58.

29. June Kronholz, "Utah Orders School to Open Its Doors—To Armed Students," *Wall Street Journal,* May 24, 2004, sec. A, A1 and A6.

30. For compelling illustrative comparative studies, see James Q. Whitman, *Harsh Justice: Criminal Punishment and the Widening Divide between America and Europe* (New York: Oxford University Press, 2003), and David Garland, *The Culture of Control: Crime and Social Order in Contemporary Society* (Chicago: University of Chicago Press, 2001). For a plausible diagnosis of its patriarchal roots, see James Gilligan, *Preventing Violence* (New York: Thames & Hudson, 2001). For alternatives, see John Braithwaite, *Restorative Justice and Responsive Regulation* (New York: Oxford University Press, 2002).

31. On ways of helping boys and men live outside patriarchy, see Terrence Real, *I Don't Want to Talk about It: Overcoming the Secret Legacy of Male Depression* (New York: Fireside, 1997), and William Pollack, *Real Boys: Rescuing Our Sons from the Myths of Boyhood* (New York: Henry Holt, 1998).

32. King, *A Testament of Hope,* 231–44.

33. See James Carroll, *An American Requiem: God, My Father, and the War that Came between Us* (Boston: Houghton Mifflin, 1996).

34. See Thomas Merton, *The Seven Storey Mountain: An Autobiography of Faith* (1948; reprint, San Diego: Harcourt Brace, 1998), 90–92, 123–24. On Merton's opposition to the Vietnam War, see *The Nonviolent Alternative* (New York: Farrar, Straus and Giroux, 1980) and *Faith and Violence: Christian Teaching and Christian Practice* (Notre Dame, IN: University of Notre Dame Press, 1968).

35. See Murray Polner and Jim O'Grady, *Disarmed and Dangerous: The Radical Lives and Times of Daniel and Philip Berrigan* (Boulder, CO: Westview Press, 1997).

36. See Daniel Berrigan, SJ, *No Bars to Manhood* (New York: Bantam, 1971).

37. See Richards, *Women, Gays, and the Constitution,* and David A. J. Richards, *Identity and the Case for Gay Rights: Race, Gender, Religion as Analogies* (Chicago: University of Chicago Press, 1999).

(EoF)

30 : 23. 23

◄ //BIBLIOGRAPHY►

//A

Abernathy, Ralph David. *And the Walls Came Tumbling Down.* New York: HarperPerennial, 1989.

Ahmed, Leila. *A Border Passage: From Cairo to America—A Woman's Journey.* New York: Farrar, Straus and Giroux, 1999.

Albright, W. E., and C. S. Mann. *The Anchor Bible: Matthew.* New York: Doubleday, 1971.

Amsterdam, Anthony G. "Thurgood Marshall's Image of the Blue-Eyed Child in *Brown*," 68 *New York University Law Review* 226–236 (1993).

Anderson, Jervis. *Bayard Rustin: Troubles I've Seen: A Biography.* New York: HarperCollins, 1997.

//B

Bainton, Roland H. *Christian Attitudes toward War and Peace: A Historical Survey and Critical Re-evaluation.* Nashville: Abingdon Press, 1960.

Baldwin, James. *Collected Essays.* Edited by Toni Morrison. New York: Library of America, 1998.

————. *Early Novels and Stories.* Edited by Toni Morrison. New York: Library of America, 1998.

Ballou, Adin. *Christian Non-resistance, in All Its Important Bearings, Illustrated and Defended.* Philadelphia: Jerome S. Ozer, 1972. Originally published in 1848 in Philadelphia by J. Miller McKim.

Banerjee, Mukulika. *The Pathan Unarmed.* Karachi, Pakistan: Oxford University Press, 2000.

Bayley, John. *Leo Tolstoy.* Plymouth, UK: Northcote House, 1997.

————. *Pushkin: A Comparative Commentary.* Cambridge: Cambridge University Press, 1971.

————. *Tolstoy and the Novel.* Chicago: University of Chicago Press, 1988.

Berrigan, SJ, Daniel. *No Bars to Manhood.* New York: Bantam, 1971.

The Bhagavad Gita. Translated by Barbara Stoler Miller. New York: Bantam Books, 1986.

The Bible (King James Version). Introduction and notes by Robert Carroll and Stephen Prickett. Oxford: Oxford University Press, 1998.

Bondurant, Joan B. *Conquest of Violence: The Gandhian Philosophy of Conflict.* Princeton: Princeton University Press, 1988. Originally published in 1958.

Bonhoeffer, Dietrich. *Letters and Papers from Prison.* Edited by Eberhard Bethge. New York: Touchstone, 1971.

Bradley, A. W., and K. D. Ewing, *Constitutional and Administrative Law,* 13th ed. Edinburgh: Pearson Education, 2003.

Braithwaite, John. *Restorative Justice and Responsive Regulation.* New York: Oxford University Press, 2002.

Branch, Taylor. *Parting the Waters: Martin Luther King and the Civil Rights Movement, 1954–63.* London: Papermac, 1988.

————. *Pillar of Fire: America in the King Years, 1963–65.* New York: Simon & Schuster, 1998.

Braude, Leo. *From Chivalry to Terrorism: War and the Changing Nature of Masculinity*. New York: Alfred A. Knopf, 2003.

Brown, Elaine. *A Taste of Power: A Black Woman's Story*. New York: Anchor Books, 1992.

Brown, Judith M. *Gandhi: Prisoner of Hope*. New Haven: Yale University Press, 1989.

Brown, Raymond E. *The Anchor Bible: The Gospel According to John I–XII*. New York: Doubleday, 1966.

Buber, Martin. *I and Thou*. Translated by Walter Kaufmann. New York: Scribner's, 1970.

Bynum, Caroline Walker. *Jesus as Mother: Studies in the Spirituality of the High Middle Ages*. Berkeley: University of California Press, 1982.

Carpenter, Edward. *Civilisation: Its Cause and Cure and Other Essays* (newly enlarged and complete edition). New York: Scribner's, 1921.

———. *From Adam's Peak to Elephanta: Sketches in Ceylon and India*. London: George Allen & Unwin, 1892.

———. *Love's Coming of Age: A Series of Papers on the Relations of the Sexes*. Chicago: Charles H. Kerr, 1912.

Carroll, James. *An American Requiem: God, My Father, and the War That Came between Us*. Boston: Houghton Mifflin, 1996.

Carson, Clayborne, and Peter Holloran, eds. *A Knock at Midnight: Inspiration from the Great Sermons of Reverend Martin Luther King, Jr.* New York: Warner Books, 2000.

Cavell, Stanley. *The Senses of Walden*. Chicago: University of Chicago Press, 1992.

Chafe, William H. *Women and Equality: Changing Patterns in American Culture*. New York: Oxford University Press, 1977.

Chappell, David L. *A Stone of Hope: Prophetic Religion and the Death of Jim Crow*. Chapel Hill: University of North Carolina Press, 2004.

Chodorow, Nancy J. *The Reproduction of Mothering: Psychoanalysis and the Sociology of Gender*. Berkeley: University of California Press, 1978.

Churchill, Winston S. *A History of the English-Speaking Peoples*. Vol. 1, *The Birth of Britain*. New York: Bantam Books, 1963.

———. *A History of the English-Speaking Peoples*. Vol. 2, *The New World*. New York: Bantam Books, 1974.

———. *A History of the English-Speaking Peoples*. Vol. 3, *The Age of Revolution*. London: Cassell, 1957.

———. *A History of the English-Speaking Peoples*. Vol. 4, *The Great Democracies*. New York: Bantam Books, 1974.

———. *Lord Randolph Churchill*. 2 vols. London: Macmillan, 1906.

———. *Marlborough: His Life and Times*. 4 vols. New York: Scribner's, 1968. Originally published in 1933.

———. *My Early Life: 1874–1904*. New York: Touchstone, 1996. Originally published in 1930.

———. *Never Give In! The Best of Winston Churchill's Speeches*. New York: Hyperion, 2003.

———. *The People's Rights*. New York: Taplinger Publishing, 1971.

———. *The River War: The Reconquest of the Sudan*. London: Four Square Books, 1960. Originally published in 1899.

———. *Savrola*. London: Beacon Books, 1957. Originally published in 1900.

———. *The Second World War*. 6 vols. Boston: Houghton Mifflin, 1948–53.

———. *The Story of the Malakand Field Force*. New York: Barnes and Noble, 1993. Originally published in 1898.

————. *The World Crisis, 1911–1918.* 2 vols. London: Odhams Press, 1938.

Collier-Thomas, Bettye, and V. P. Franklin, eds. *Sisters in the Struggle: African American Women in the Civil Rights–Black Power Movement.* New York: New York University Press, 2001.

Conquest, Robert. *Stalin: Breaker of Nations.* New York: Penguin, 1991.

Conrad, Joseph. *Heart of Darkness.* London: Penguin, 1995. Originally published in 1902.

————. *Notes on Life and Letters.* McLean, VA: IndyPublish.com, n.d. Originally published in 1920.

————. *The Secret Sharer and Other Stories.* New York: Dover, 1993.

Crawford, Vicki L., Jacqueline Anne Rouse, and Barbara Woods, eds. *Women in the Civil Rights Movement.* Bloomington: Indiana University Press, 1993.

Daube, David. *The New Testament and Rabbinic Judaism.* Peabody, MA: Hendrickson, 1998.

Davies, W. D. *The Setting of the Sermon on the Mount.* Cambridge: Cambridge University Press, 1964.

Davis, Angela. *An Autobiography.* New York: International Publishers, 1988. Originally published in 1974.

deGruchy, John W., ed. *The Cambridge Companion to Dietrich Bonhoeffer.* Cambridge: Cambridge University Press, 2002.

Dinnerstein, Dorothy. *The Mermaid and the Minotaur: Sexual Arrangements and Human Malaise.* New York: Harper & Row, 1976.

Donald, David Herbert. *Lincoln.* New York: Simon & Schuster, 1995.

Dyson, Michael Eric. *I May Not Get There with You: The True Martin Luther King, Jr.* New York: Touchstone, 2001.

Ellsberg, Robert, ed. *Gandhi on Christianity.* Maryknoll, NY: Orbis Books, 1991.

Enright, Dominique, comp. *The Wicked Wit of Winston Churchill.* London: Michael O'Mara Books, 2001.

Erikson, Erik H. "The Galilean Sayings and the Sense of 'I.'" *Yale Review* 70, no. 3 (1981): 321–47.

————. *Gandhi's Truth: On the Origins of Militant Nonviolence.* New York: W. W. Norton, 1993.

Evans, Sara. *Personal Politics: The Roots of Women's Liberation in the Civil Rights Movement and the New Left.* New York: Vintage Books, 1980.

Ewing, K. D., and C. A. Gearty. *The Struggle for Civil Liberties: Political Freedom and the Rule of Law in Britain, 1914–1945.* Oxford: Oxford University Press, 2001.

Fiorenza, Elisabeth Schussler. *In Memory of Her: A Feminist Theological Reconstruction of Christian Origins.* New York: Crossroad Publishing, 2002.

————. *Jesus: Miriam's Child, Sophia's Prophet.* New York: Continuum, 1994.

————, ed. *Searching Scriptures.* Vol. 1, *A Feminist Introduction.* New York: Crossroad Publishing, 1993.

————. *Searching the Scriptures.* Vol. 2, *A Feminist Commentary.* New York: Crossroad Publishing, 1994.

Fischer, Louis. *Gandhi: His Life and Message for the World.* New York: Penguin, 1982.

Flusser, David. *Jesus.* Jerusalem: Hebrew University Magnes Press, 2001.

————. *Judaism and the Origins of Christianity.* Jerusalem: Hebrew University Magnes Press, 2001.

Foner, Philip S., ed. *The Life and Writings of Frederick Douglass.* Vol. 2. New York: International Publishers, 1950.

255

Foster, R. F. *Lord Randolph Churchill: A Political Life.* Oxford: Clarendon Press, 1981.

Foxhall, Lin, and John Salmon, eds. *When Men Were Men: Masculinity, Power and Identity in Classical Antiquity.* London: Routledge, 1998.

Fredriksen, Paula. *From Jesus to Christ.* 2nd ed. New Haven: Yale University Press, 2000.

———. *Jesus of Nazareth, King of the Jews: A Jewish Life and the Emergence of Christianity.* New York: Alfred A. Knopf, 2000.

Freeman, Joanne B. *Affairs of Honor: National Politics in the New Republic.* New Haven: Yale University Press, 2001.

Freud, Sigmund. "'Civilized' Sexual Morality and Modern Nervous Illness." In *The Standard Edition of the Complete Psychological Works of Sigmund Freud,* vol. 9 (1906–1908), ed. James Strachey, 181–204. London: Hogarth Press, 1959.

———. *On the Universal Tendency to Debasement in the Sphere of Love.* In *The Standard Edition of the Complete Psychological Works of Sigmund Freud,* vol. 11 (1910), ed. James Strachey, 177–90. London: Hogarth Press, 1975.

Furbank, P. N. *E. M. Forster: A Life.* San Diego: A Harvest Book, 1978.

Furet, Francois. *The Passing of an Illusion: The Idea of Communism in the Twentieth Century.* Translated by Deborah Furet. Chicago: University of Chicago Press, 1999.

Gandhi, Manubehn. *Bapu—My Mother.* Ahmadabad, India: Navajivan Publishing House, 1949.

Gandhi, Mohandas K. *An Autobiography: The Story of My Experiments with Truth.* Translated by Mahadev Desai. Boston: Beacon Press, 1993.

———. *The Bhagavad Gita According to Gandhi.* Translated by John Strohmeier. Berkeley: Berkeley Hills Books, 2000.

———. *The Collected Works of Mahatma Gandhi.* Vol. 9, September 1908–November 1909. Delhi, India: The Publications Division. 1963.

———. *The Collected Works of Mahatma Gandhi.* Vol. 10, November 1909–March 1911. Delhi, India: The Publications Division, 1963.

———. *Hind Swaraj and Other Writings.* Edited by Anthony J. Parel. Cambridge: Cambridge University Press, 2000.

———. *Non-violent Resistance (Satyagraha).* Mineola, NY: Dover, 2001.

———. *Satyagraha in South Africa.* Translated from the Gujarati by Valji Govindji Desai. Ahmadabad, India: Navajivan Publishing House, 1928.

Gandhi, Rajmohan. *The Good Boatman: A Portrait of Gandhi.* New Delhi: Penguin, 1995.

Garfield, Deborah M., and Rafia Zafar, eds. *Harriet Jacobs and "Incidents in the Life of a Slave Girl."* Cambridge: Cambridge University Press, 1996.

Garland, David. *The Culture of Control: Crime and Social Order in Contemporary Society.* Chicago: University of Chicago Press, 2001.

Garrison, William Lloyd. *Selections from the Writings and Speeches of William Lloyd Garrison.* Boston: R. F. Wallcut, 1852.

———. *Thoughts on African Colonization.* New York: Arno Press and the New York Times, 1968. Originally published in 1832.

Garrow, David J. *Bearing the Cross: Martin Luther King, Jr., and the Southern Christian Leadership Conference.* New York: Quill/William Morrow, 1986.

Genovese, Eugene D. *Roll, Jordan, Roll: The World the Slaves Made.* New York: Vintage Books, 1974.

Giddings, Paula. *When and Where I Enter: The Impact of Black Women on Race and Sex in America.* New York: William Morrow, 1984.

Gilligan, Carol. *The Birth of Pleasure*. New York: Alfred A. Knopf, 2002. Revised as *The Birth of Pleasure: A New Map of Love*. New York: Vintage Books, 2003.

———. *In a Different Voice: Psychological Theory and Women's Development*. Cambridge, MA: Harvard University Press, 1982.

Gilligan, James. *Preventing Violence*. New York: Thames & Hudson, 2001.

———. *Violence: Reflections on a National Epidemic*. New York: Vintage Books, 1997.

Gilmore, David D., ed. *Honour and Shame and the Unity of the Mediterranean*. Washington, DC: American Anthropological Association, 1987.

Goldstein, Joshua A. *War and Gender: How Gender Shapes the War System and Vice Versa*. Cambridge: Cambridge University Press, 2001.

Grant, Jacquelyn. *White Women's Christ and Black Women's Jesus: Feminist Christology and Womanist Response*. Atlanta: Scholars Press, 1989.

Gregg, Richard B. *The Power of Nonviolence*. New York: Schocken Books, 1971. Originally published in 1935.

Green, Martin. *The Origins of Nonviolence: Tolstoy and Gandhi in Their Historical Settings*. University Park: Pennsylvania State University Press, 1986.

———. *Tolstoy and Gandhi, Men of Peace: A Biography*. New York: Basic Books, 1983.

Green, Richard. *The "Sissy Boy Syndrome" and the Development of Homosexuality*. New Haven: Yale University Press, 1987.

Greenberg, Kenneth S. *Honor and Slavery*. Princeton: Princeton University Press, 1996.

Guha, Ramachandra. *An Anthropologist among the Marxists and Other Essays*. Delhi, India: Permanent Black, 2001.

Gustafson, Richard F. *Leo Tolstoy: Resident and Stranger*. Princeton: Princeton University Press, 1986.

Hallie, Philip P. *Let Innocent Blood Be Shed: The Story of the Village of Le Chambon and How Goodness Happened There*. New York: Harper & Row, 1979.

Haskins, James. *Bayard Rustin: Behind the Scenes of the Civil Rights Movement*. New York: Hyperion Books, 1997.

Hauerwas, Stanley. *The Peaceable Kingdom: A Primer in Christian Ethics*. Notre Dame, IN: University of Notre Dame Press, 1983.

———. *With the Grain of the Universe: The Church's Witness and Natural Theology*. Grand Rapids, MI: Brazos Press, 2001.

Hawthorne, Nathaniel. *The Scarlet Letter*. New York: Penguin, 1983. Originally published in 1850.

Hedges, Chris. *War Is a Force That Gives Us Meaning*. New York: Public Affairs, 2002.

Herman, Judith. *Trauma and Recovery*. New York: Basic Books, 1997.

Heschel, Abraham J. *The Prophets*. New York: Perennial Classics, 2001.

Heyn, Dalma. *The Erotic Silence of the American Wife*. New York: A Plume Book, 1997.

Higginbotham, Evelyn Brooks. *Righteous Discontent: The Women's Movement in the Black Baptist Church, 1880–1920*. Cambridge, MA: Harvard University Press, 1993.

Howe, Daniel Walker. "Henry David Thoreau on the Duty of Civil Disobedience," an inaugural lecture delivered before the University of Oxford on May 21, 1990. Oxford: Clarendon Press, 1990.

Hunter-Gault, Charlayne. *In My Place*. New York: Vintage Books, 1993.

Ignatieff, Michael. *The Warrior's Honor: Ethnic War and the Modern Conscience*. New York: Henry Holt, 1997.

Jacobs, Harriet A. *Incidents in the Life of a Slave Girl.* Edited by Jean Fagan Yellin. Cambridge, MA: Harvard University Press, 1987. Originally published in 1861.

James, Lawrence. *The Rise and Fall of the British Empire.* New York: St. Martin's Griffin, 1994.

Jenkins, Roy. *Churchill: A Biography.* New York: Farrar, Straus and Giroux, 2001.

———. *The British Liberal Tradition: From Gladstone to Young Churchill, Asquith, and Lloyd George—Is Blair Their Heir?* Toronto: University of Toronto Press, 2001.

Jeremias, Joachim. *The Sermon on the Mount.* London: Athlone Press, 1961.

Joshi, Pushpa. *Gandhi on Women.* Ahmadabad, India: Navajivan Publishing House, 1988.

Juergensmeyer, Mark. *Terror in the Mind of God: The Global Rise of Religious Violence.* Berkeley: University of California Press, 2000.

Kalven, Harry, Jr. *The Negro and the First Amendment.* Chicago: University of Chicago Press, 1965.

Kapur, Sudarshan. *Raising Up a Prophet: The African-American Encounter with Gandhi.* Boston: Beacon Press, 1992.

Karl, Frederick R. *Joseph Conrad: The Three Lives.* New York: Farrar, Straus and Giroux, 1979.

Kaufmann, Walter. *Critique of Religion and Philosophy.* Princeton: Princeton University Press, 1958.

Kertzer, David I. *Sacrifices for Honor: Italian Infant Abandonment and the Politics of Reproductive Control.* Boston: Beacon Press, 1993.

King, Karen L. *The Gospel of Mary of Magdala: Jesus and the First Woman Apostle.* Santa Rosa, CA: Polebridge Press, 2003.

King, Martin Luther Jr. *A Testament of Hope: The Essential Writings of Martin Luther King, Jr.* Edited by James M. Washington. San Francisco: Harper & Row, 1986.

Kluger, Richard. *Simple Justice: The History of "Brown v. Board of Education" and Black America's Struggle for Equality.* New York: Vintage Books, 1977.

Koestler, Arthur. *Darkness at Noon.* Translated by Daphne Hardy. New York: Bantam Books, 1968. Originally published in 1941.

Koonz, Claudia. *Mothers in the Fatherland: Women, the Family, and Nazi Politics.* New York: St. Martin's Press, 1987.

———. *The Nazi Conscience.* Cambridge, MA: Belknap Press, 2003.

Kronholz, June. "Utah Orders School to Open Its Doors—To Armed Students." *Wall Street Journal,* May 24, 2004, sec. A, A1 and A6.

Langmuir, Gavin I. *History, Religion, and Anti-Semitism.* Berkeley: University of California Press, 1990.

———. *Toward a Definition of Anti-Semitism.* Berkeley: University of California Press, 1990.

Laqueur, Walter. *The Dream That Failed: Reflections on the Soviet Union.* New York: Oxford University Press, 1994.

Leeming, David. *James Baldwin: A Biography.* New York: Alfred A. Knopf, 1994.

Lewis, Bernard. *What Went Wrong? Western Impact and Middle Eastern Response.* Oxford: Oxford University Press, 2002.

Ling, Peter J., and Sharon Monteith. *Gender in the Civil Rights Movement.* New York: Garland Publishing, 1999.

Litwack, Leo F. *Been in the Storm So Long: The Aftermath of Slavery.* New York: Vintage Books, 1979.

Lodge, David. *Consciousness and the Novel: Connected Essays.* Cambridge, MA: Harvard University Press, 2002.

Lopez, Donald S., Jr. *The Story of Buddhism: A Concise Guide to Its History and Teachings.* San Francisco: Harper, 2001.

Maalouf, Amin. *In the Name of Identity: Violence and the Need to Belong.* Translated by Barbara Bray. New York: Arcade Publishing, 2000.

Makiya, Kanan. *Cruelty and Silence: War, Tyranny, Uprising, and the Arab World.* New York: W. W. Norton, 2002.

Mandelker, Amy. *Framing Anna Karenina: Tolstoy, the Woman Question, and the Victorian Novel.* Columbus: Ohio State University Press, 1993.

Margalit, Avishai. "The Suicide Bombers." *New York Review of Books* 50, no. 1 (January 16, 2003): 36–39.

Martin, Ralph G. *Jennie: The Life of Lady Randolph Churchill.* Vol. 1, *The Romantic Years, 1854–1895.* New York: New American Library, 1970.

———. *Jennie: The Life of Lady Randolph Churchill.* Vol. 2, *The Dramatic Years, 1895–1921.* New York: New American Library, 1972.

Mayer, Henry. *All on Fire: William Lloyd Garrison and the Abolition of Slavery.* New York: St. Martin's Griffin, 1998.

McNeil, Genna Rae. *Groundwork: Charles Hamilton Houston and the Struggle for Civil Rights.* Philadelphia: University of Pennsylvania Press, 1983.

McPherson, James M. *The Abolitionist Legacy: From Reconstruction to the NAACP.* Princeton: Princeton University Press, 1975.

Mehta, Ved. *Mahatma Gandhi and His Apostles.* New Haven: Yale University Press, 1976.

Meier, John P. *A Marginal Jew: Rethinking the Historical Jesus.* 3 Vols. New York: Doubleday, 1991–2001.

Mernissi, Fatema. *Islam and Democracy: Fear of the Modern World.* Translated by Mary Jo Lakeland. Cambridge, MA: Perseus, 1992.

———. *The Veil and the Male Elite: A Feminist Interpretation of Women's Rights in Islam.* Cambridge, MA: Perseus, 1991.

Merton, Thomas. *Faith and Violence: Christian Teaching and Christian Practice.* Notre Dame, IN: University of Notre Dame Press, 1968.

———. *The Nonviolent Alternative.* New York: Farrar, Straus and Giroux, 1980.

———. *The Seven Storey Mountain: An Autobiography of Faith.* San Diego: Harcourt Brace, 1998. Originally published in 1948.

Miller, William Ian. *Bloodtaking and Peacemaking: Feud, Law, and Society in Saga Iceland.* Chicago: University of Chicago Press, 1990.

———. *Humiliation and Other Essays on Honor, Social Discomfort, and Violence.* Ithaca, NY: Cornell University Press, 1993.

Mitchell, Juliet. *Mad Men and Medusas: Reclaiming Hysteria* (New York: Basic Books, 2000).

Monk, Ray. *Ludwig Wittgenstein: The Duty of Genius.* New York: Free Press, 1990.

Mottley, Constance Baker. *Equal Justice under Law.* New York: Farrar, Straus and Giroux, 1998.

Murdoch, Iris. *Metaphysics as a Guide to Morals.* New York: Allen Lane, 1992.

———. *The Sovereignty of Good.* New York: Routledge, 1992.

Murthy, B. Srinivasa. *Mahatma Gandhi and Leo Tolstoy Letters.* Long Beach, CA: Long Beach Publications, 1987.

Naipaul, V. S. *India: A Wounded Civilization.* New York: Vintage Books, 1978.

The New Oxford Annotated Bible. New York: Oxford University Press, 1991.

Niebuhr, Reinhold. *Moral Man and Immoral Society: A Study in Ethics and Politics.* Louisville, KY: Westminster John Knox Press, 2001. Originally published in 1932.

Nietzsche, Friedrich. *On the Genealogy of Morals.* Translated by Douglas Smith. Oxford: Oxford University Press, 1996.

Nisbett, Richard E., and Dov Cohen. *Culture of Honor: The Psychology of Violence in the South.* Boulder, CO: Westview Press, 1996.

Oliver, Dawn, and Gavin Drewry. *The Law and Parliament.* London: Butterworths, 1998.

Olson, Lynne. *Freedom's Daughters: The Unsung Heroines of the Civil Rights Movement from 1830 to 1970.* New York: Scribner's, 2001.

Orwell, George. *A Collection of Essays.* San Diego: A Harvest Book, 1981.

Parekh, Bhikhu. *Colonialism, Tradition, and Reform: An Analysis of Gandhi's Political Discourse.* Rev. ed. New Delhi: Sage Publications, 1999.

————. *Gandhi: A Very Short Introduction.* Oxford: Oxford University Press, 1997.

Patterson, Orlando. *The Rituals of Blood: Consequences of Slavery in Two American Centuries.* Washington, DC: Civitas, 1998.

Peristiany, J. G., ed. *Honour and Shame: The Values of Mediterranean Society.* Chicago: University of Chicago Press, 1966.

Pipes, Daniel. *Militant Islam Reaches America.* New York: W. W. Norton, 2002.

Pollack, William. *Real Boys: Rescuing Our Sons from the Myths of Boyhood.* New York: Henry Holt, 1998.

Polner, Murray, and Jim O'Grady. *Disarmed and Dangerous: The Radical Lives and Times of Daniel and Philip Berrigan.* Boulder, CO: Westview Press, 1997.

Potter, David. *The Impending Crisis, 1848–1861.* Edited by Don E. Fehrenbacher. New York: Harper & Row, 1976.

Pushkin, Alexander. *Eugene Onegin.* Translated by Charles Johnson with an introduction by John Bayley. London: Penguin, 1979.

Rahula, Walpola. *What the Buddha Taught.* New York: Grove Press, 1974.

Rampersad, Arnold, ed. *Richard Wright: Later Works.* New York: Library of America, 1991.

Rasmussen, Larry. *Dietrich Bonhoeffer—His Significance for North Americans.* Minneapolis, MN: Fortress Press, 1990.

Rauschenbusch, Walter. *Christianity and the Social Crisis.* Louisville, KY: Westminster/John Knox Press, 1991. Originally published in 1907.

Real, Terrence. *I Don't Want to Talk about It: Overcoming the Secret Legacy of Male Depression.* New York: Fireside, 1997.

Reddick, L. D. *Crusader without Violence: A Biography of Martin Luther King, Jr.* New York: Harper & Brothers, 1959.

Richards, David A. J. *Conscience and the Constitution: History, Theory, and Law of the Reconstruction Amendments.* Princeton: Princeton University Press, 1993.

————. *Foundations of American Constitutionalism.* New York: Oxford University Press, 1989.

————. *Free Speech and the Politics of Identity.* Oxford: Clarendon Press, 1999.

————. *Identity and the Case for Gay Rights: Race, Gender, Religion as Analogies.* Chicago: University of Chicago Press, 1999.

————. *A Theory of Reasons for Action.* Oxford: Clarendon Press, 1971.

————. *Toleration and the Constitution.* New York: Oxford University Press, 1986.

————. *Tragic Manhood and Democracy: Verdi's Voice and the Powers of Musical Art.* Brighton, UK: Sussex Academic Press, 2004.

————. *Women, Gays, and the Constitution: The Grounds for Feminism and Gay Rights in Culture and Law.* Chicago: University of Chicago Press, 1998.

Robnett, Belinda. *How Long? How Long? African-American Women in the Struggle for Civil Rights*. New York: Oxford University Press, 1997.

Rolland, Romain. *Mahatma Gandhi*. Translated by Catherine D. Groth. New Delhi: Publications Division, 1990.

———. *Tolstoy*. Translated by Bernard Miall. Port Washington, NY: Kennikat Press, 1911.

Roy, Arundhati. *War Talk*. Cambridge, MA: South End Press, 2003.

Ruddick, Sara. *Maternal Thinking: Toward a Politics of Peace*. Boston: Beacon Press, 1989.

Ruether, Rosemary Radford. *Sexism and God-Talk: Toward a Feminist Theology*. Boston: Beacon Press, 1993.

Ruskin, John. *Unto This Last*. Edited by Clive Wilmer. London: Penguin, 1997.

Rustin, Bayard. *Down the Line: The Collected Writings of Bayard Rustin*. Chicago: Quadrangle Books, 1971.

———. *Strategies for Freedom: The Changing Patterns of Black Protest*. New York: Columbia University Press, 1976.

Salter, William Mackintire. *Ethical Religion*. Boston: Roberts Brothers, 1891.

Sanders, E. P. *The Historical Figure of Jesus*. London: Allen Lane, 1993.

———. *Jesus and Judaism*. Philadelphia: Fortress Press, 1985.

Schiavone, Aldo. *The End of the Past: Ancient Rome and the Modern West*. Translated by Margery J. Schneider. Cambridge, MA: Harvard University Press, 2000.

Schulke, Glip, and Penelope Ortner McPhee. *King Remembered*. New York: W. W. Norton, 1986.

Scott, James G. *Domination and the Arts of Resistance: Hidden Transcripts*. New Haven: Yale University Press, 1990.

Shirer, William L. *Gandhi: A Memoir*. New York: Washington Square Press, 1979.

Shridharani, Krishnalal. *War without Violence: A Study of Gandhi's Method and Its Accomplishments*. New York: Harcourt Brace, 1939.

Spierenburg, Pieter. *Men and Violence: Gender, Honor, and Rituals in Modern Europe and America*. Columbus: Ohio State University Press, 1998.

Stern, Daniel N. *The Interpersonal World of the Infant: A View from Psychoanalysis and Developmental Psychology*. New York: Basic Books, 1985.

Sundquist, Eric J. *To Wake the Nations: Race in the Making of American Literature*. Cambridge, MA: Harvard University Press, 1993.

Thomas à Kempis. *The Imitation of Christ*. Edited by Paul M. Bechtel. Chicago: Moody Press, 1984.

Thoreau, Henry D. *Reform Papers*. Edited by Wendell Glick. Princeton: Princeton University Press, 1973.

———. *Walden*, in *Henry David Thoreau*, ed. Robert F. Sayre, 321–588 (New York: Library of America, 1985)..

Tolstaya, Tatyana. *Pushkin's Children: Writings on Russia and Russians*. Translated by Jamey Gambrell. Boston: Houghton Mifflin, 2003.

Tolstoy, Leo, *Anna Karenina: A Novel in Eight Parts*. Translated by Richard Pevear and Larissa Volokhonsky. New York: Viking, 2000.

———. *Childhood, Boyhood, Youth*. Translated by Rosemary Edmonds. London: Penguin, 1964.

———. *Confession*. Translated by David Patterson. New York: W. W. Norton, 1983.

———. *The Four Gospels Harmonized and Translated*. Vol. 1, Translated by Leo Wiener. Boston: Dana Estes, 1904.

———. *The Four Gospels Harmonized and Translated.* Vol. 2, Translated by Leo Wiener. New York: Colonial Press, 1904.

———. *The Gospel in Brief.* Translated by Isabel Hapgood. Lincoln: University of Nebraska Press, 1997.

———. *Great Short Works.* Translated by Louise and Aylmer Maude, with an introduction by John Bayley. New York: Perennial Library, 1967.

———. *I Cannot Be Silent: Writings on Politics, Art, and Religion by Leo Tolstoy.* Edited and Translated by W. Gareth Jones. Bristol, UK: Bristol Press, 1989.

———. *The Kingdom of God Is within You: Christianity Not as a Mystic Religion but as a New Theory of Life.* Translated by Constance Garnett. Lincoln: University of Nebraska Press, 1984. Originally published in 1894.

———. *My Religion; On Life; Thoughts on God; On the Meaning of Life.* Translated by Leo Wiener. Boston: Dana Estes, 1904.

———. *The Sebastopol Sketches.* Translated by David McDuff. London: Penguin, 1986.

———. *War and Peace.* Translated by George Gibian. Norton Critical Edition. 2nd ed. New York: W. W. Norton, 1996.

———. *What Then Must We Do?* Translated by Aylmer Maude. Devon, UK: Green Books, 1991.

Troyat, Henri. *Tolstoy.* Translated by Nancy Amphoux. New York: Grove Press, 1967. Originally published in French in 1965.

Tsuzuki, Chushichi. *Edward Carpenter, 1844–1929: Prophet of Human Fellowship.* Cambridge: Cambridge University Press, 1980.

Varshney, Ashutosh. *Ethnic Conflict and Civic Life: Hindus and Muslims in India.* New Haven: Yale University Press, 2002.

Vermes, Geza. *The Changing Faces of Jesus.* New York: Viking Compass, 2001.

———. *Jesus and the World of Judaism.* London: SCM Press, 1983.

———. *Jesus the Jew: A Historian's Reading of the Gospels.* Philadelphia: Fortress Press, 1981. Originally published in 1973.

———. *The Religion of Jesus the Jew.* Minneapolis, MN: Fortress Press, 1993.

Villard, Fanny Garrison. *William Lloyd Garrison on Non-resistance.* New York: Nation Press Printing, 1924.

Washington, Joseph R., Jr. *Black Religion: The Negro and Christianity in the United States.* Boston: Beacon Press, 1964.

Werth, Alexander, trans. *The Diary of Tolstoy's Wife, 1860–1891.* New York: Payson and Clarke, 1928.

Whitman, James Q. *Harsh Justice: Criminal Punishment and the Widening Divide between America and Europe.* New York: Oxford University Press, 2003.

Wildavsky, Aaron. *The Nursing Father: Moses as a Political Leader.* Tuscaloosa: University of Alabama Press, 1984.

Wilson, A. N. *Jesus: A Life.* New York: Fawcett Columbine, 1992.

———. *Tolstoy: A Biography.* New York: W. W. Norton, 1988.

Wilson, Douglas L. *Honor's Voice: The Transformation of Abraham Lincoln.* New York: Alfred A. Knopf, 1998.

Witherell, Elizabeth Hall, ed. *Henry David Thoreau: Collected Essays and Poems.* New York: Library of America, 2001.

Witherington III, Ben. *Women and the Genesis of Christianity.* Cambridge: Cambridge University Press, 1990.

Wolpert, Stanley. *Gandhi's Passion: The Life and Legacy of Mahatma Gandhi*. Oxford: Oxford University Press, 2001.

Woodward, C. Vann, and Elisabeth Muhlenfeld. *The Private Mary Chesnut: The Unpublished Civil War Diaries*. New York: Oxford University Press, 1984.

Woolf, Virginia. *Three Guineas*. San Diego: Harcourt Brace, 1938.

Wyatt-Brown, Bertram. *Southern Honor: Ethics and Behavior in the Old South*. New York: Oxford University Press, 1982.

Yoder, John Howard. *The Original Revolution: Essays on Christian Pacifism*. Scottdale, PA: Herald Press, 1998.

Young, Andrew. *An Easy Burden: The Civil Rights Movement and the Transformation of America*. New York: HarperCollins, 1996.

//p. 265

INDEX

RN: The Index on pages 265 to 271 will not be read. End RN. 20:37.48 (EOF)